IN SEARCH OF DIGNITY

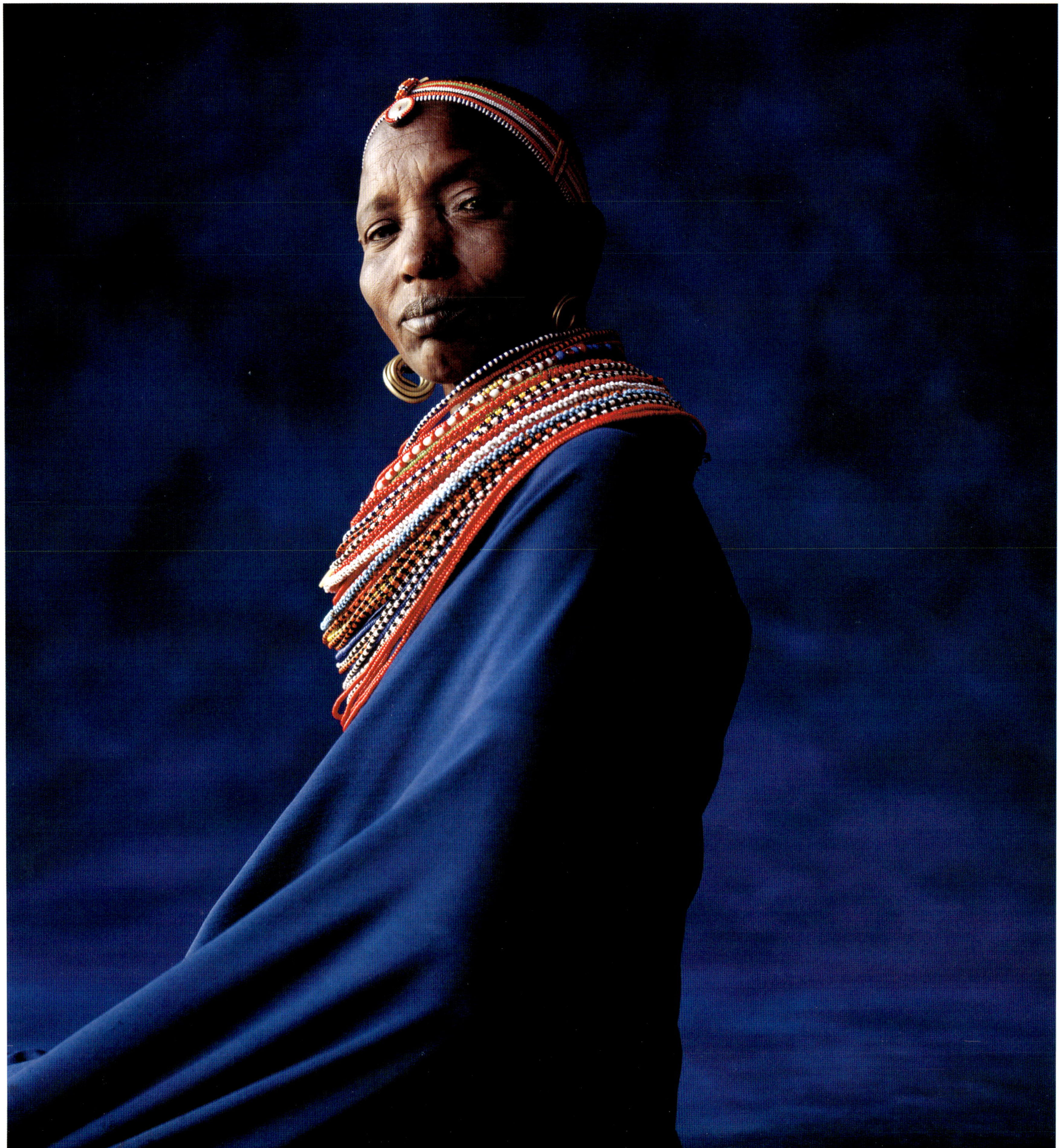

JANIFER LEPARALEEN,
TWENTY-SEVEN,
SAMBURU.
MARALAL, KENYA.

IN SEARCH OF DIGNITY

PHOTOGRAPHS BY
GÜNTER PFANNMÜLLER

ESSAYS BY WILHELM KLEIN

PREFACE BY WADE DAVIS

APERTURE

FOREWORD

WADE DAVIS

On first impression there is, at least for the anthropologist, something vaguely disturbing about the format and premise of this exquisite book. Dignity, after all, is not a trait of a people, it is a quality of an individual, and within any culture there are those who possess it and those who do not. It is elusive and impossible to quantify, but not difficult to find, in the streets of our cities or in the remote reaches of distant lands. The person of dignity, whether he or she is an elder of the Rendille, a shaman of the Barasana, a wandering sadhu, minstrel prince, or a banker in New York, is radiant, alive, with a presence of being that, like a magnet, draws one to their side. One seeks to walk in their shadow, to bathe in the glow of their integrity.

The notion that dignity is something that must be searched for, or that we ought be surprised in any way to encounter its presence among peoples who are exotic only to us, as indeed we are to them, is curious indeed. The authors also tread on sensitive ground in their style and choice of format and technique. Photography and anthropology came of age in the same decade, and throughout the nineteenth century, in particular, the camera as a tool served to exaggerate the exoticism of the other, to widen the chasm that lay between cultures, and reinforce a social Darwinian scheme that invariably placed Victorian England at the top of a cultural ladder to success. As scientists measured the breasts and skull sizes of a host of native subjects, what Michael Taussig has charitably called the "penis school of physical anthropology," cameras were always present to record in profile and frontal view the stunned faces of the subjects, isolated always against a neutral backdrop that lent to the scene the dark façade and illusion of scientific objectivity. It is difficult even today to view any portrait, however beautiful, of an indigenous person shot in isolation against such a backdrop, without recalling this sordid history when scholars indulged in the anthropometric mismeasure of man.

The portable studio with its neutral canvas palette, without texture or history, is also reminiscent of the painted backdrops of the frontier photographers of the American West who captured and froze Geronimo and Sitting Bull in defeat, their stoic indifference and resigned nobility less a characteristic of a people, as these images have led us to believe, than the result of a century of impossible grief. Edward Curtis viewed photography as a salvage operation, posing his subjects with the explicit intention of recording the last vestiges of what he viewed as a doomed world. His sepia images fade like the land itself. But even Curtis within the frame of his lens provided some context to the lives he documented. Here in the photographs we have form alone, portraits as stylish as those in an elegant fashion magazine.

Ironically, what in the end redeems these images, and elevates them to the sublime, is the intensity and mindfulness of the collaborators, artists whose sensitivities are obvious and whose deliberate decision to embrace this method, even at risk of comparison to the past, has allowed them to transcend the inherent limitations of the technique. What results is a stunning evocation of place and history, mysteriously revealed not in detail or scenery but in the jewel-like quality of the images themselves, the sheer beauty of the light, the wonder of a glance or smile that isolates the germ of a people, the essence of the individuals so exquisitely portrayed, the very spirit of the culture that gave them birth. Rarely has so much been revealed by available light.

In studying these portraits, of dancing girls from Rajasthan, Karo hunters from Ethiopia, a Samburu warrior of the grasslands of northern Kenya, remember that each individual has a history, a network of kin ties, a place in a social organization that links father to son, sister to cousin, husband to wife. In short, a role to play in the saga of a people. Every man and woman here portrayed grew up circumscribed by rules, touched by the wild, blessed by the cult of the seed, the magic of the hunt, the healing power of plants. In temples and fields, on mountain slopes, in the shadowy world of dreams, they learned the ways of the spirits, the texture of the soul, the meaning of stars. Rivers run through their homelands, forests provide shelter from a harrowing sky, the air is dense with the intoxicating possibilities of life. In houses of grass and stone, children are born, youths come of age, lovers couple, and elders are nursed into the realm of the dead.

These then are the faces of humanity, a small sampling of the range of the human imagination as brought into being by culture. Study these images and recall what is being lost as we drift from a polychromatic world of diversity toward a monochromatic world of monotony. When your father and mother were born there were perhaps six thousand languages spoken on Earth. A language, of course, is more than a cluster of words, it is the flash of the human spirit, the vehicle through which the soul of a culture enters the material realm. Today, of the languages still spoken, fully half are not being taught to schoolchildren—effectively they are already dead—and only three hundred are spoken by more than one million people. In another century, only a few hundred may survive. What we are losing is the diversity of the human experience, and thus the capacity of humanity to cope with the common problems that confront us all.

Consider then these photographs, the product of a long and sincere labor, as a gift, laid down before your eyes as a reminder of a harsh reality and a nascent hope. There is a fire burning over the earth, taking with it plants and animals, cultures, languages, ancient skills and visionary wisdom. Quelling this flame and reinventing the poetry of diversity is the most important challenge of our times.

IN SEARCH OF DIGNITY

THE TIMELESS FACE OF HUMANITY

What a piece of work is a man! How noble in reason, how infinite in faculty, in form and moving how express and admirable, in action how like an angel, in apprehension how like a god—the beauty of the world, the paragon of animals!

—*William Shakespeare,* Hamlet

Most people are only vaguely aware that every person, independent of nationality, class, or race is endowed with dignity. It is an elusive quality because it is often obscured by poverty, bigotry, and pride. To perceive it, we need to look at the fate of humankind from beyond our habitual point of view. A radical perspective would take us back to the nascence of life itself, to a quality that transcends the purely physical and chemical. Then it is not life alone we perceive but a quality more precious and mysterious than that which merely distinguishes the animate from the inanimate—the awareness of being alive. It is that wondrous sense of being that vivifies humanity's dignity. It is this we were in search of—not in a rational but in an intuitive, though systematic, way.

When we look into a mirror or into the face of our neighbor we see an individual who is sometimes fearful or haughty, a person molded by the social and political codes of our time. More often than not, these modes and manners keep us from seeing his essentially spiritual nature. Only in rare moments of love, piety, courage, or devotion can we glance through the veil of our day-to-day existence and perceive the grace within. These moments, however, are short-lived, and our routine perspective takes over again. This is when photography comes in, when we freeze and capture the fleeting moment through the shutter of our camera. Then this inexplicable something, this mysterious sense of being that is beyond the control of science, becomes fixed, ready to be explored by our intellect and absorbed by our emotions.

When we open this book we encounter such photographs—images of the eternal face of humanity. Strung as if across time, the images in this book are examples of the enduring essence of humanity. This is revealed as much in the faces of those living at the dawn of time as in the spiritual luminosity on the faces of devout Asian monks and hermits.

These photographs bring you eye to eye with tribal people from the Rift Valley whose cultural traditions and patterns of daily life have not changed over thousands of years. They show herders who live in an unbroken tradition of interdependence with their animals, and peasants who still see themselves as an integral part of the soil they perennially turn over. These photographs are of people who are alive today, but who could have lived at any time in human history. Many of them radiate what the religiously inclined amongst us would interpret as the presence of God.

LIGHT IS THE KEY Light makes the world comprehensible. Light is energy and color; light is warmth. Light influences our moods, and it is in the full light of day that we gather the strength to face the unknown; the inevitable fate of our individual existence. Light is the sustaining potion of life. Light is also the medium of photography—the key to our endeavor.

Such was the focus when we set out to design our first portable studio. We knew that capturing and making visible what is not a reflection but an innate quality that emerges from within a person demands a special use of light. We had to create a situation in which light neither overwhelmed nor inhibited the appearance of this subtle property. Available, untainted, reflected light filtering in from one side had to spread and create a light dome inside a cubicle, the dimensions of which had to be at least ten times bigger than the photographed space.

There was a second problem we had to overcome. It is a human propensity to project customary viewpoints onto what we see. It is a problem of values, preconceptions, and prejudice. With this in mind, we knew that we had to avoid common sights that were likely to already be categorized in our minds and in the minds of the eventual viewers of the photographs. We were aware that prejudice lay not only in the mind of the beholder but also in the person photographed. Thus we had to look for people outside industrialized societies who still live in harmony with nature, or for others for whom spiritual awareness is the true base of life's evolvement. We consciously avoided photographing people from western contemporary society. This is not to imply that comparable human dignity or a spiritual sense of being is not present in contemporary western sensibility. It is simply that our conditioning would have made it more difficult for us to perceive it within them.

We knew that we could not bring the people, many of whom represent our fast-fading past, to our state-of-the-art studio in Germany. We therefore set out to take the studio to the people who live at what is called "the ends of the earth."

Six field trips brought us into three regions: civilization's cradle in the Ethiopian and Kenyan Rift Valley, the remote hills of the Golden Triangle in northern Myanmar and northern Thailand, and the isolated Thar Desert of northwest India.

According to statistics, the societies in these regions are the least "modern" on earth, insofar as their use of tools and technology has been consistent for several thousand years. We were not sure if knowing this would hamper our endeavor, for this fact, too, evolves from a western conception of progress.

However, light came to our rescue. One of the many—to us similar-looking—people outside the studio would, upon entering it, be transformed as if by a magic wand. The nameless and indistinguishable—the consistently ill-fated peasant—became unique. Not only did we sense it instantly; it also left its mark on film.

In hindsight we can see that photographing hundreds of people in dozens of villages and camps and being overwhelmed by their hospitality, humility, and openness, could have led us to romanticize the experience. However, beneath the undisputedly romantic ideas that initially inspired our travels, there has always been a sober professionalism accompanied by hard work and a dogged determination to overcome innumerable obstacles. The people we met were on the threshold of modernity, with similar desires to those that beset the members of more technologically advanced societies. They were less developed in a western sense, but impressively adapted to their harsh environments. Most importantly, their generally innocent attitude allowed them to enter the studio without any preconceptions. This made it much easier for us to approach them, and to capture on film what would have been elusive in a businesslike atmosphere.

After years of traveling and experimenting with three prototypes of portable studios, we learned to harness the light we were looking for and ended up with this average equation in photographic terms: a Hasselblad with a 120 mm lens, Kodak Ektachrome 100 ASA film, 1/8th sec. at an aperture of F4. It sounds simple, yet it requires closely controlled light in the cubicle, where the appearance of subtle colors borders on the magical.

Compared with the many-faceted reflections of light that are usually in our field of vision, the gentle and steady light inside the portable studio assumes a serene quality. As in meditation, where the empty mind is the fertile ground for insights beyond the superficial, the contemplative light inside the studio permits the emergence of delicate shades of color that are usually hidden behind a staccato of superfluous secondary images. Poised in this light, the subject seems disengaged from his or her physical surroundings, while a shallow depth of focus that centers on the eyes magnifies a quality that transcends the physical. At once individuality, tribal affiliation, gender, and historical moment become secondary. What stands revealed is the intrinsic, mysterious and enduring beauty that rests in the human heart—the beauty of life itself.

We had ventured out to catch a glimpse of this beauty, and when we returned we were awed by our experience and by the photographs in this book.

JOURNEYS THROUGH TIME Often when you attempt to pinpoint the exact moment that motivated and stimulated your thoughts and activities for a long-term project, you realize that things don't exist in isolation. There is always a thread leading to something else, which lies even farther back. Yet sometimes an inspirational moment, the proverbial falling star, can be grasped. In our case it happened during a starry night in the early 1980s. Pfanni (as Günter Pfannmüller is known to his friends and associates) and I were sitting on the battered platform of a Burmese WWII truck. We had just crossed the Ava Bridge on our way back to Mandalay. After a day of photographing in the Sagaing hills we were in a euphoric mood. Somehow we felt that we were in an exceptional situation.

The country then known as Burma was still off the beaten track, and few foreigners made it beyond Rangoon. General Ne Win's government was not interested in letting travelers disturb his people with whom he had embarked on the 'Burmese Way to Socialism.' A stay of seven days was the longest open to non-diplomatic visitors—not enough time to see more than Pagan and Mandalay. We circumvented this restriction by using two passports each, one set of which was always at the Bangkok embassy. While we left most of our equipment in Burma, every seven days we flew to Thailand for two days. From Thailand we returned to Burma to continue from where we had left off. After having produced the *Insight Guide* on this "forgotten land," we were now collecting material for a coffee-table book. We were entirely fascinated. Even after traveling most of the world, we found Upper Burma exceptional. The influence of history and religion on its people, and the breathtaking landscape throughout which they moved like "dispossessed princes" had caught us unaware.

As so often happened on the way back to the hotel, we were discussing the day's events. The moonlit temples and pagodas mirrored in the tranquil waters of the Irrawaddy danced in front of our eyes. There is a point of saturation when beauty and well-being is insurmountable, and this was such a moment. You wrestle for words—but there are none, and you know that what you caught on film was more than just a sunlit landscape or the image of another human being, it was an intangible sense of spirituality.

What was it that shone through our days, that distinguished these gentle people from those which we had known all our lives? The word that came to mind was dignity, something that had nothing to do with the pride that comes from accomplishments. The dignity we encountered during those weeks in Upper Burma was timeless—a dignity that can only be found where people live in close communion with nature, unaware of and unaffected by the shrill political theater around them.

When asking ourselves how we could catch this timeless essence, the idea of the portable studio came to our mind. Later, at the bar of the old Mandalay Hotel and after a few rum sours shaken with egg whites by Francis, our friendly Indian bartender, Pfanni started to draw the first sketches into his notebook. For nearly a decade we harbored the idea but there were so many other things to do. Then in 1988 there was the bloody military takeover that changed Burma into Myanmar, Rangoon into Yangon, and kept us from returning for a couple of years. It was five years later, in 1993, when we had the rare chance to travel the upper reaches of the Irrawaddy, passing through the defiles north of Mandalay and entering Kachin State, that the idea came up again.

In the meantime, Pfanni had refined the design of the studio, and it was during the autumn of 1993 that the prototype, measuring thirteen-by-twenty-six-by-thirteen feet and weighing less than one hundred and

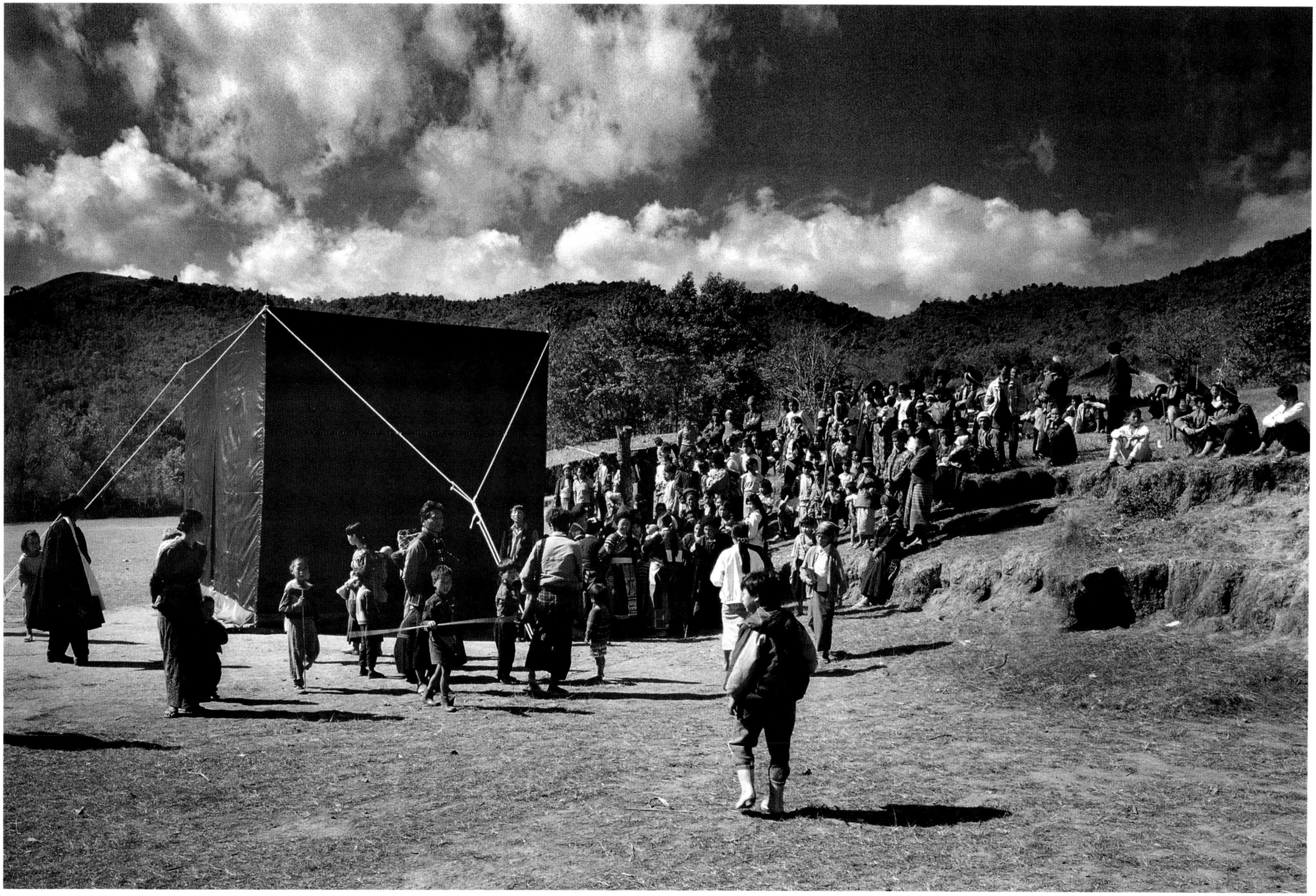

THE PORTABLE STUDIO IN PAIN PYIT, SHAN STATE, MYANMAR.

thirty pounds, was ready. For want of time we had been unable to test the newly designed studio back in Frankfurt, but over the following years we found out the hard way that it would not have mattered much. The climatic conditions in Germany are rather different from those we were about to encounter. Since then we have battled winds that would have converted the tent into a balloon had we not been able to dismantle it instantly. There were unforgettable rain storms that appeared as surprisingly as they disappeared, leaving the tent and us shattered after just a few minutes of heavy downpour. Seasoned by past travels, we were a tested team. Pfanni and I were joined by my wife, Renate, who was to become our camp manager, and by Sabine Seitz, Pfanni's junior partner in his Frankfurt studio, who was organizing the logistics of our endeavor. During each of our field trips we hired local drivers, translators, and handymen, and at times created a team of up to ten people.

STILL AT STAKE: DIGNITY AND HUMAN RIGHTS We asked for permission to go up to Myitkyina and received it. Less than a month after the war there ended, our studio stood on the wide, windswept field where the animistic Manao Festival was taking place for the first time after more than thirty years. We came at the right time, to the right place, and with the right equipment to experience the joyous reunion of the Kachin tribes—a celebration for which they had waited nearly two generations. The Kachin tribes of the Golden Triangle had been cut off from the rest of the world for decades. While jets and Internet communication made the world smaller, the Kachin tribes remained enclosed in the far-off hills of their tribal worlds as if in time capsules.

It was our experience among these people that widened our perspective. We came back once more to Myanmar in 1995 to head for the Sagaing province and the equally remote Shan and Chin Hills. While the Yangon junta was the focus of worldwide criticism due to human rights violations, we were photographing people who had withstood the oppression of the Burmese kings in the past and who seemed to be unaffected by the awful situation that had developed elsewhere in the country. Though the different peace and armistice agreements that pacified the region were more than welcomed by the people we met, from a political point of view the quarrel between the Bamar majority and the hill tribes along the border was far from over.

Our visit coincided with the ripening of the crop, and we sensed their unabashed joy in finally harvesting the golden yield of their paddy fields without fear of outside interference. The serenity and calmness in the *kyaungs* (the Buddhist monasteries) taught us that we were on the right path in our search. In our travels through northern Myanmar, the indescribable faculty in human beings to withstand tyranny and find peace was affirmed.

As we searched for dignity we were also documenting the tribes of the Golden Triangle. The Trans-Salween area was out of reach due to the drug war the Wa tribe was fighting. We had to approach the region through the hills of northern Thailand to photograph tribes that could not be reached from the Myanmar side. Most of these tribes live on windswept hillcrests amid an environment destroyed by decades of slash-and-burn agriculture. They are poor and forgotten by the governments in Bangkok and Yangon, but their poverty is only material. They, like the tribes of northern Myanmar, radiated a humanity hard to come by in any of the big cities.

WHERE HUMANITY EMERGED Over the years of photographing in the hills of Southeast Asia we realized that what we had started rather haphazardly would now have to be systematized, and would have to include similar images from two other distinct human environments: people living in tropical jungles and people living in savannas and deserts.

Consequently, the autumn of that same year brought us to Ethiopia. We came for the Rift Valley, a geological formation with towering mountains, acacia plains dotted with azure lakes, and low-lying, steaming-hot equatorial lowlands.

We went to the Omo, to the north of Lake Turkana. It is the ethnographers' cradle of mankind, where some of the tribes live in even greater seclusion than the hill tribes of the Golden Triangle. Their lives differ little from that of their forebearers thousands of years ago. They are hunters and gatherers and move their homes with the seasons. We started with the Mursi, a tribe that has retained ancient traditions, such as women stretching their lips with clay lip-plates.

With the soldiers of the Mengistu army recently dispersed, their Kalashnikovs cheaply for sale all over the country, and with the clan war in Somalia spilling into Ethiopia's Oromo region, it was a dangerous endeavor. More than once we had to rapidly break camp to avoid the bandits and secessionists who make this region between Sudan, Kenya, and Somalia one of the most insecure in the world.

Yet it was a successful trip, so entirely enjoyable that we left our equipment in Addis Ababa, sure to come back six months later. We did return, and picked up right where we had left off. This time we set up our studio with the Tsemays, the Karos, the Hamers, and the Boranas in Ethiopia, then moved across the border of Kenya to the Samburus, south of Lake Turkana. Despite the rapid technological development in the western world, this border region between Ethiopia and Kenya has seen no change. One could be in a Bronze Age environment, if it were not for the diverse wars at the Horn of Africa and the guns carried by every male older than sixteen. In this semi-desert, the tribes as well, with their huge herds of cattle have not changed, neither in appearance nor in manners. They are true representatives of our pastoral forebearers, and they are perfect examples of people living with dignity and in harmony with their environment.

SHAPED BY THE DESERT While moving with half a ton of equipment across some of the most inhospitable terrain in the world, we often met people who had never seen photographs of themselves. We were most touched by the wise and knowledgeable elders. Their faces were the most expressive, and their dignity seemed to stem directly from their interactions with nature and their perceptions of their place in the order of the universe.

It didn't take long before we realized we had to deepen this aspect of our search, and we knew that it had to be in India. There was a special occasion coming up. It so happened that in November 1998, concurrent with the Pushkar Camel Fair in the Rajasthan desert, there was also the Urs Festival at Ajmer, less then seven-and-a-half miles away. At both, one an auspicious Hindu gathering and one an important Muslim festival, hundreds of thousands of visitors were expected, and in the midst of them holy men from all over northern India.

For fourteen days we were engulfed in the frenzied religious life of India, moving our studio from the camel campgrounds of Pushkar to the heart of the pilgrimage route to Ajmer's Sufi saint, Khwaja Moinuddin Chisti. The following week found us in the solitude of the Rann of Kutch, not more than twenty-four miles from the Pakistan border—a region where the Indian and Pakistani armies are on constant alert. We were moving through northern India's most parched region with a family of nomadic Rabari herders. It was there that the circle closed. While sitting around an open fire with people who as a rule sleep under the stars without tents, Pfanni and I remembered the night under a similar sky when it all started on the platform of a Burmese lorry.

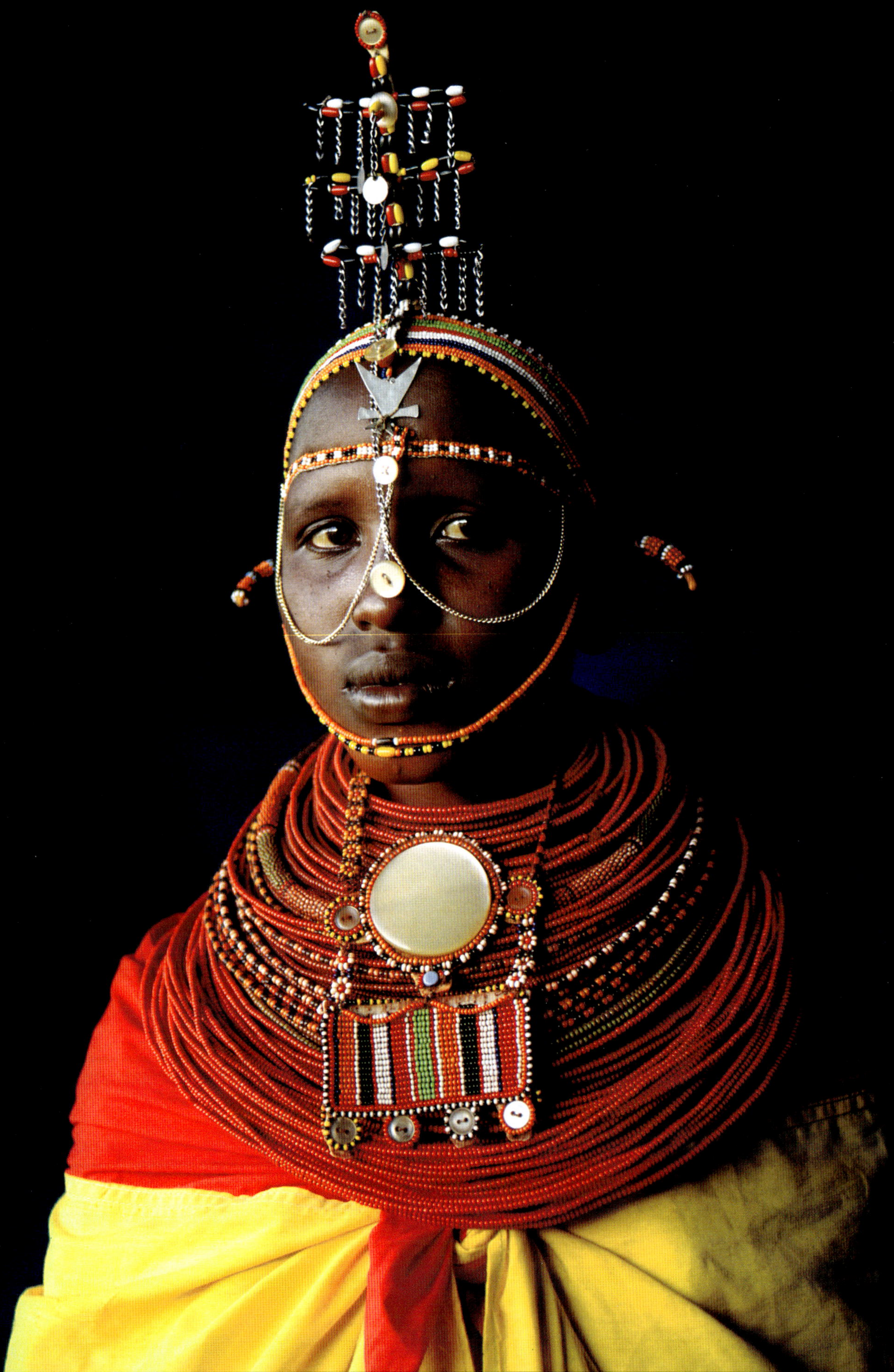

MAGIDA, SIXTEEN, SAMBURU. MARALAL, KENYA.

ROOTS

TRIBES OF THE RIFT VALLEY

Had we been systematic, our quest would have started in Africa. But before 1995 the Horn of Africa, where we expected to find people living as our ancestors did thousands of years ago, was much too unsafe to move in with all our equipment. Though the socialist dictator, Mengistu Haile Mariam, had fled Ethiopia in 1991, the clan war in Somalia swept into the Ogaden and Oromo provinces of Ethiopia, and made traveling in the south and the east of the country extremely perilous. By 1996, however, we were ready to face whatever would happen. Aki Haddis, our contact in Addis Ababa, was optimistic and convinced us it was the right time to go. Some of the drivers of his trekking company had recently been in the Omo region, and pronounced it safe.

Two of them came with us—Getu, a half-Oromo, half Amharic young man who seemed perpetually upbeat, and the older Workayu, who had driven a tank for Mengistu's army during the recent Ogaden war. They knew that this was not to be a nine-to-five job that ended when we reached our destination. They were our mechanics, porters, cooks, translators and watchmen. Of our two Mercedes Jeeps, only one had four-wheel drive; the time we spent pulling each other through knee deep mud and up precipitous trails is legendary. If ever our staying power was tested, it was on this journey. Our two drivers did such a fine job that in hindsight we know that without them we would never have succeeded.

It was later that we had to deal with the odds. We started our journey at a leisurely pace. On the way south from Addis Ababa to Arba Minch we camped at Lake Langano and Lake Abiyata—a Rift Valley fantasyland embedded between mountains that rise in the east to over thirteen thousand feet. For the first few days our trip was more of a luxury safari than a field trip—spaghetti with pesto and a 1989 Barolo for a dinner al fresco, while not sixty yards from our mess thousands of flamingos prepared themselves noisily for the night. An East African sunset did the rest to mesmerize us—anyone who has seen the silhouettes of aging acacia trees against a burning sky knows what we are talking about. We also had the pleasure of staying overnight at Arba Minch. The lodge there, the Bekele, is a jewel. Situated high on a knoll between Lake Abaya and Lake Chamo, it provides a spectacular view of lakes and rolling hills. After a light African shower, the flowers, bushes, and trees started to emit a fragrance that contained all the perfumes of the world; a fragrance that paralyzed the brain. We became totally captivated by this extraordinary sensuous experience. When night fell it was this fragrance rather than the visual imprints that marked the day. A few days later life looked very different. Our cars were stuck on what was more of a rocky animal track than a road. For the first time, and not the last, we had to offload all our equipment and make the cars pull each other up an escarpment before reloading them again. No wonder it took us a week to reach the Omo.

We set out to photograph the Dorse in a place called Chinche, high up in the mountains beyond Arba Minch. After having set up the studio, and before we could earnestly start photographing, we realized that these people were the most unreliable and light-fingered we had so far encountered. We were constantly making sure that none of our indispensable gear was stolen—a terrible experience for Sabine, who felt responsible for over two thousand pieces of equipment.

We had to leave the place quickly. It wasn't that the Dorses were intimidating, they were just too deft at picking up any odd small item and disappearing with it into the crowd. Before we realized it, even the antenna and the rearview mirror of one of the Mercedes had been unscrewed and removed.

We were still too close to civilization. It was time to move on across the Woyto bridge, the needle's eye through which you slip to find yourself three thousand years back in time, onto the other side of the river.

An hour later we found the Tsemays. From out of nowhere they came to the wind-wheel-driven watering hole at Luka. While their cattle drank they exchanged gossip. We had found our people, and our interlude with the Dorses was soon forgotten.

In spite of all the hardships of their pastoral lives, the Tsemays appeared to live in paradisiacal innocence. One of the girls, nine-year-old Insaka Dulo, had just collected some plants and to us, seemed like a symbol of purity and virtue. Koke-Kale, a twenty-one-year-old warrior, indicated his eagerness to be photographed. He had just killed a wild buffalo and therefore was eligible to wear an ostrich feather in his hair. For the first time we were confronted with the narcissism of the East African warriors. Koke-Kale could not lift his eyes from the Polaroid we gave him; it was obvious that he was absorbed with the image of himself. We would see similar scenes again and again with the Karos, the Hamer, and the Samburus. They all loved the Polaroids—and the rearview mirrors of our Jeeps.

That evening a tremendous wind-funnel swept across our camp, missing our tents by just a few odd meters. Had it hit our tents, we would have had to pack up for good. Africa proper was simultaneously welcoming and warning us.

Later, at Jinka, we prepared ourselves for what was to be the most difficult and evasive tribe we expected to encounter—the Mursi. There we also met David Freund, a young Israeli who had just finished his military service and was more or less strolling across East Africa. Since he also wanted to visit the Mursis, we made space for him in one of our cars. He was great company, a bright and intelligent human being with whom we shared our Mursi experiences. When he left us, he walked off across the bush as unperturbed as he came, with his one plastic Evian water bottle sticking out of his tiny knapsack. Six months later, when we were back at the Omo, we heard what had happened to him and realized it could have easily happened to us. He was taken hostage by the Afars and was in their custody for months. Then, one night he escaped and walked stoically for forty-three miles across the desert, was seen once more at a watering hole, and has since disappeared and been declared dead by the authorities.

The Mursis were not where they were supposed to be—their village was deserted. Their spring had dried up and they wanted to avoid the constant harassment by the Bodi, a tribe that lives to the northeast of them. Our guide, a ranger from the Mago National Park who spoke the language of the Mursi, suggested that we drive on for another fifty-six miles toward the Omo river. Somewhere along its shore, he said, we should find them.

It took us fourteen hours to cross the Ngalibong Mountains. Our cars repeatedly sank axle-deep in mud. Together with a Toyota packed with a dozen Mursis, we fought our way along the difficult path. The Mursis kept cutting a new track through the thorn bushes with their bandas while the rest of us were pushing and pulling the cars onto higher ground. By two in the morning, in the light of a full moon, we reached a provisional Mursi settlement on the Omo.

The next morning we set up our studio on the shore high above the crocodile infested river, and for two days we made some of our best photographs ever. Of the tribes in Africa, the Mursi adhere most closely to some of the oldest traditional customs. Women like Nakita Olegole (page 38), still wear huge clay lip-plates and ear-plates, and many of the men still wear body paint instead of clothing (Baikadai Ndunka, page 40).

What started in a good atmosphere began to sour when the Mursis realized that they could be paid for posing and use the money to buy ammunition for their Kalashnikovs. Officially they can own guns, but the trading of bullets is illegal. Soon some Kenyan traders arrived, and deals were done in front of our studio while both parties chewed the intoxicating *qat* leaf. We had experienced the effect of *qat* in Yemen, and it was no different here. By two in the afternoon the quarrels had started and we had to dismantle our studio as fast as we could. Seeing these agitated people brandishing their guns, it was obvious that anything could happen at any moment. But there was no escape. It had been raining the night before, and the only track out of the village was impassable.

When we packed the next day we realized that the red sack containing the films we had used to photograph the Mursis with was gone. It must have been stolen by one of the Mursi women while we were taking the last photographs. There was no long discussion. Again the *qat* started to have its effect on the men, and following the advice of the ranger, despite the condition of the track, we had to make our exit as fast as possible. It was a very grim day.

Six months later we were back in Turmi, a center of the Hamer in the south. At the caravansary were three Israelis. We talked with them about David Freund. They told us what had happened to him, and at the same time gave us a red sack filled with 'the films that the Mursis had stolen from David.' Some of those very photographs are included in this book.

This story unfurled in many unexpected ways. When we left the year before we had offered 500 birr (the currrency in Ethiopia, equivalent to $60 U.S. dollars, or the price of a Kalashnikov rifle), to whoever could come up with the films. We finally paid the money to a man in Jinka who somehow managed to remove the rolls of film from the head of a Mursi woman where they substituted for months as curlers. A month later the Mursis robbed a Scandinavian traveler. They didn't take his camera or anything else, just his films. Inspired by our 500 birr offer, they assumed that films are the most valuable objects a foreigner carries.

After leaving the Mursis via a twelve hour ordeal through a mud track, we stayed a night at the Mago Park. Here we took our first bath since Jinka in the clear water of the Mago River. The next morning we continued to Roussos Camp. Nassos Roussos is a living legend in Ethiopia. He is maybe the last true 'White Hunter' of East Africa, a man straight from a Hemingway novel. Nassos is of Greek descent and together with his American wife, Susan, he runs a hunting and conservation camp on the Omo. After the ordeal with the Mursis, his palisaded encampment with clean bungalows in the shade of huge trees was a sanctuary where we could organize our things and make new plans.

Roussos Camp is not far from the Karo village Kolcho, which lies high up on a cliff three hundred and thirty feet above the Omo. These Kolcho Karos and the Karos from Dus, a village about twelve miles to the north, were the reason we decided to come back six months later. The Karo tribe is in its last generation, with a life-style and culture that will not survive this century. A certain wistfulness lay over this encounter. There are not enough of them to survive as a distinctive tribe; their culture is too vulnerable to withstand outside influences. Their faces sometimes overflowed with happiness and pride, and at times they emanated sadness. Their appearance was like a fin de siècle performance—joy without future and sadness in vain.

We returned via Turmi and the weekly Hamer market. To our western eyes, the Hamer were among the most beautiful people of Southern Ethiopia; a tribe with huge herds of cattle, aggressive young warriors, and confident young women.

We returned to Ethiopia in May 1996 to the news that Workayu, our reliable 'tank-driving' companion, had just died of an unknown fever. While mourning at the loss of our friend, we soon found out that Sirak who took his place was equally fit for the job. We continued photographing the gentle Karos with their graffiti-like body paintings, and the ferocious-looking Hamer warriors with their exemplary spirit of freedom. These were some of the best times we spent in Africa. The people we photographed came as close as possible to the idea we had envisioned. Old Karo warriors like Dore Lale (page 31), Bori Gadi (page 25), and young women like Gao (page 26), or Marija (page 32), were outstanding examples of human beings who left intense imprints on both our films and in our minds.

We followed the Hamer tribesmen and their huge cattle herds into the savanna, where we photographed them in their awesome environment. In spite of their fierce appearance they turned out to be gentle and hospitable people. When they move across the wide plain they carry with them only a loincloth, a cowhide for cover, a stick, a Kalashnikov, a calabash, and a little wooden headrest. One gets a sense that they would not trade in their spirit of freedom and sense of being alive for any other lifestyle.

We left Susan and Nassos with much regret and continued eastward along dried-out riverbeds and tracks where no one had driven since before the last rainy season. We were warned about the dangers; this stretch of land is where all the contraband from Kenya moves through, and the people we would meet there would probably be following self-made laws. We realized this when we arrived in Yarbello. Our passé-partout papers issued by the Ministry of Information in Addis were of no use. For what we wanted to do we needed additional confirmation from the Council of the Oromo People, which was going to convene in a few days.

Groups of bandits and a renegade fraction of the Oromo Liberation Front were moving across the country, and we were repeatedly informed about the cars they had robbed on the main road to Kenya. Finally we were

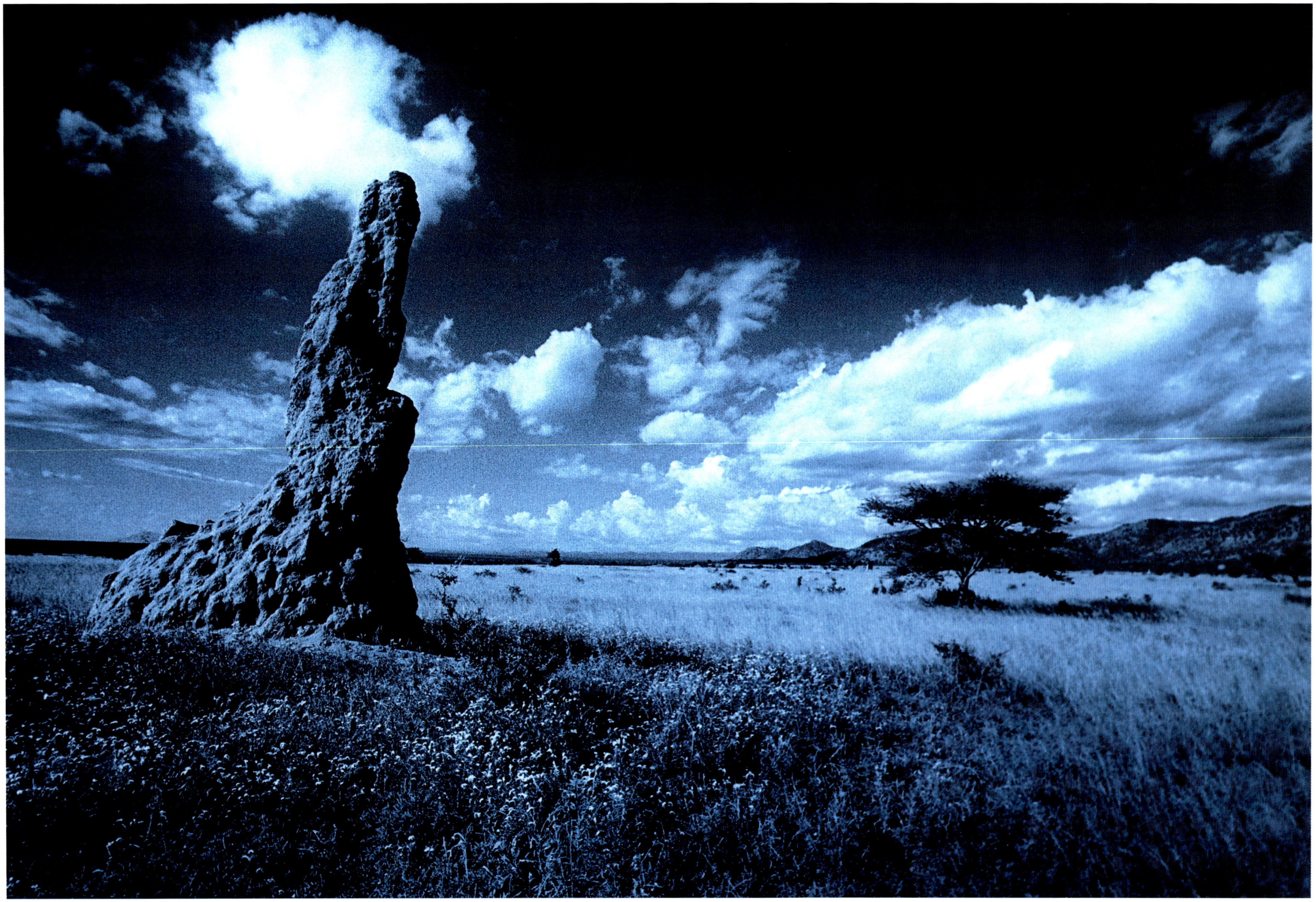

SAVANNA ALONG THE OMO RIVER, THE CRADLE OF MANKIND, ETHIOPIA.

able to leave Yarbello after getting permission to set up our studio in an unused storage camp of the Care organization, deep in the Boranas' country near Dubuluk. Our timing proved to be ideal in that the next morning a bomb exploded on Yarbello's main road not far from our 'hoteele,' killing a handful of innocent market visitors.

Except for an old watchman, the Care camp was vacant and we were obliged to bring our own security staff along. We hired Antana and Jatani, two armed militiamen in Yarbello, and had to buy their daily rations of *qat* as part of their official salary. Though our guards were armed with submachine guns, we were all in agreement that in the case of an incident we would not want them to resist.

Once again we hired a well-regarded local as liaison and translator. In Cheru we had found a Borana who spoke English, so we were not dependent on Amharic as an intermediate language. He was well-respected and made it easy for us to interact with the otherwise unapproachable Boranas. During the long evenings around the campfire he acquainted us with the finer ceremonial details of a Borana's life and told us long stories of his clan.

We photographed the Boranas in their villages (at Dabasa Wario, page 45), and at the camp (page 44), but after a week our situation was similar to our experience with the Mursis the year before. We had to leave as fast as possible, not because of the Boranas, but because after hearing rumors that the OLF (Oromo Liberation Front) was in the vicinity, our two militiamen left us on short notice.

We hurried on to the Kenyan border. After learning how to expedite the process from the truck drivers, we crossed within twenty-four hours. Once again, the situation in North Kenya was similar to that in Southern Ethiopia. The main road south could only be negotiated in a convoy and with a military escort. We also learned that there were tribal skirmishes going on between the Turkanas and the Samburus along the southern shore of Lake Turkana, our next destination. Therefore we spontaneously opted to continue to Maralal, the informal center of the Samburus. It took us another three days of driving over washboard roads, but it was worth it.

The Samburus are herders and follow patterns of life similar to the Hamer and the Masai. There, too, it is their young and proud warriors, the *morans*, who give color to their tribal customs. Since the Kenyan government has more control over their outback than the Ethiopian government, there are no visible handguns. As in the old days, the warriors are still armed with spears.

We set up our base at the Yare Camp at the outskirts of Maralal. The camp is run by a Scot, Malcolm Gascoigne—a figure as well known in northern Kenya as Nassos Roussos is in Ethiopia. Malcolm acquainted us with Stephen, a Samburu *moran* who spoke good English. Stephen arranged a conference with the elders of his clan. We had arrived at the end of the eight-year tenure of this generation of *morans*. They were more than willing to be photographed in their *moran* splendor (pages 46 through 49), a tradition which they would soon have to give up when they marry and become householders, the colorless elders of the clan.

The Samburus were the last tribe we wanted to photograph before ending our trip at Nairobi. There was no hurry, and with Malcolm and Stephen's help we were soon accomplishing our goal. Stephen's *moran* peers, Koynante, Lgolunyi, and Topia, all acknowledged lion killers, showed up at the studio (page 48), along with the young women, Naidasha, Sitimi, and Matanet (page 50). When stepping into our studio, these people seemed to have just stepped out of a mythical past.

After days of photographing we spent delightful evenings in their company around the open fire listening to firsthand stories of lions killed with just a spear, endless treks with cattle over parched land, and searches for water holes while surviving on a mixture of blood and urine. Listening to them talk was like hearing voices from the past. And now, sometimes, when looking at the photographs, it is like looking across time into the faces of our ancestors.

Traveling through East Africa, from Addis Ababa to Nairobi, moving off the main highway from one tribe to the next, is still like time-traveling. It is a journey into the world of the hunters and gatherers, pastoralists, and nomadic farmers. Political difficulties, rough traveling conditions, and a smack of danger keep out those who travel only in comfort. The others, however, will find along the Rift Valley what cannot be found in this intensity, variety, and beauty anywhere else in the world.

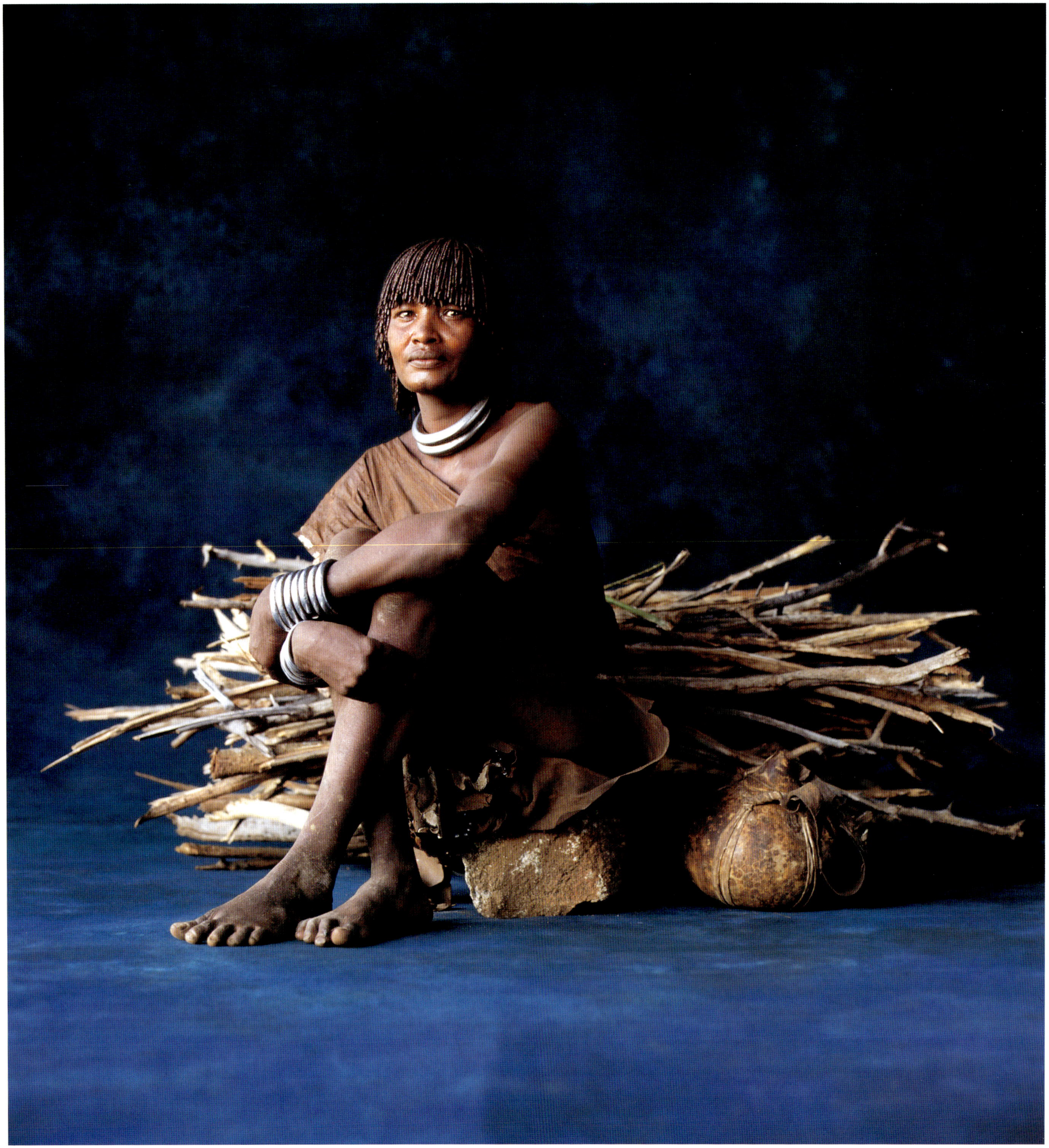

MARLE LUNGO,
TWENTY-NINE, HAMER.
TURMI, ETHIOPIA.

Marle Lungo came to the Turmi market with a huge bundle of firewood she had collected in the bush. She will use it to barter or, if she's lucky, to get hold of a few birr (the Ethiopian currency).

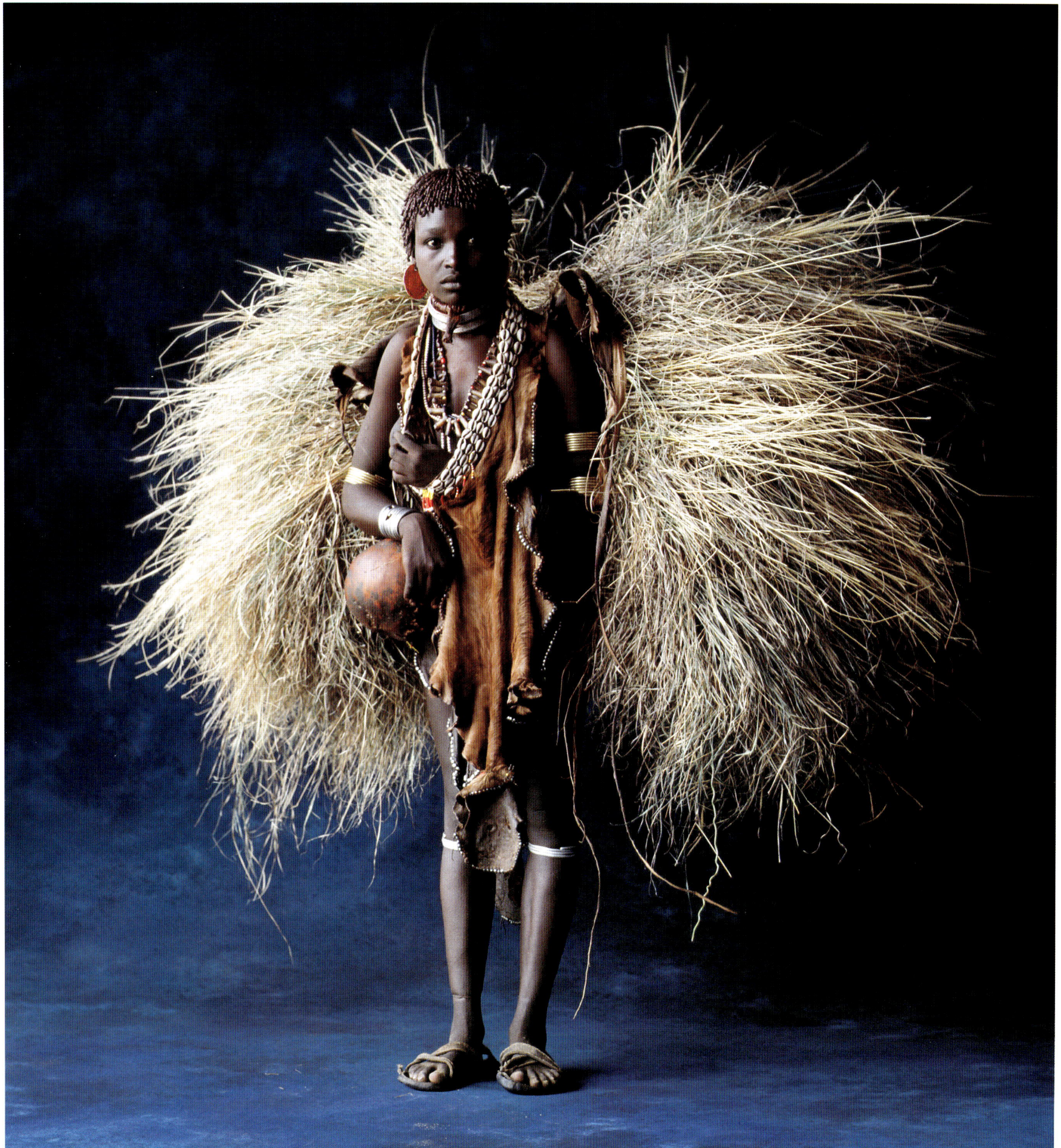

ALO MANA,
TWENTY-FIVE, HAMER.
TURMI, ETHIOPIA.

Alo Mana arrived at the Turmi market with a huge load of dried grass to exchange for a few necessities she can only get at Turmi. There is no other market for more than sixty miles.

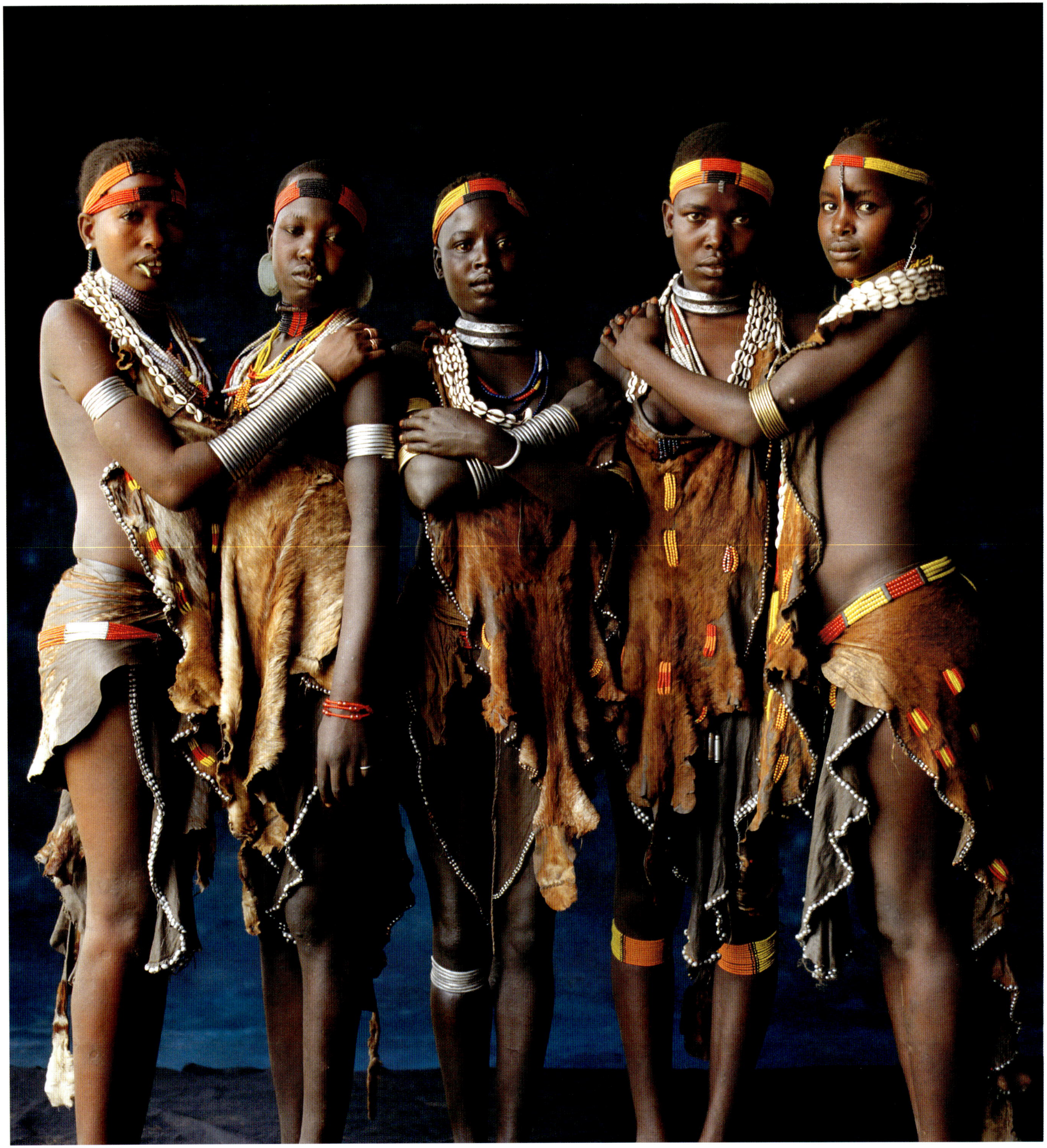

LEFT TO RIGHT:
BUNA, SIXTEEN; GABUSCHE, SEVENTEEN; SHOSHO, SEVENTEEN; AILO, SIXTEEN; AND LISO, FOURTEEN; HAMER. TURMI, ETHIOPIA.

Buna, Gabusche, Shosho, Ailo, and Liso are unmarried. It takes many hours to walk across the bush that encloses Turmi, but going to the market is a welcome opportunity to meet others.

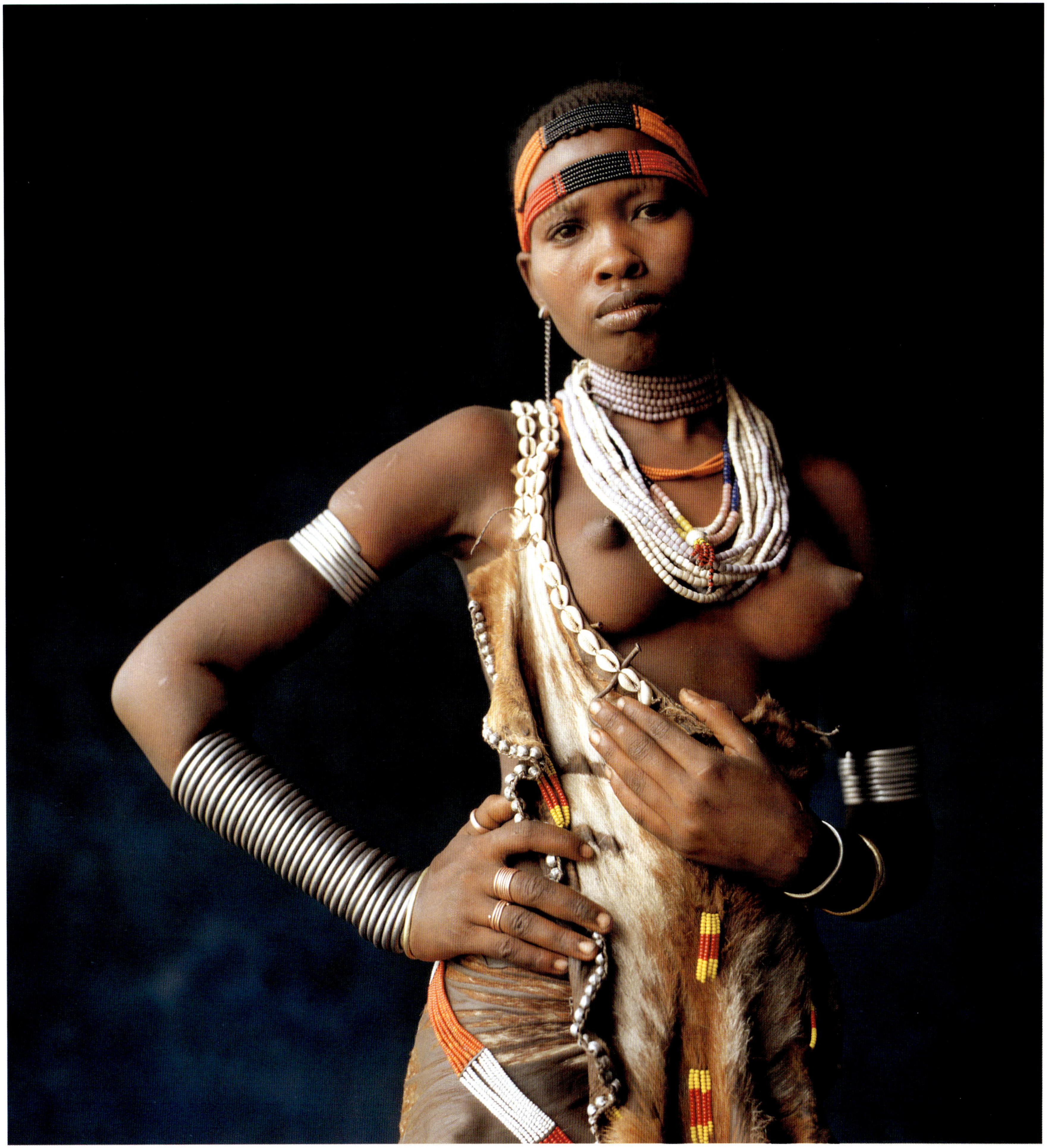

BUNA, SIXTEEN, HAMER.
TURMI, ETHIOPIA.

For Buna, as for other women in the remote tribal region of southwestern Ethiopia, it is natural to be bare-breasted. The many bracelets and necklaces women wear signify that they come from a wealthy clan with many cattle.

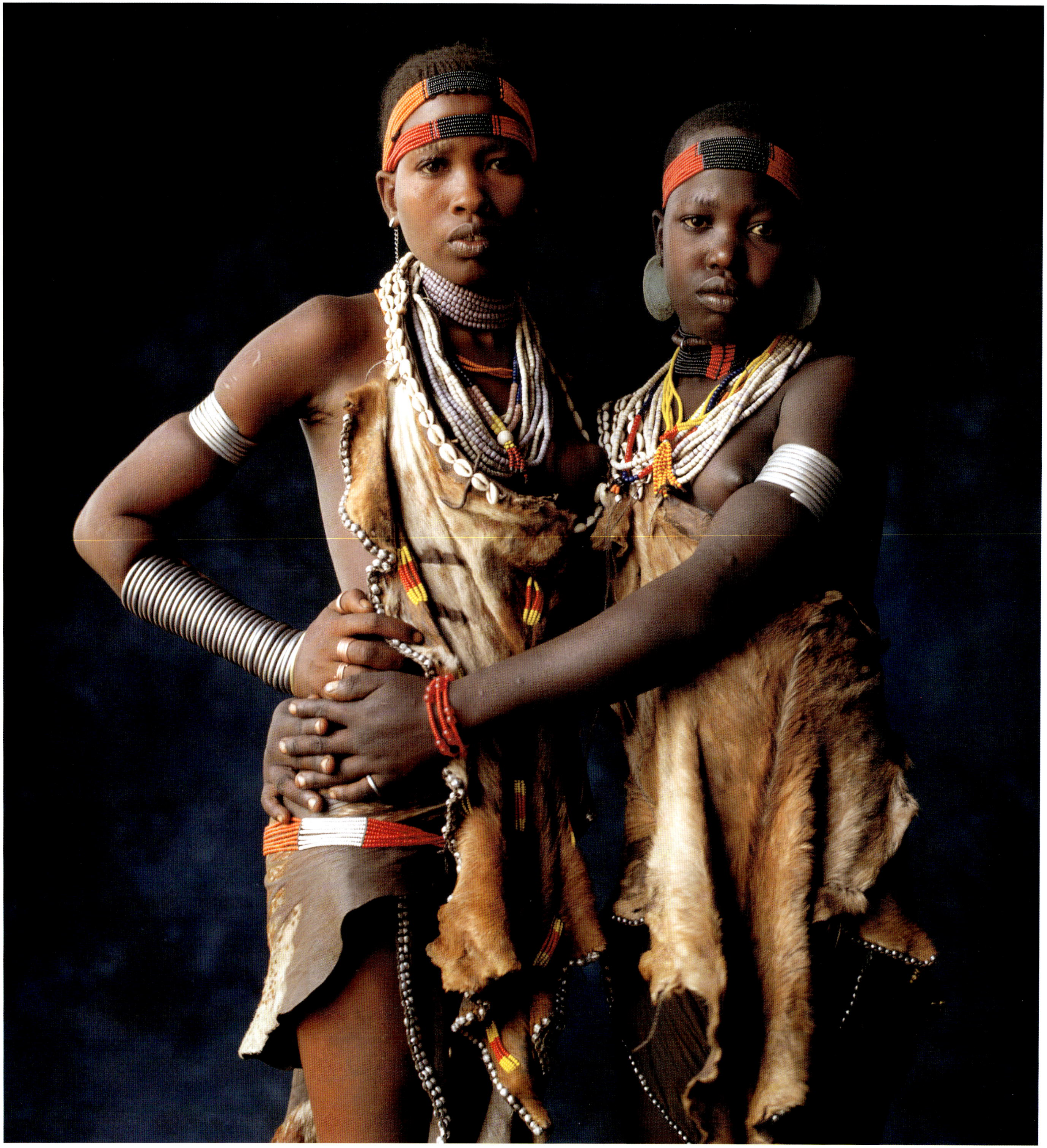

BUNA, SIXTEEN, GABUSCHE, SEVENTEEN, HAMER. TURMI, ETHIOPIA.

Buna and Gabusche were two of the dozens of young Hamer women who came to the Monday market at Turmi. Turmi is a village with one road, one tree, a police station, and a few caravansaries. Coming from their nomadic encampments in the savanna, these young women consider the trip to Turmi a visit to the "big city."

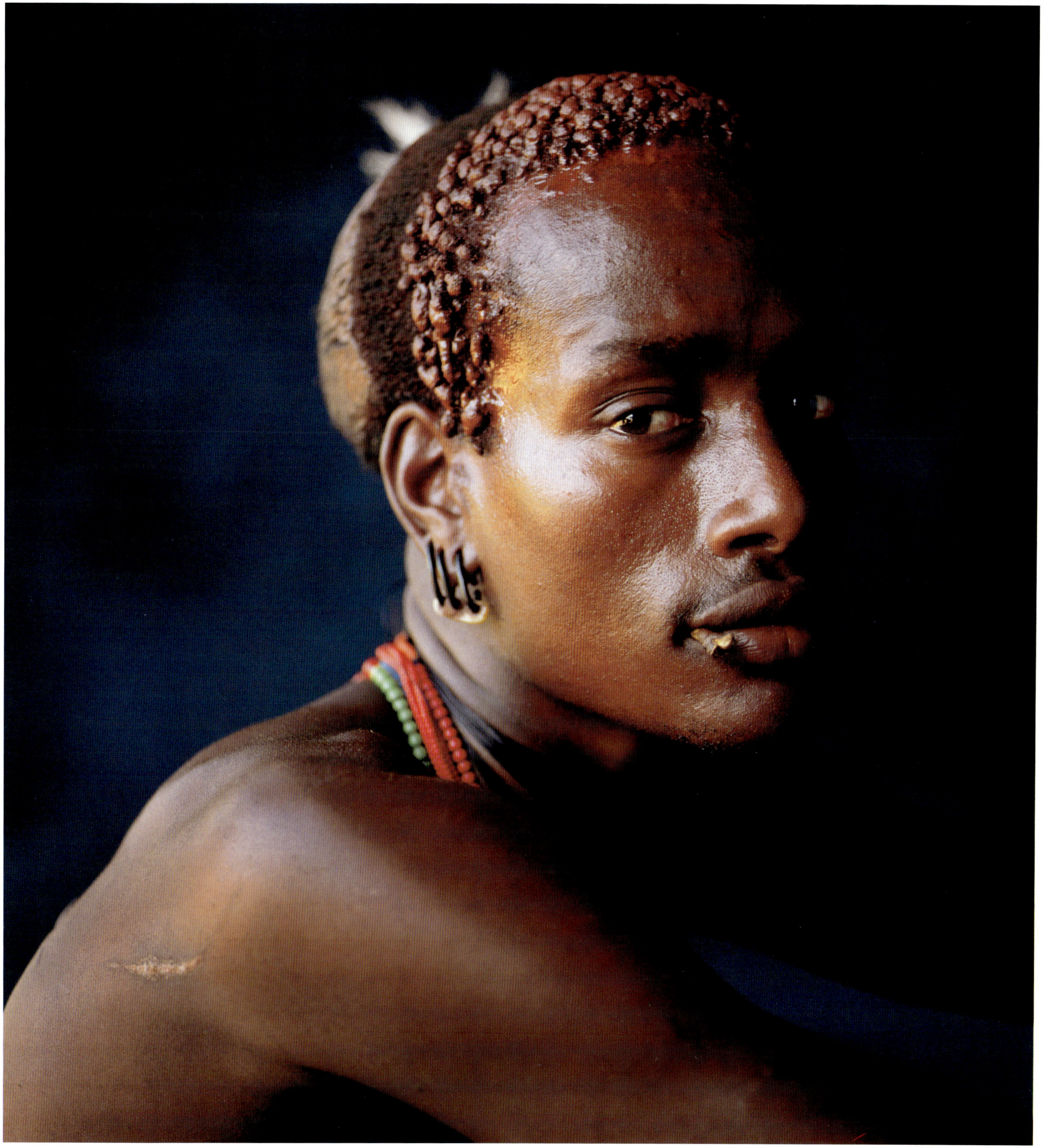

TAGASHU COLI,
TWENTY-THREE, HAMER.
TURMI, ETHIOPIA.

Tagashu Coli is a Hamer cattle herder. Like most of his peers, he spends his time with the cattle in the savanna. When out with the herd, he carries a calabash for water, a stick, a small wooden stool (which doubles as a headrest), and a cowhide to protect him from the rain. He is chewing on a piece of wood with medicinal properties that keep his teeth and gums healthy.

BORI GADI, SIXTY, HUNTER, KARO. ROUSSOS CAMP, ETHIOPIA.

Bori Gadi is one of the elders of the small Karo tribe. The Karos are settled in villages along the Omo. They plant some crops on the steep embankment of the river. They exchange their crops for milk, blood, and meat with the Hamer tribe, with whom they share the land peacefully.

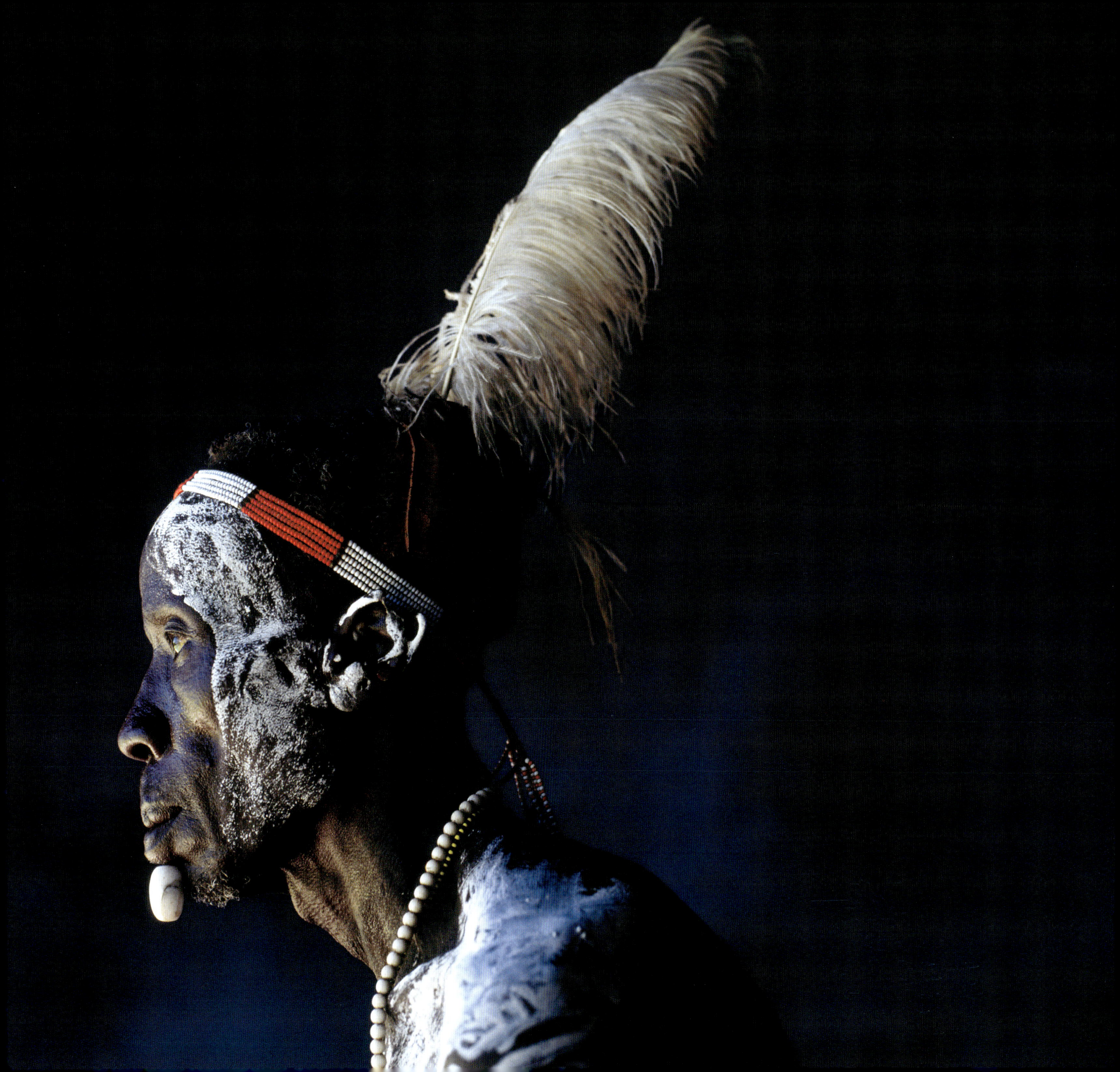

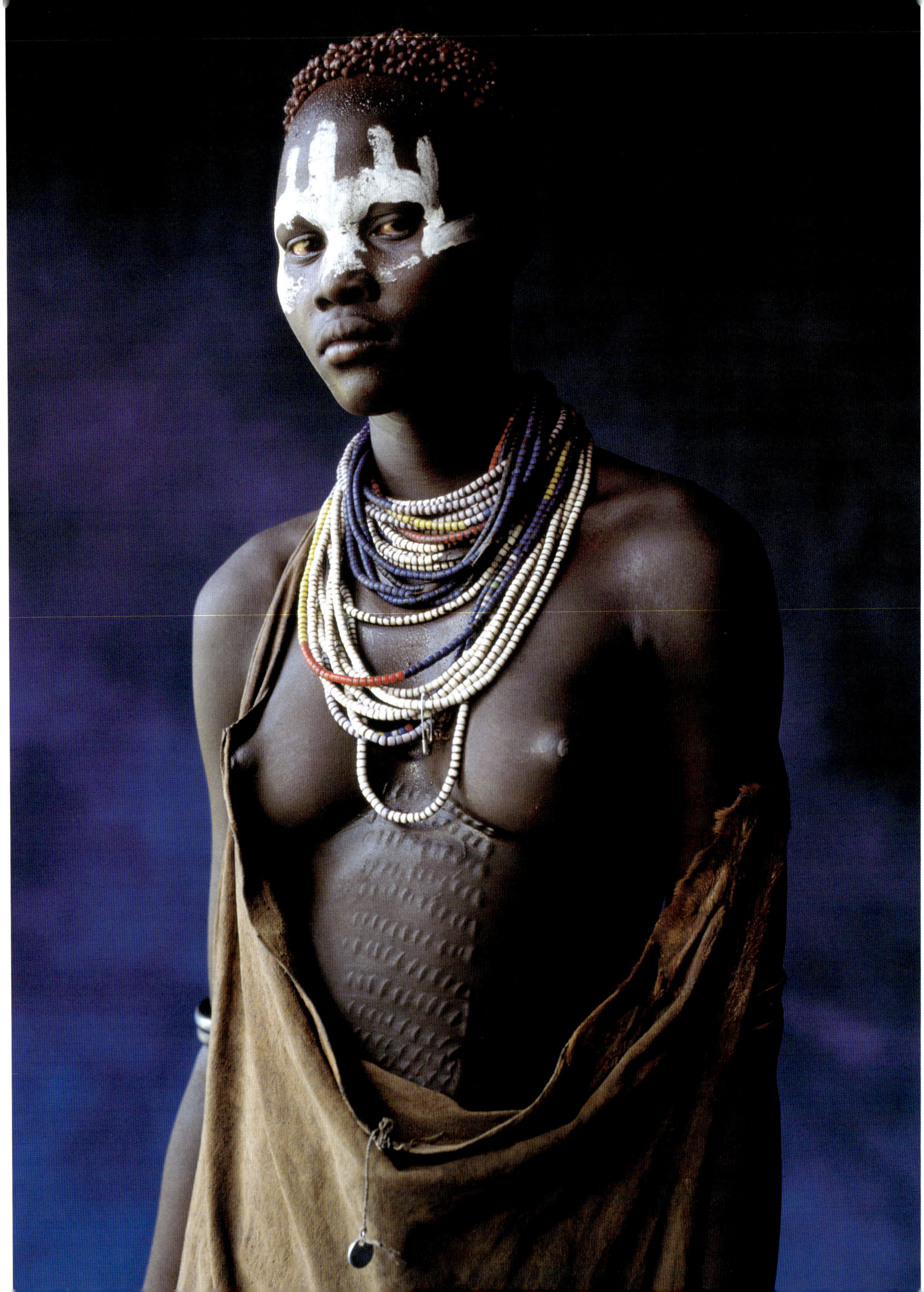

GAO, SEVENTEEN, KARO.
DUS, ETHIOPIA.

Gao lives in the small Karo village of Dus. The Karo tribe is near extinction, with fewer than four thousand tribe members left. They live along the Omo River, growing sorghum, which they then use for barter with the Hamer herders.

OPPOSITE: MUNTE, TWENTY-TWO, AND GAO, SEVENTEEN, KARO. ROUSSOS CAMP, ETHIOPIA.

Munte and Gao use paint to decorate their bodies. A simple iron nail is inserted through a permanent hole to adorn the lower lip.

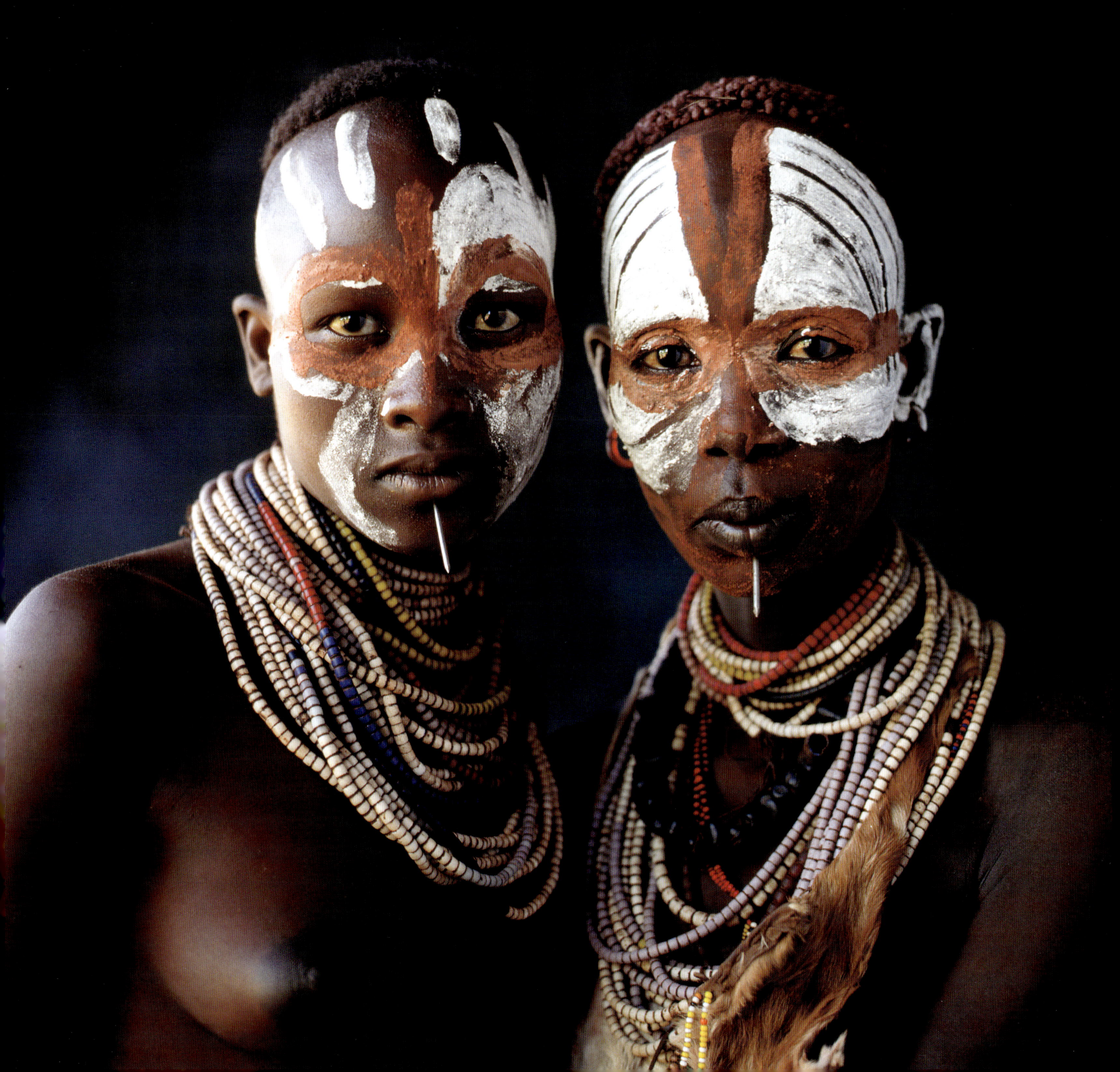

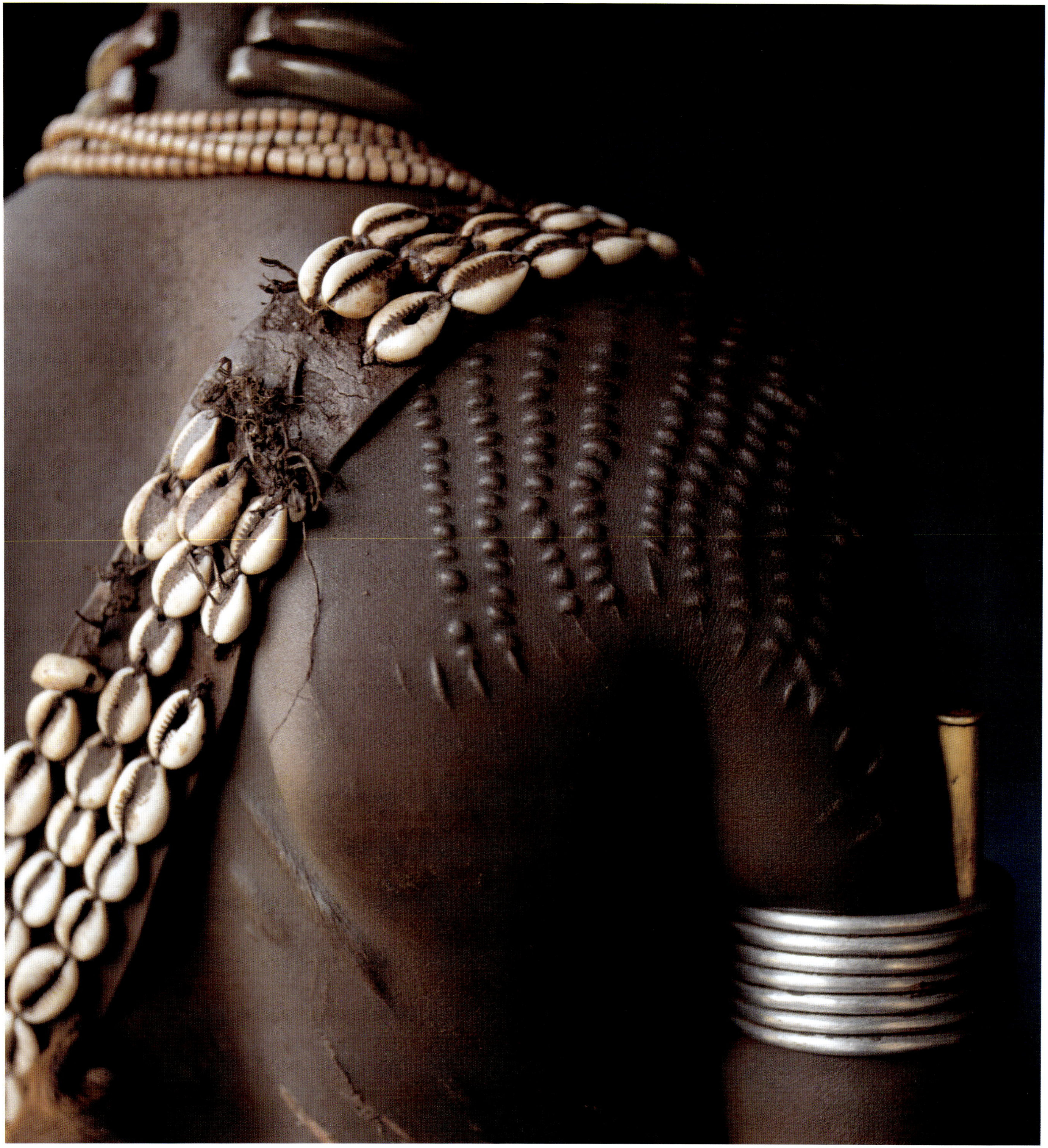

BEREGI, FIFTEEN, HAMER. TURMI, ETHIOPIA.

Beregi's body is decorated here in the typical fashion of Hamer women. The painful body decoration was applied by her older brother; it is proof of her ability to endure pain in her initiation into womanhood.

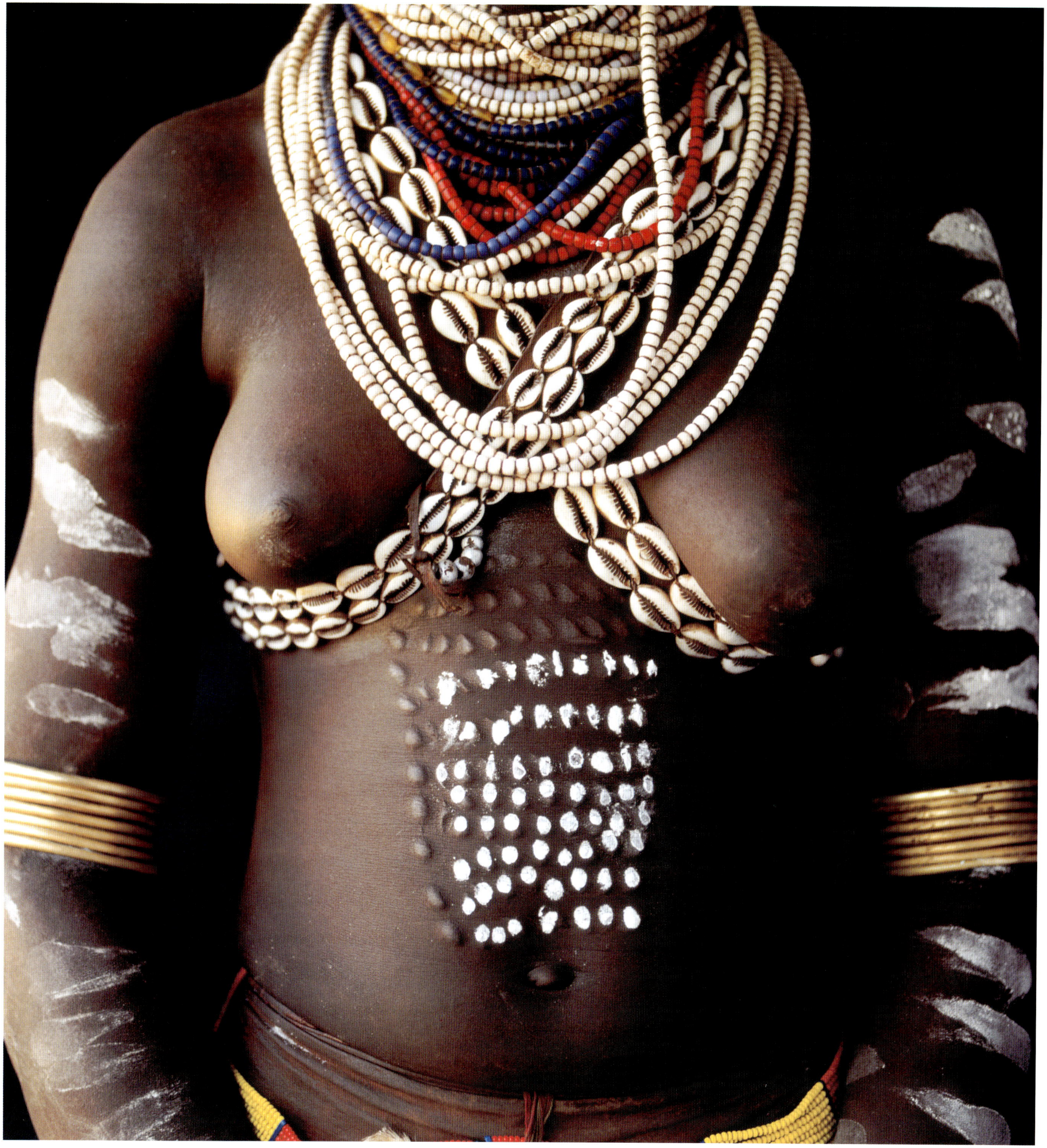

BUNU, FIFTEEN,
KARO. ROUSSOUS CAMP,
ETHIOPIA.

Bunu has small shells inserted into her skin at the solar plexus. This is seen as both a sign of how much pain she can endure and a beautification of the body.

WHEN A TRIBE DISAPPEARS FROM THE FACE OF THE EARTH, IT IS MORE THAN THE DISAPPEARANCE OF AN ENDANGERED CULTURE. THEIR PEOPLE WILL LIVE ON BIOLOGICALLY, BUT SOMETHING ELSE WILL HAVE VANISHED, AN ENTITY THAT IS AS EPHEMERAL AS AN IDEA, FLEETING AS THE FRAGRANCE OF A FLOWER. IT IS THE END OF A DANCE PERFORMANCE ON AN EVER CHANGING STAGE.

DORE LALE, FIFTY, KARO, HUNTER. ROUSSOS CAMP, ETHIOPIA.

The face of Dore Lale reflects the situation of his tribe. There is a sadness in the face of the elders that speaks to the decline of their tribal culture. Only the young are still enthusiastic and confident; the elders see no future for the Karo.

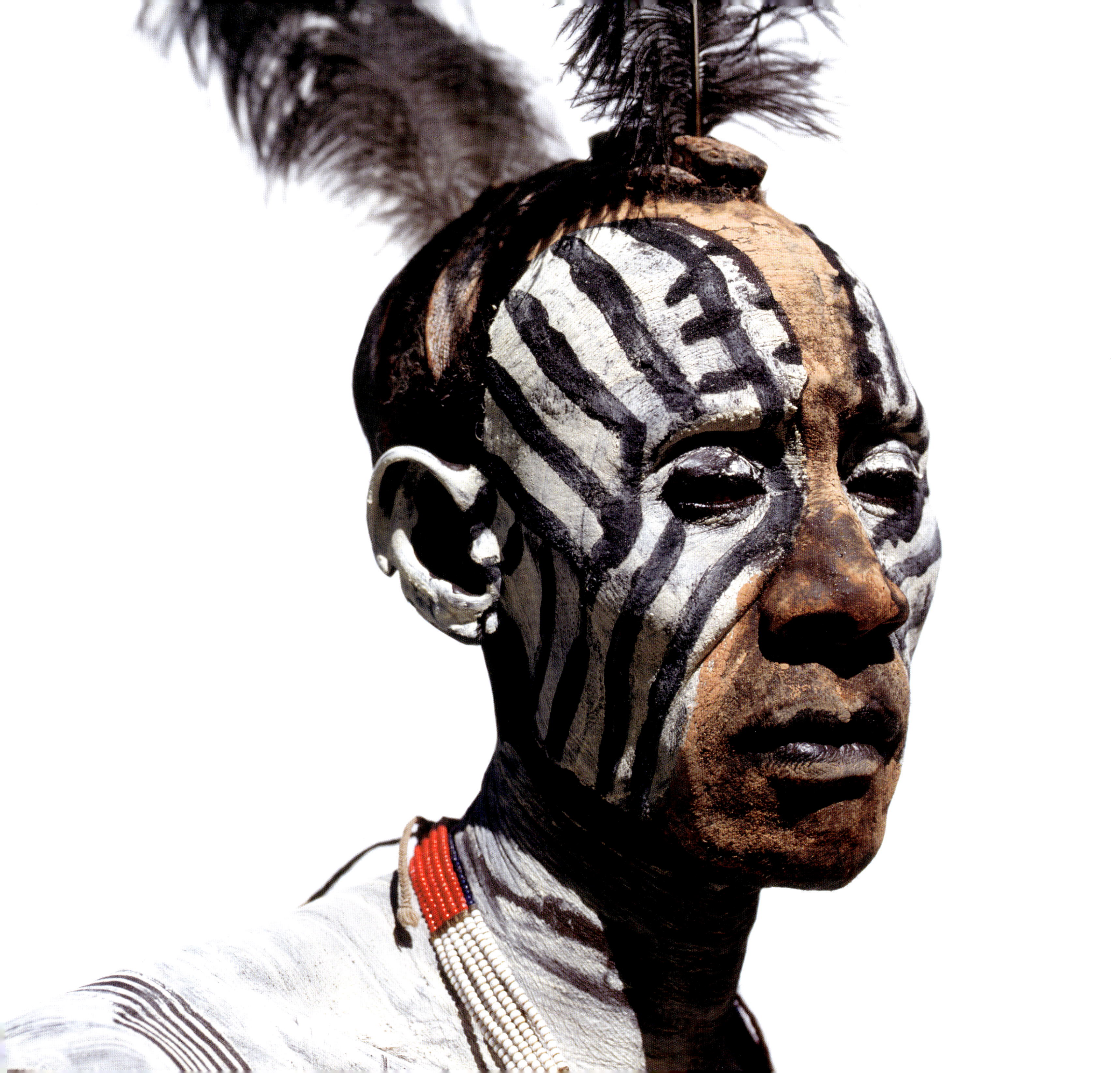

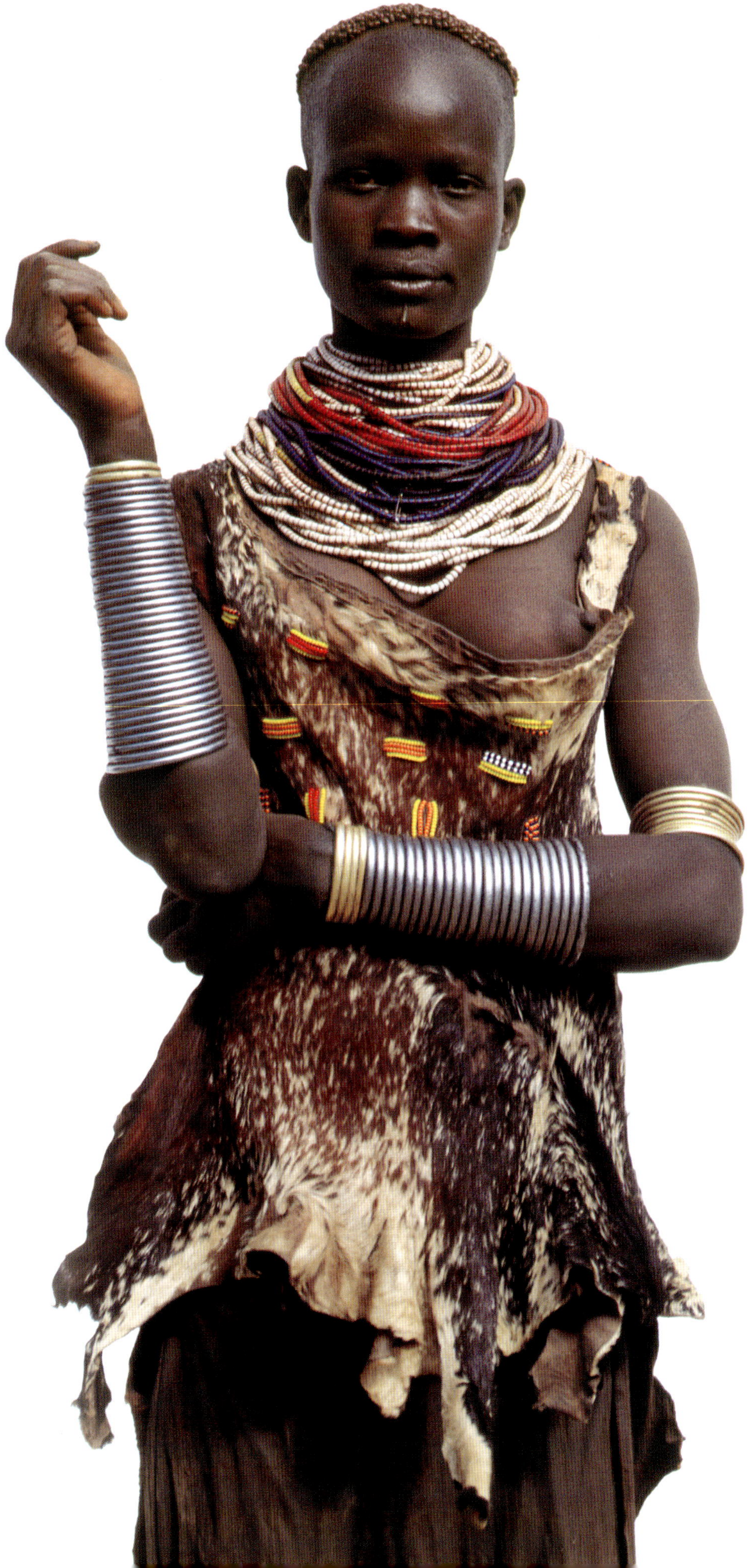

MARIJA, TWENTY-THREE, KARO. ROUSSOS CAMP, ETHIOPIA.

Marija, who is not yet married, is dressed like her peers, in a sheepskin and a variety of necklaces and bracelets. Most young married women we saw in the Karo villages were pregnant or had just borne a child.

OPPOSITE, LEFT TO RIGHT: DINA, EIGHTEEN; DULU, THIRTY; KOPINI, THIRTY; GURMARE, TWENTY-FIVE; AND OKADA, THIRTY-FIVE; HAMER, HERDERS. NEAR KOLCHO, ETHIOPIA.

We met Dina, Dulu, Kopini, Gurmare, and Okada as they were moving through the savanna with a herd of a few hundred cattle. It is the duty of the young men to stay with the herd. Okada and Guame were already full-fledged warriors, having gone through the tribe's "cattle jump" initiation, in which young Hamer men prove their strength and agility.

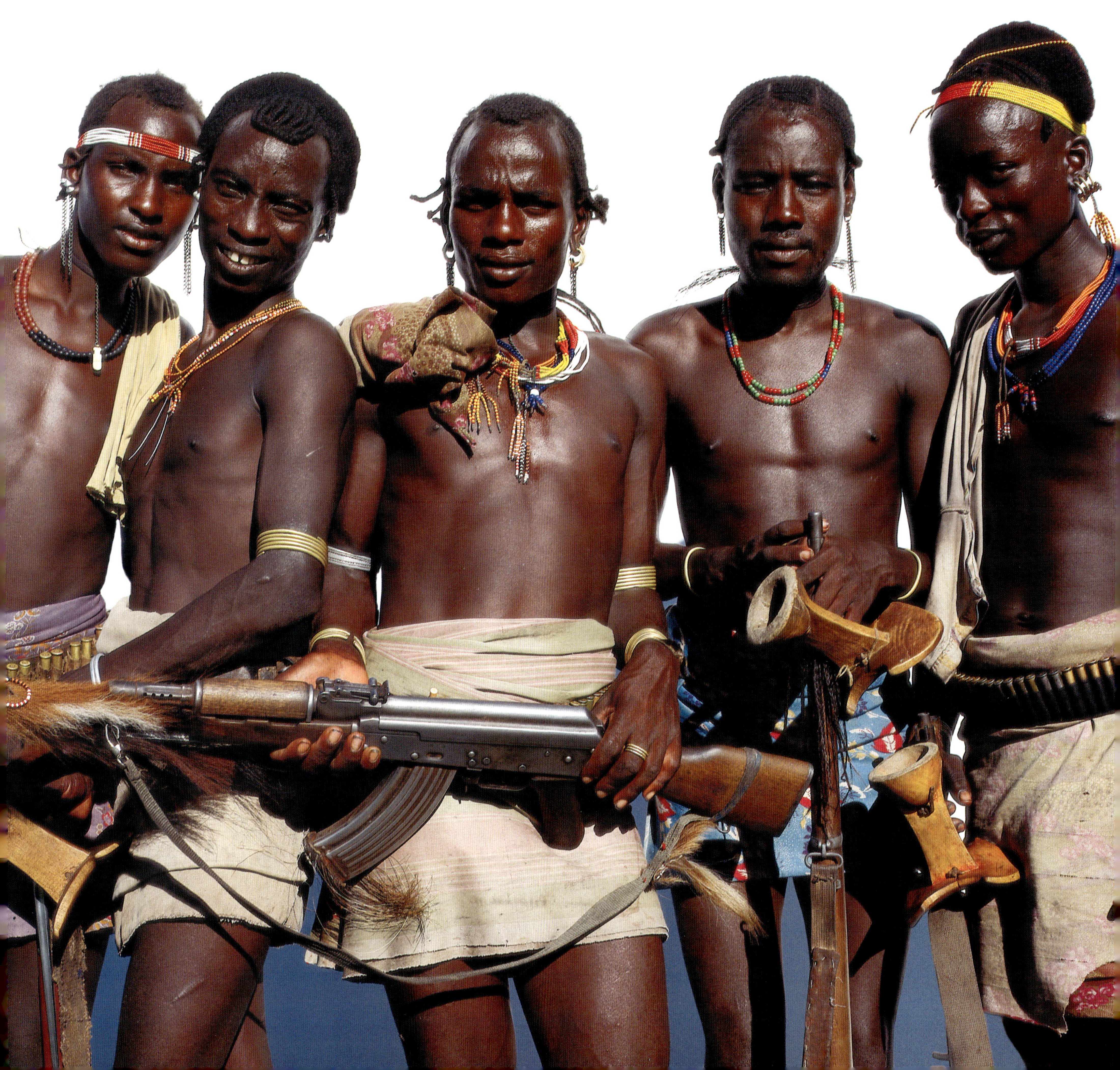

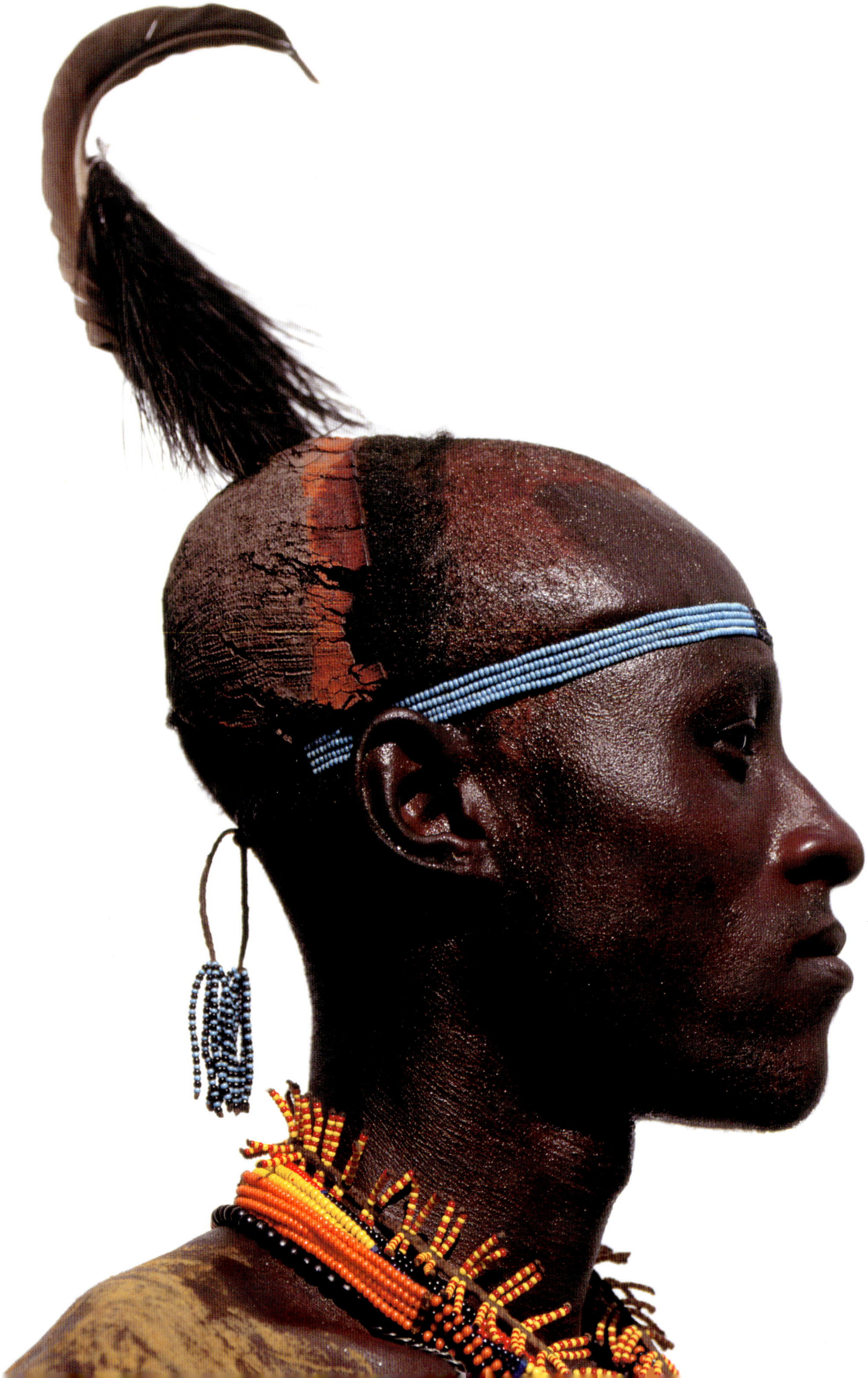

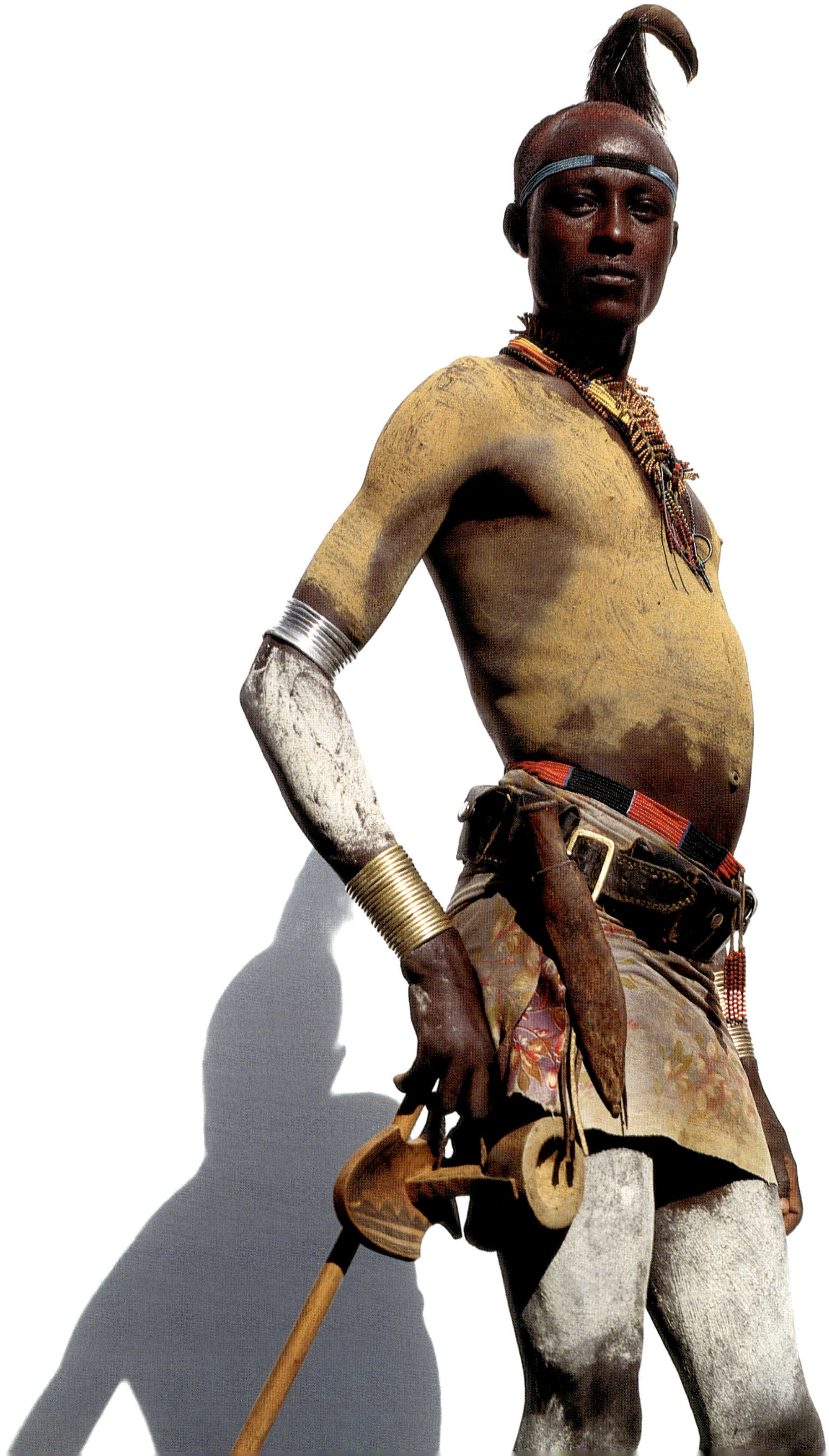

OPPOSITE AND THIS PAGE:
LALE AREDA, THIRTY-FIVE,
KARO, FARMER AND HUNTER.
KOLCHO, ETHIOPIA.

Lale Areda is fully dressed for the day. The color on his body is an adornment, yet it also protects him from the mosquitoes and the raging sun. He is ready to leave for the endless grasslands that surround his village. The Karo rarely hunt with a spear, as guns are readily available. As a result, the younger generation has not acquired the traditional hunting skills of their fathers.

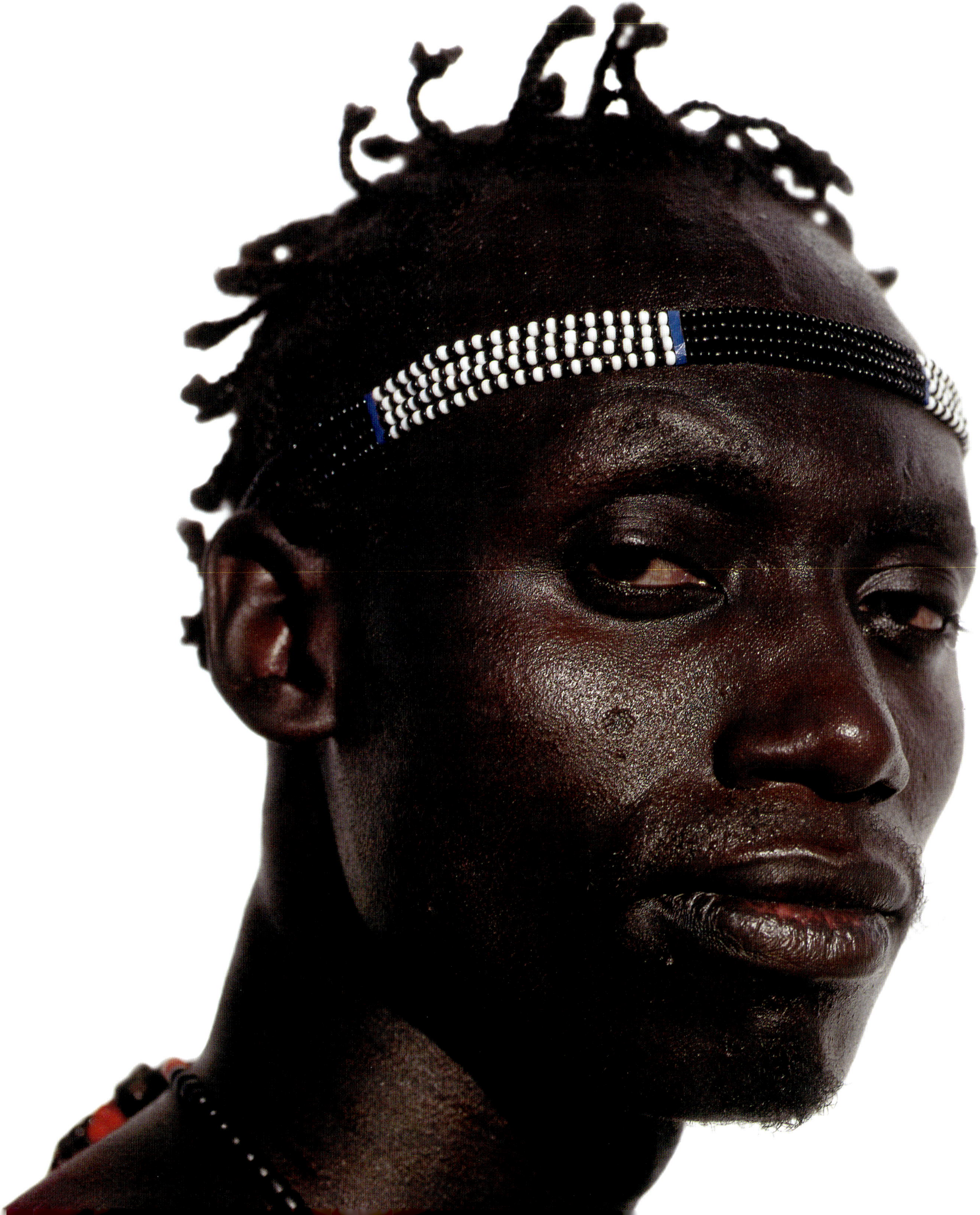

A MAN'S FACE AS A RULE SAYS MORE, AND MORE INTERESTING THINGS, THAN HIS MOUTH, FOR IT IS A COMPENDIUM OF EVERYTHING HIS MOUTH WILL EVER SAY, IN THAT IT IS THE MONOGRAM OF ALL HIS THOUGHTS AND ASPIRATIONS.

—ARTHUR SCHOPENHAUER

AJA, TWENTY-TWO, KARO.
KOLCHO, ETHIOPIA.

Aja joined the Ethiopian army in order to escape the seclusion of his remote village. When he returned, he could not adapt to the slow-moving pace of village life. When we left, he begged us to take him to the main north-south road. He wanted to hike to Addis Ababa.

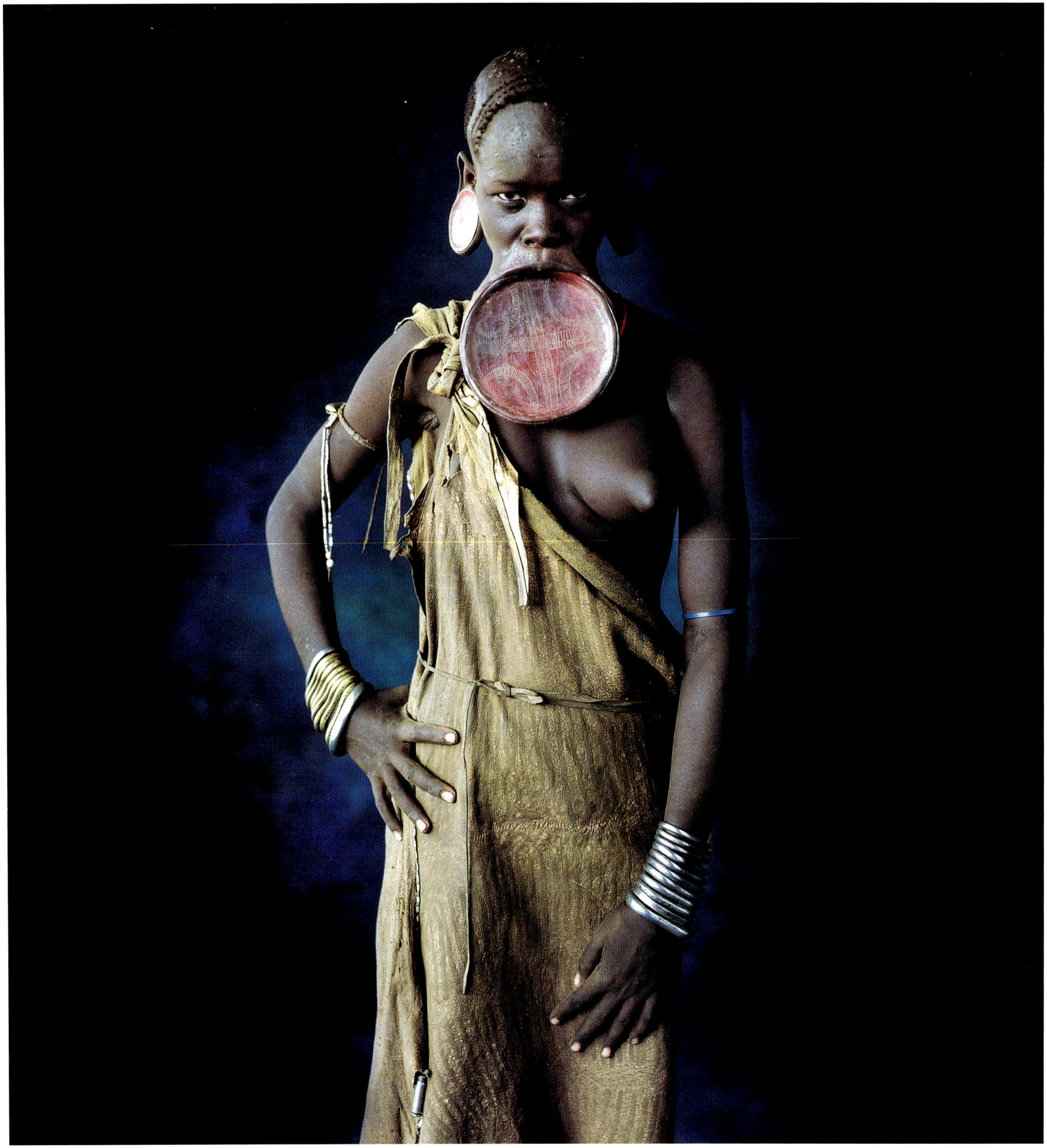

NAKITA OLEGOLE,
SEVENTEEN, MURSI.
MAKARO, ETHIOPIA.

Mursi women wear huge clay plates in their lower lips. When they are young, the lip is slit open; as they grow older, gradually larger and larger clay plates are inserted. Mursi men and women consider large lip-plates an enhancement to a woman's beauty.

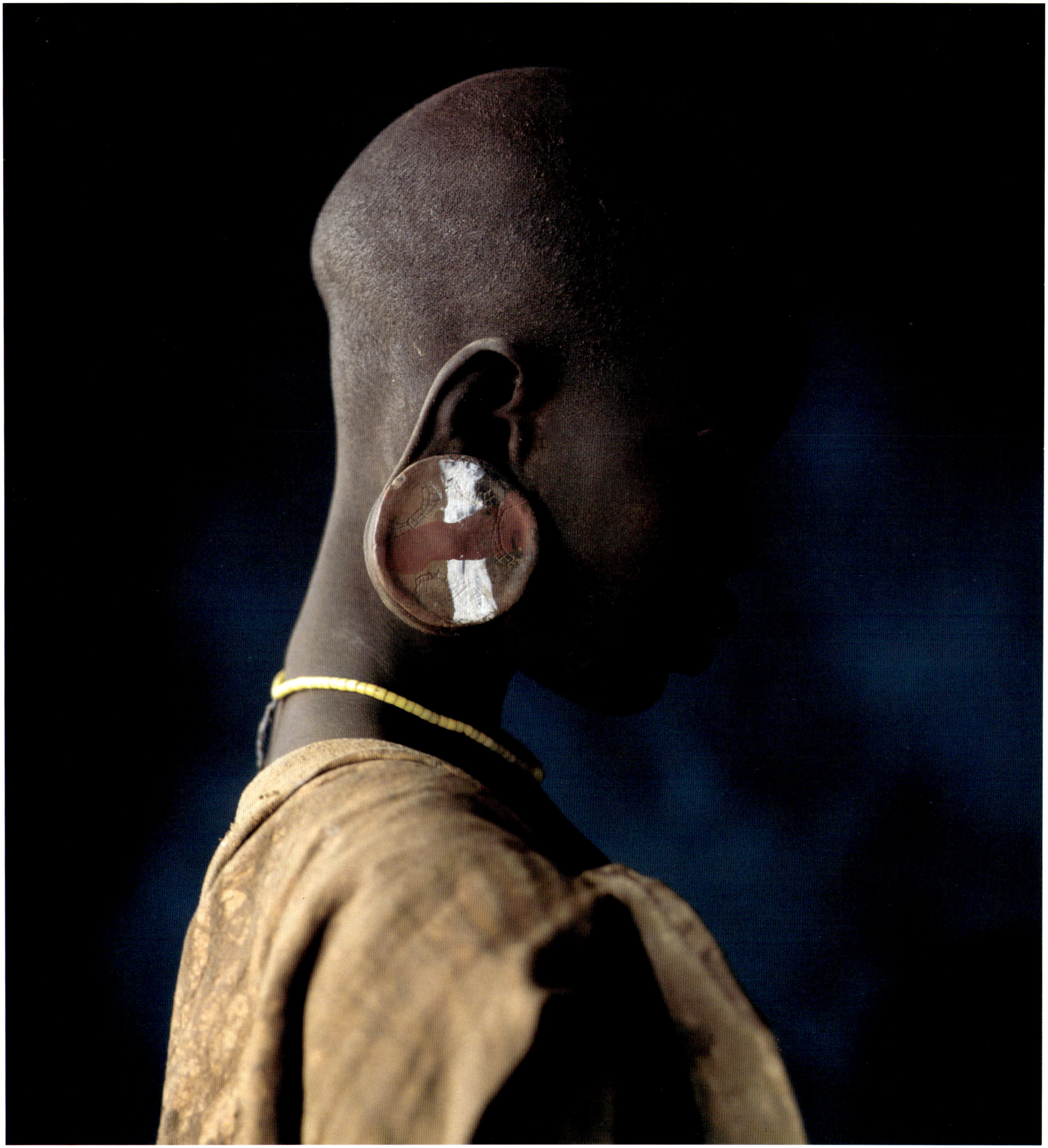

NABOKE, FIFTEEN, MURSI.
MAKARO, ETHIOPIA.

Mursi women also prize huge clay ear-plates, inserted into a slit in the earlobes when they are little girls. Gradually larger plates are inserted until they reach a diameter of up to four inches.

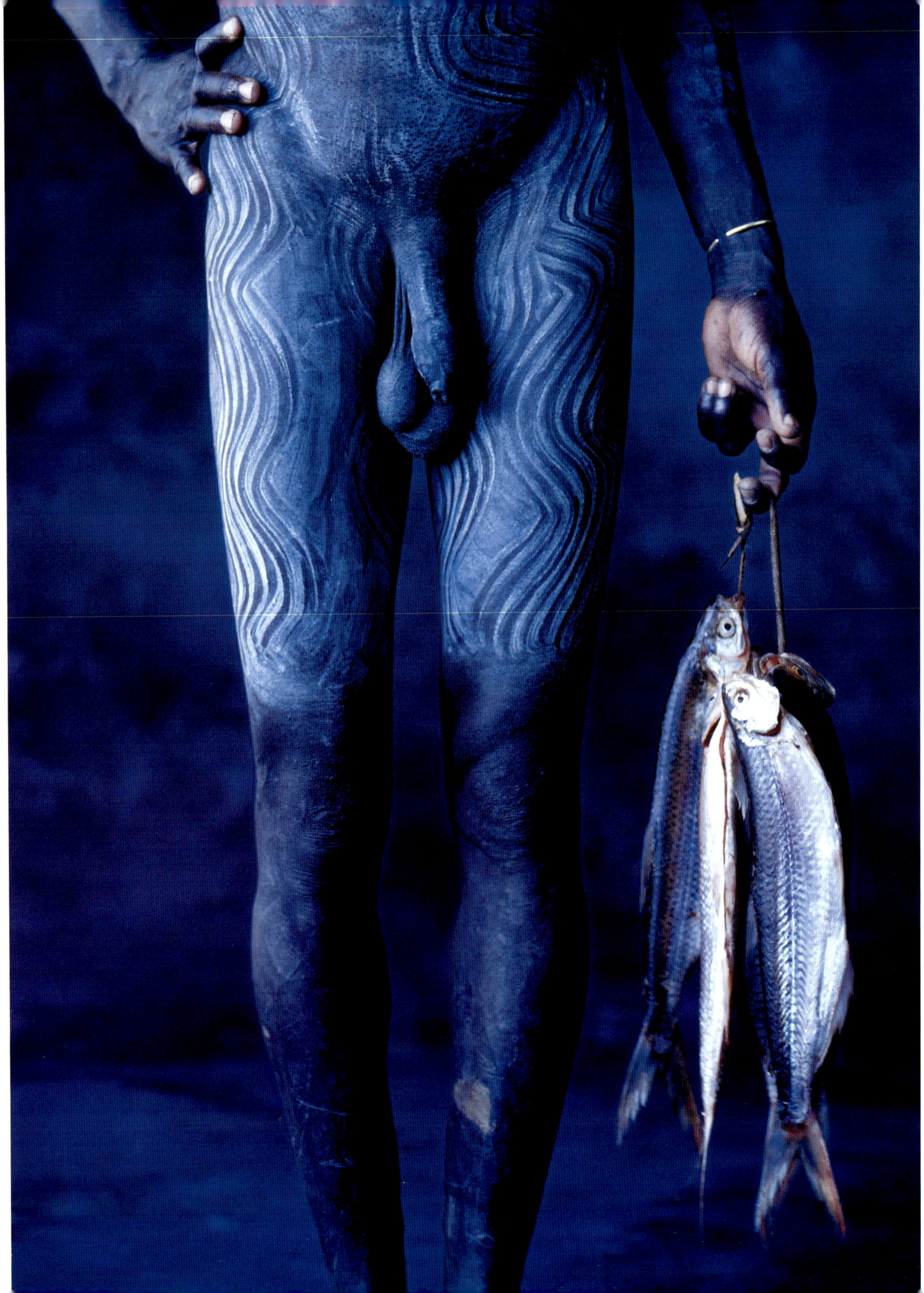

MURSI BODY PAINTING.

The Mursis are some of the most isolated people in East Africa. They are a very shy people. They are nomadic, moving along the Omo River to the west of Jinka. Often, Mursi men wear no clothes at all. Instead, they paint their bodies with intricate designs.

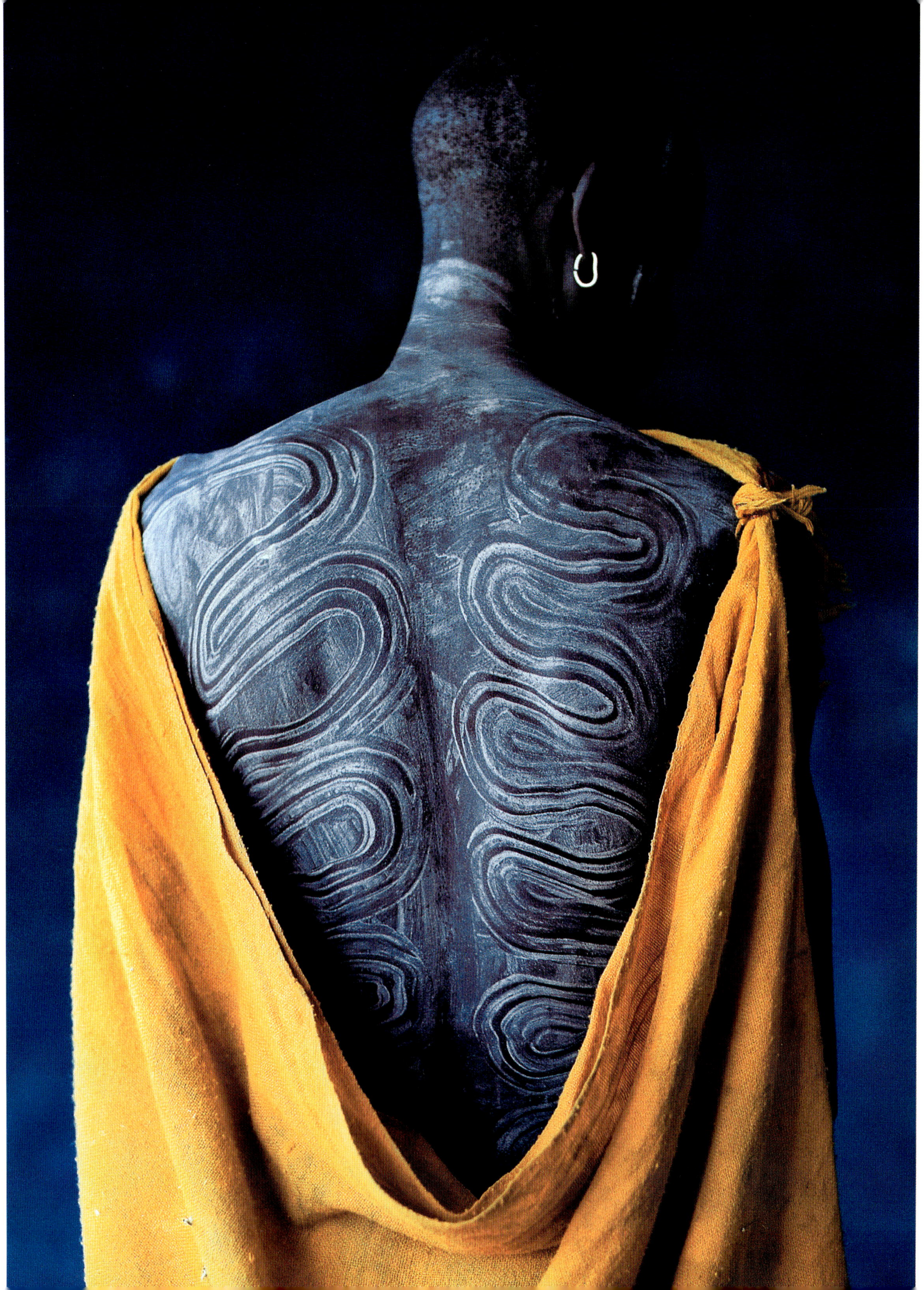

MURSI BODY PAINTING.
MAKARO, ETHIOPIA.

Every morning we watched the Mursi paint intricate patterns on one another's bodies with lime. Body painting is often the sole substitute for garments.

KUIJE, NINETEEN, KARO. ROUSSOS CAMP, ETHIOPIA.

Kuije, a Karo girl from the village of Kolcho, will see many changes during her lifetime. The old tribal customs are deteriorating. Her future husband will not be able to hunt successfully given the depletion of wildlife on the savanna. Young men have returned from the army bringing new ideas to the village. Contact with other cultures is changing the traditional customs followed by older members of the community.

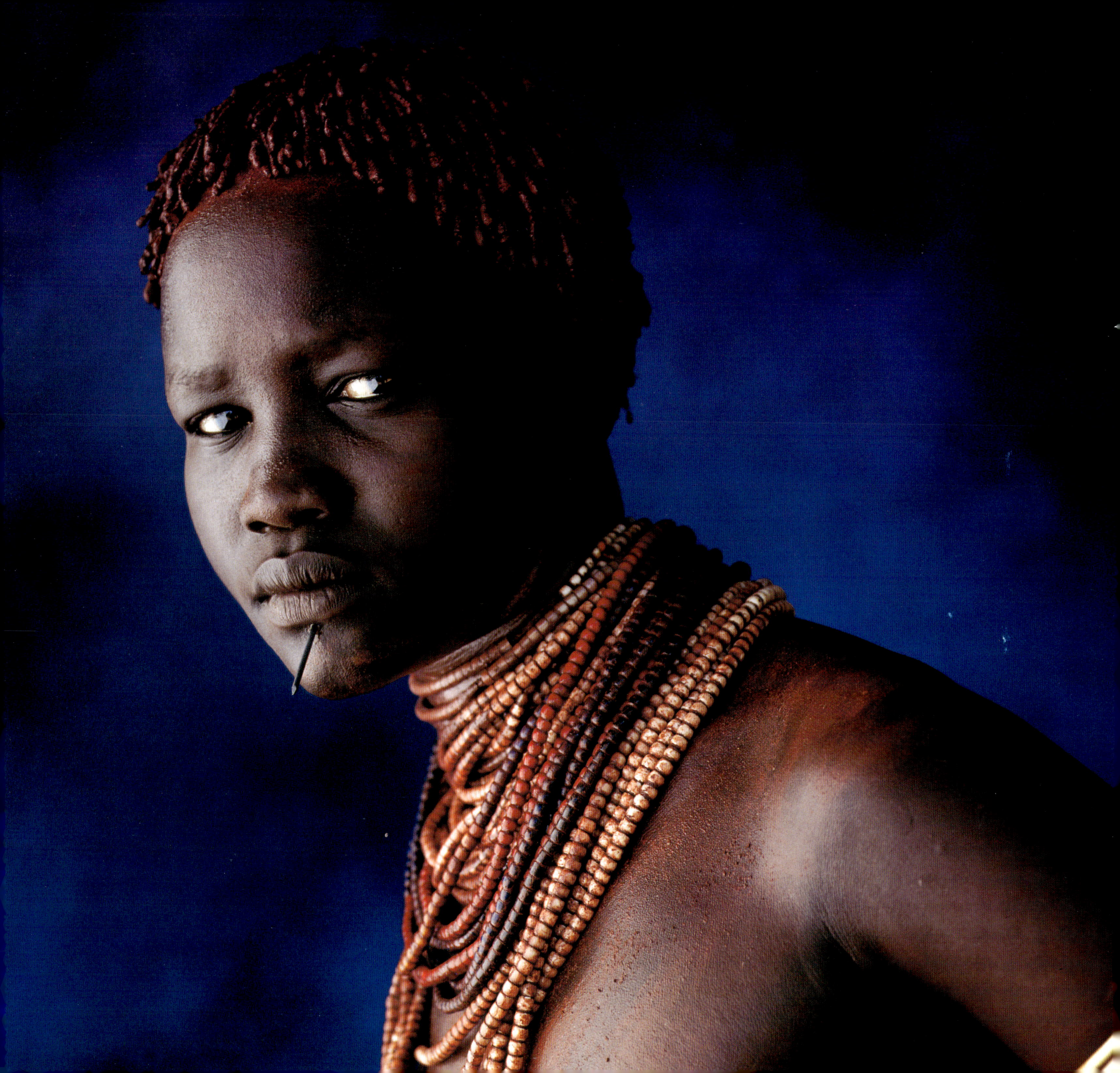

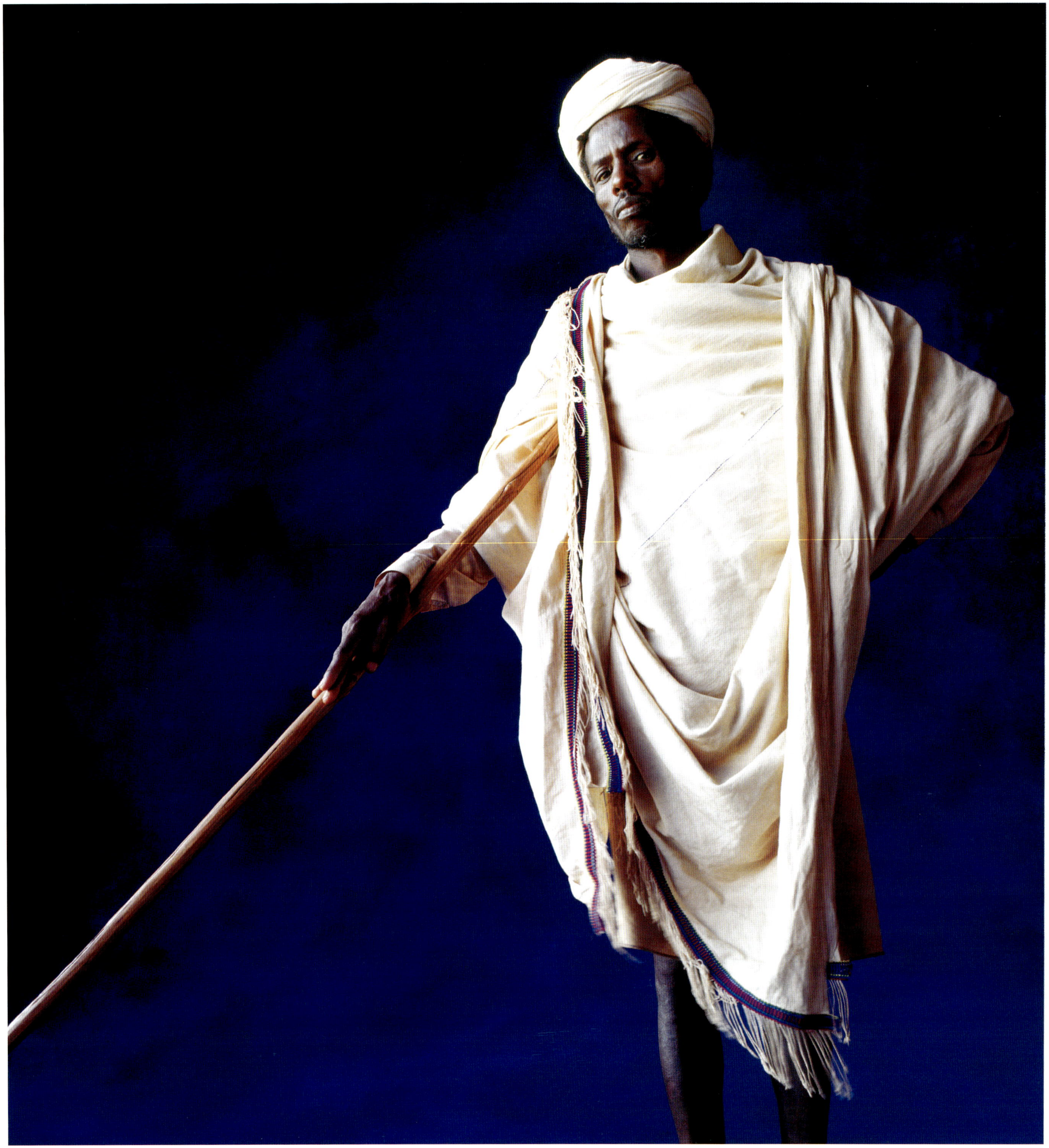

KIYO WARIO, FORTY-EIGHT, HERDER, BORANA. DUBULUK, ETHIOPIA.

The Borana own cattle, sheep, and goats. They resemble Somalis and share many of their tribal customs. The region in Southern Ethiopia where they live receives only twenty inches of rain per year. It is only through the knowledge of age-old grazing routes and a system by which the clans equitably share the available water that they can survive in such a harsh environment.

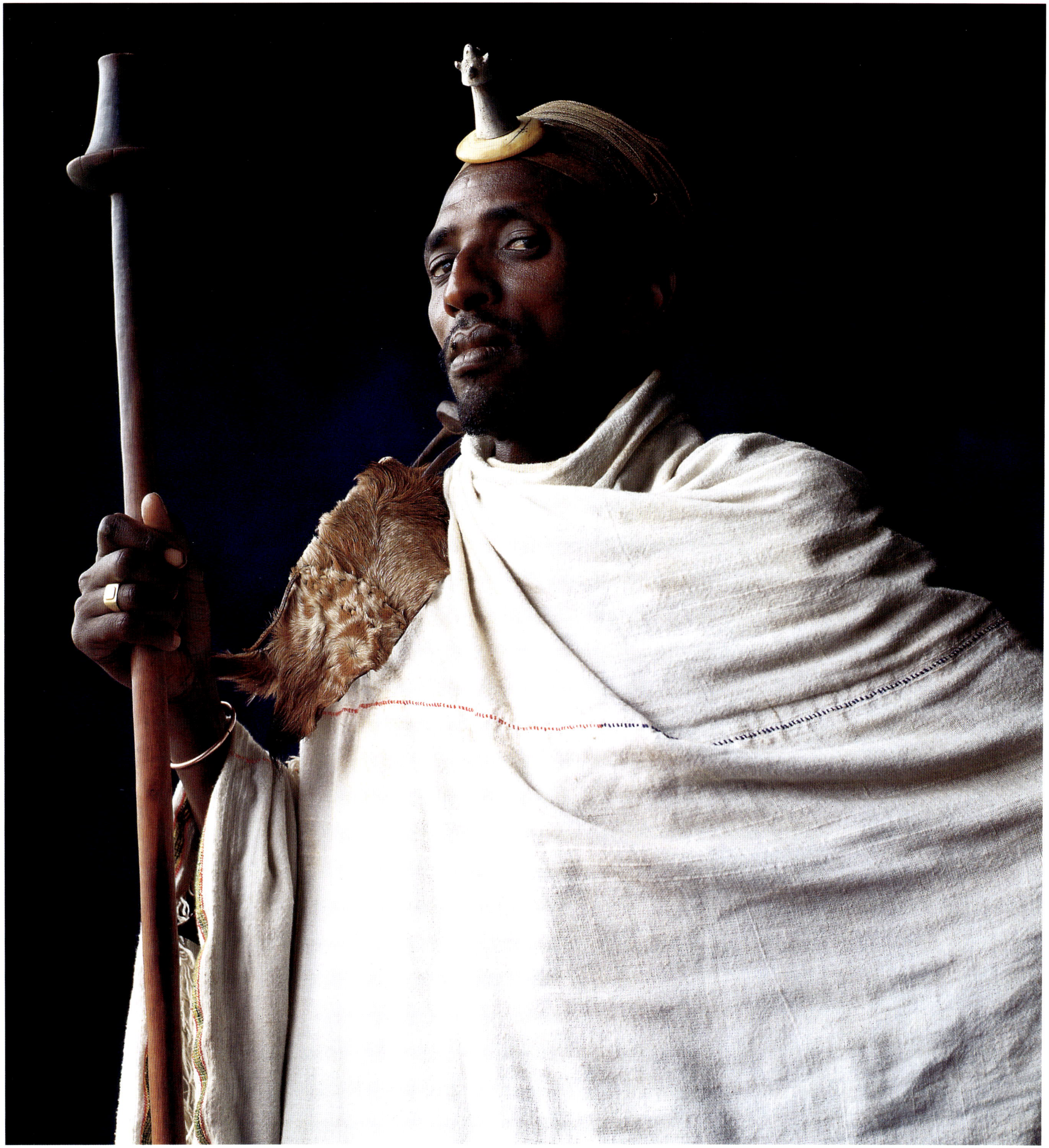

WAGO DABASA, THIRTY-TWO, BORANA, HERDER. DABASA WARIO, ETHIOPIA.

On his forehead Wago Dabasa wears a *kaltacha*, a phallic symbol. This is a custom from former times when Borana men cut off the penises of their slain enemies and returned to their clan proudly wearing them on their foreheads.

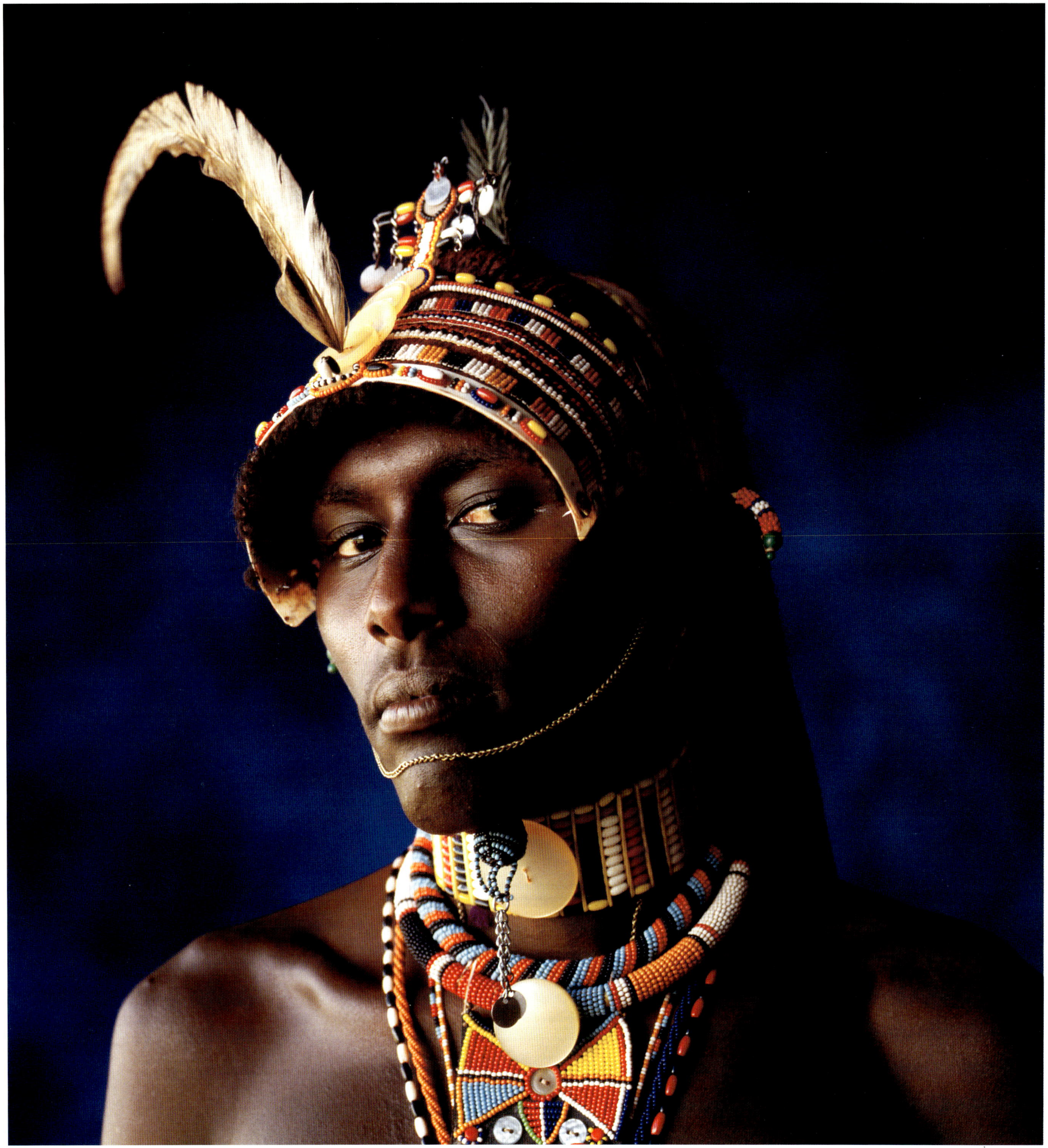

KOYNANTE, TWENTY-FOUR, *MORAN*, SAMBURU. MARALAL, KENYA.

Koynante's days as a warrior will soon be over and he will then have to dismantle his colorful uniform. When he marries, his father will give him his inheritance in cattle. As long as Koynante himself does not have a *moran* (warrior) son, he will pay other *morans* to take his herd to pasture.

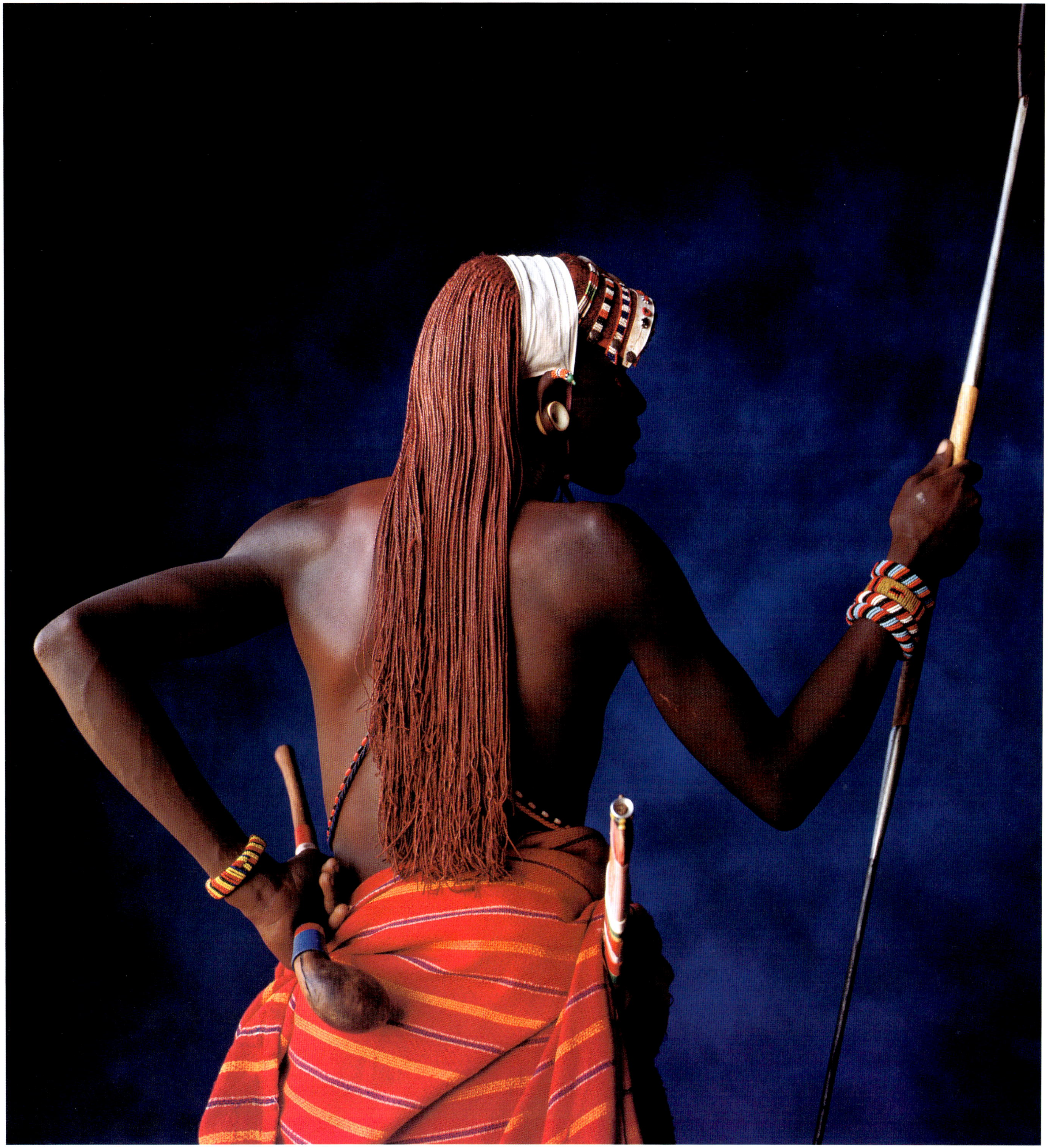

LLACHERDA, TWENTY-SIX, *MORAN*, SAMBURU. MARALAL, KENYA.

Llacherda takes great pride in his long plaited hair. Each day *morans* spend hours braiding one another's hair into fine long strings and keeping them in shape. They are colored with a natural ochre dye. The eight years during which they are *morans* are the peak years in the life of every male Samburu.

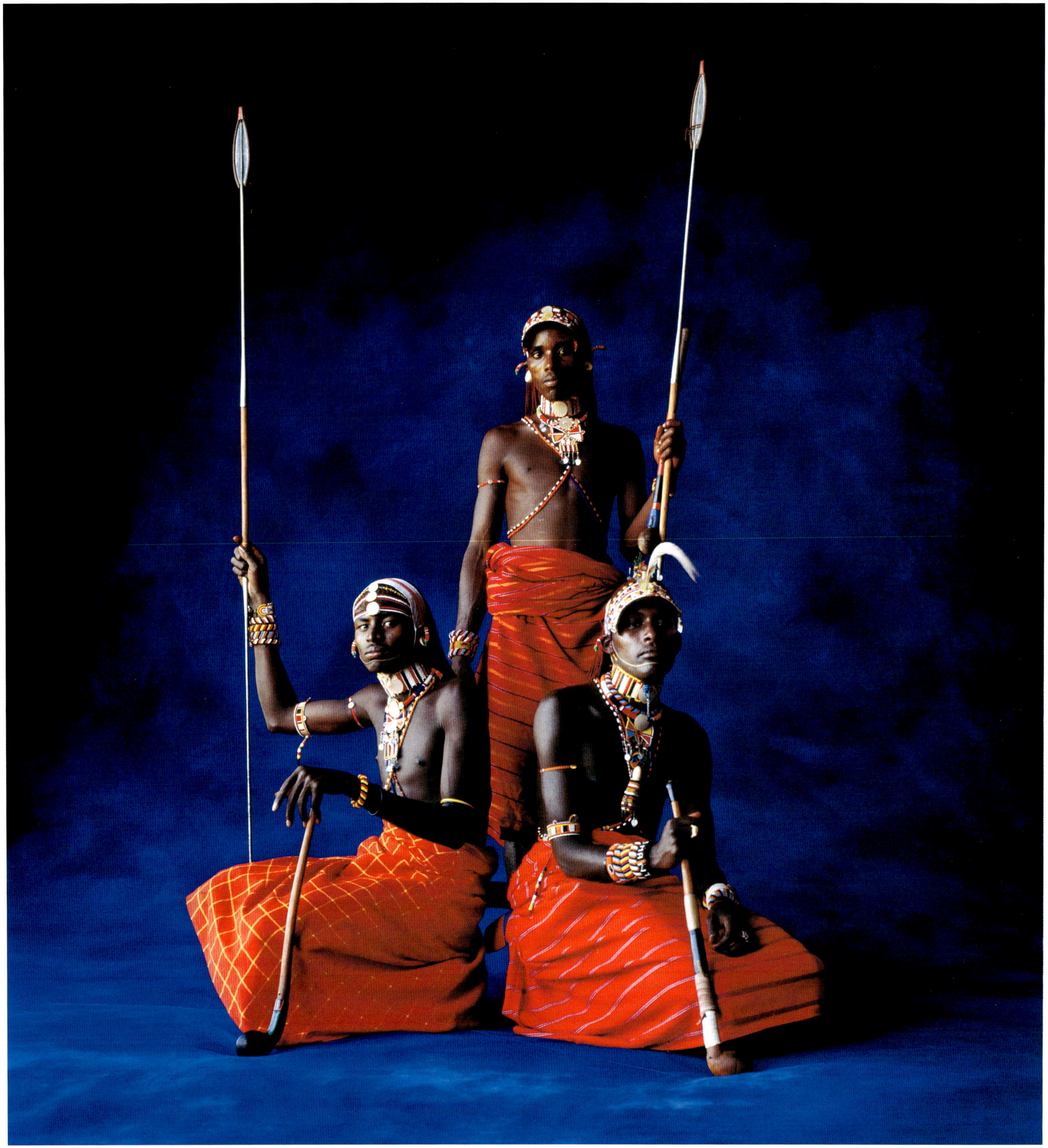

LEFT TO RIGHT: KOYNANTE, TWENTY-FOUR; LLACHERDA, TWENTY-SIX; TOPIA, TWENTY-THREE; *MORANS*, SAMBURU. MARALAL, KENYA.

Koynante, Llacherda, and Topia are Samburu *moran* warriors. Every eight years a new age group takes over and the old ones become householders. For Samburu men, the assumption of the clan's fighting and herding duties from the previous generation is the most important ceremony of their lives.

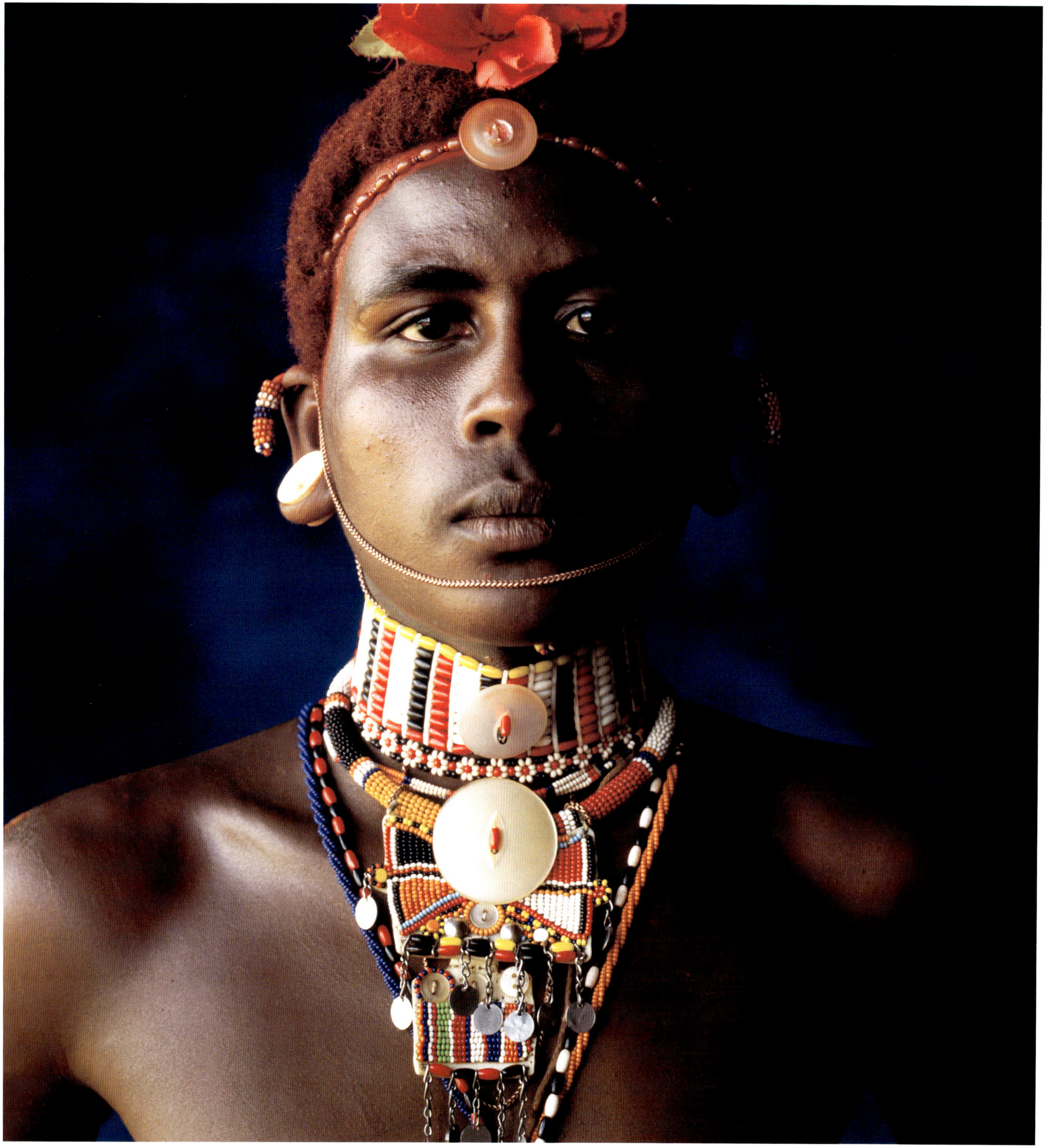

NDOLO, TWENTY, *MORAN*, SAMBURU. MARALAL, KENYA.

Ndolo is a Samburu warrior with elaborate head and neck adornments. Only *morans* are permitted to embellish their heads and necks, according to an ancient dress code specifically for warriors. Once they become elders, they will be obliged to wear the common, colorless household clothing.

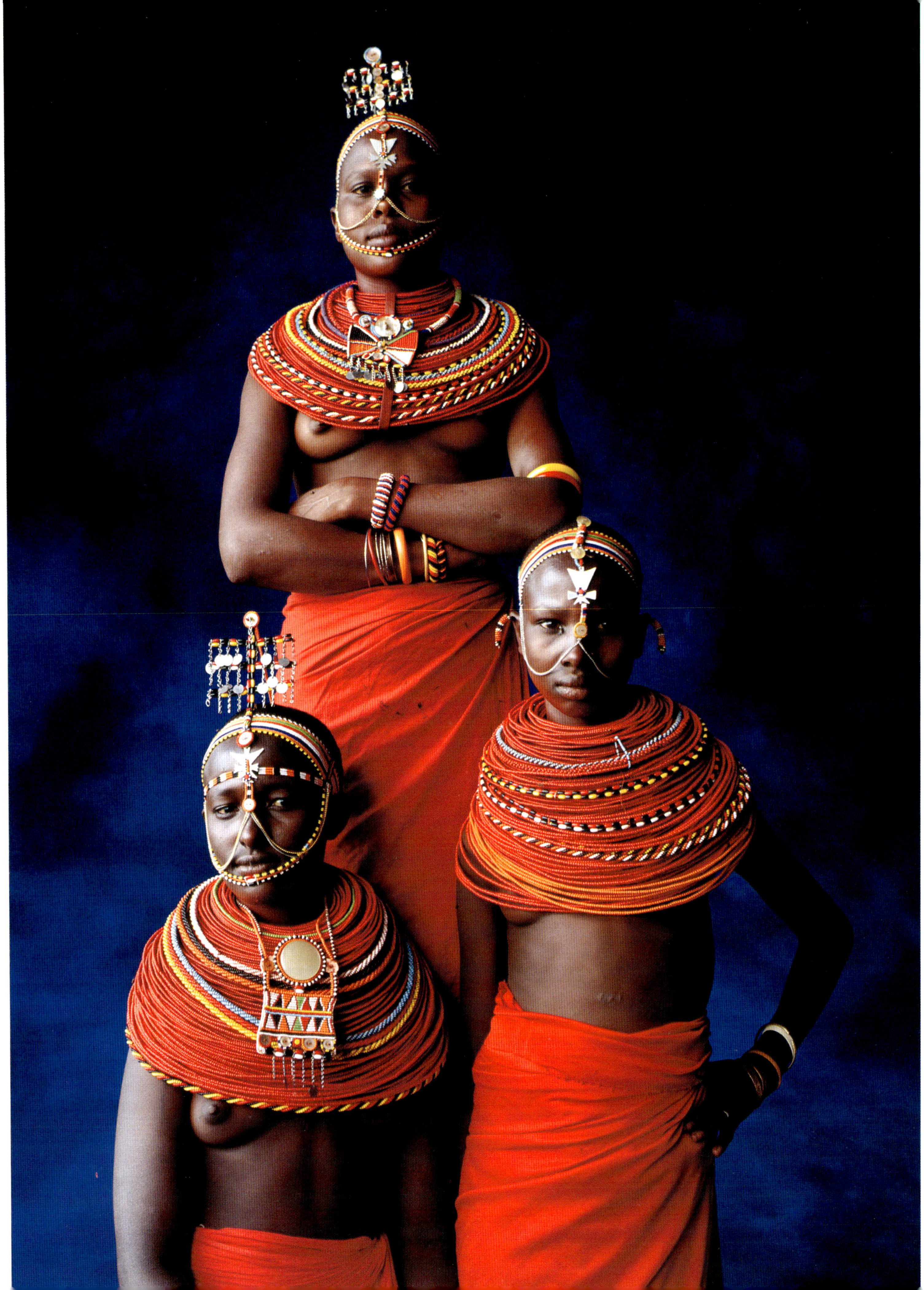

LEFT TO RIGHT:
NAIDASHA, FIFTEEN;
SITIMI, SEVENTEEN;
AND MATANET,
THIRTEEN; SAMBURU.
MARALAL, KENYA.

Until they get married, Samburu girls live a relatively free life. Naidasha, Sitimi, and Matanet wear the red outfit of unmarried women. Like the young men of their age group who are about to become warriors, the girls dress and adorn themselves with a variety of tribal jewelry.

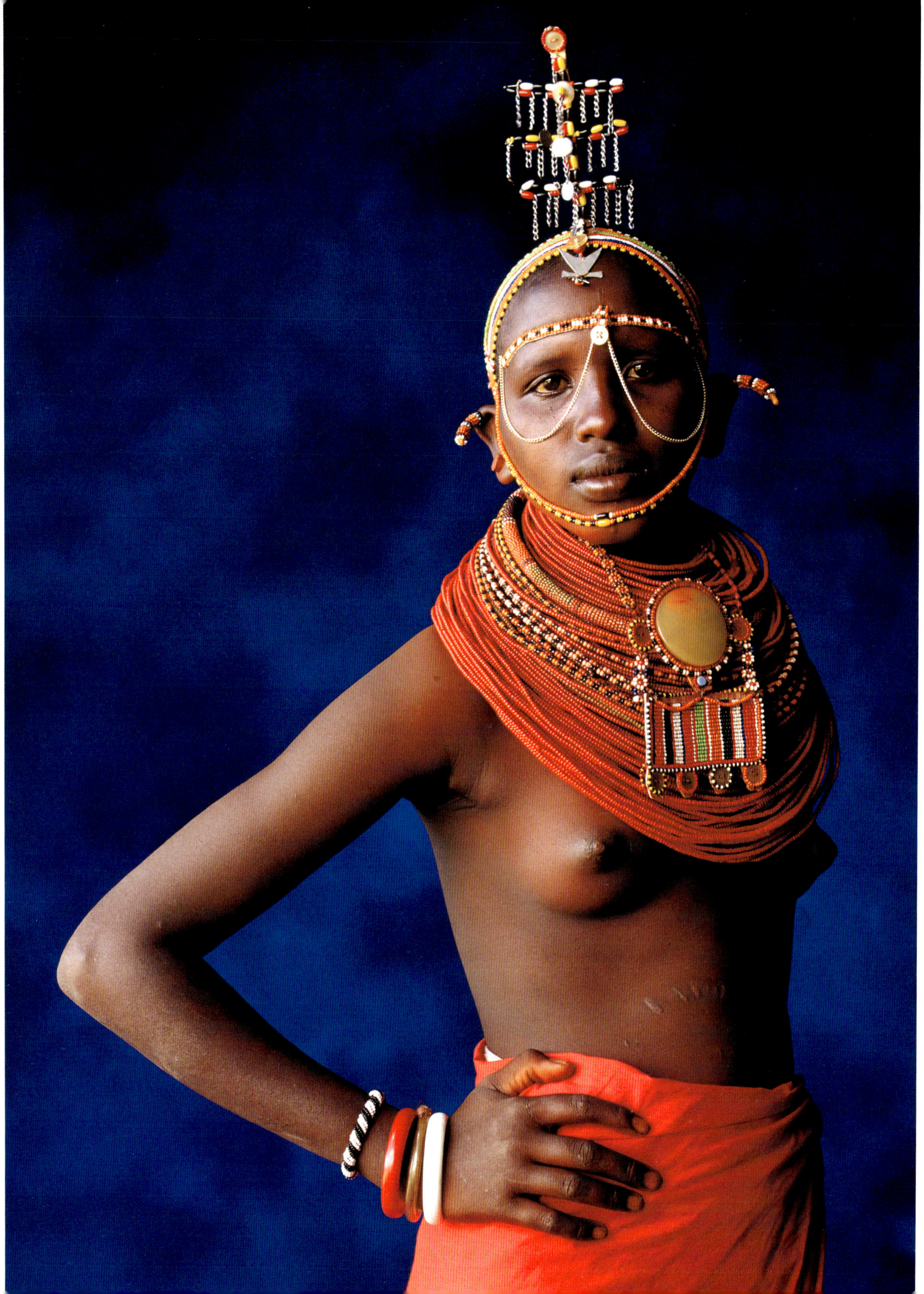

MAGIDA, SIXTEEN, SAMBURU. MARALAL, KENYA.

Magida is an unmarried Samburu. She adorns her neck with beads on wire. These adornments can weigh up to twelve pounds, and Samburu girls start to wear them from the age of five. They first receive them from their fathers, then from their *moran* boyfriends, and later from their husband. Once married, Magida will build the hut where she and her husband will raise their children.

WHEN STEPPING INTO OUR STUDIO, THESE PEOPLE SEEMED TO HAVE JUST STEPPED OUT OF A MYSTICAL PAST. LISTENING TO THEM TALK WAS LIKE HEARING VOICES FROM THE PAST. AND NOW, SOMETIMES, WHEN LOOKING AT THE PHOTOGRAPHS, IT IS LIKE LOOKING ACROSS TIME INTO THE FACES OF OUR ANCESTORS.

MACHUCH LENGUPAE,
THIRTY-SIX, SAMBURU.
MARALAL, KENYA.

As her blue coat signifies, Machuch Lengupae is married. According to ancient tribal tradition, Samburu women are circumcised before they are married.

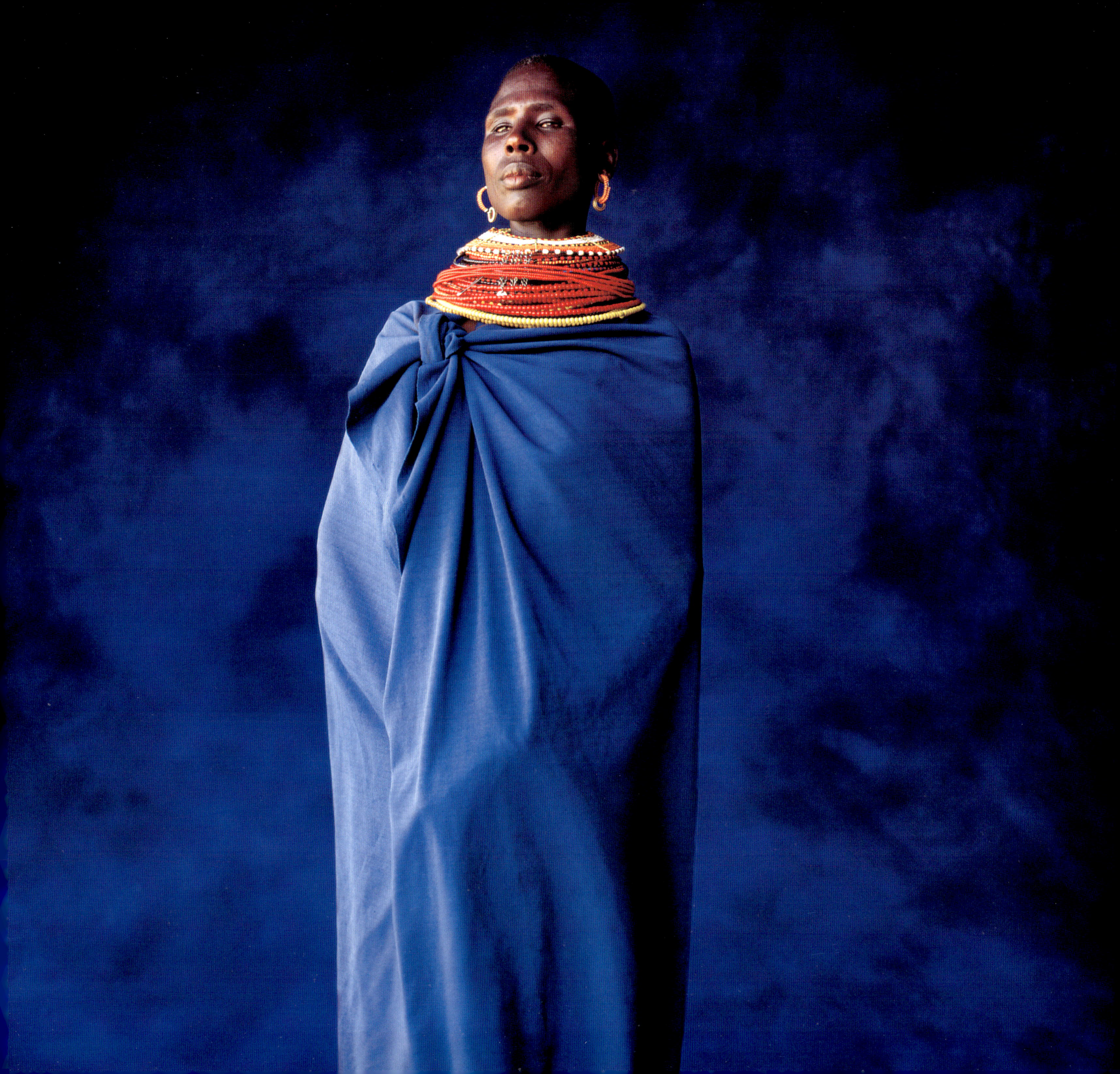

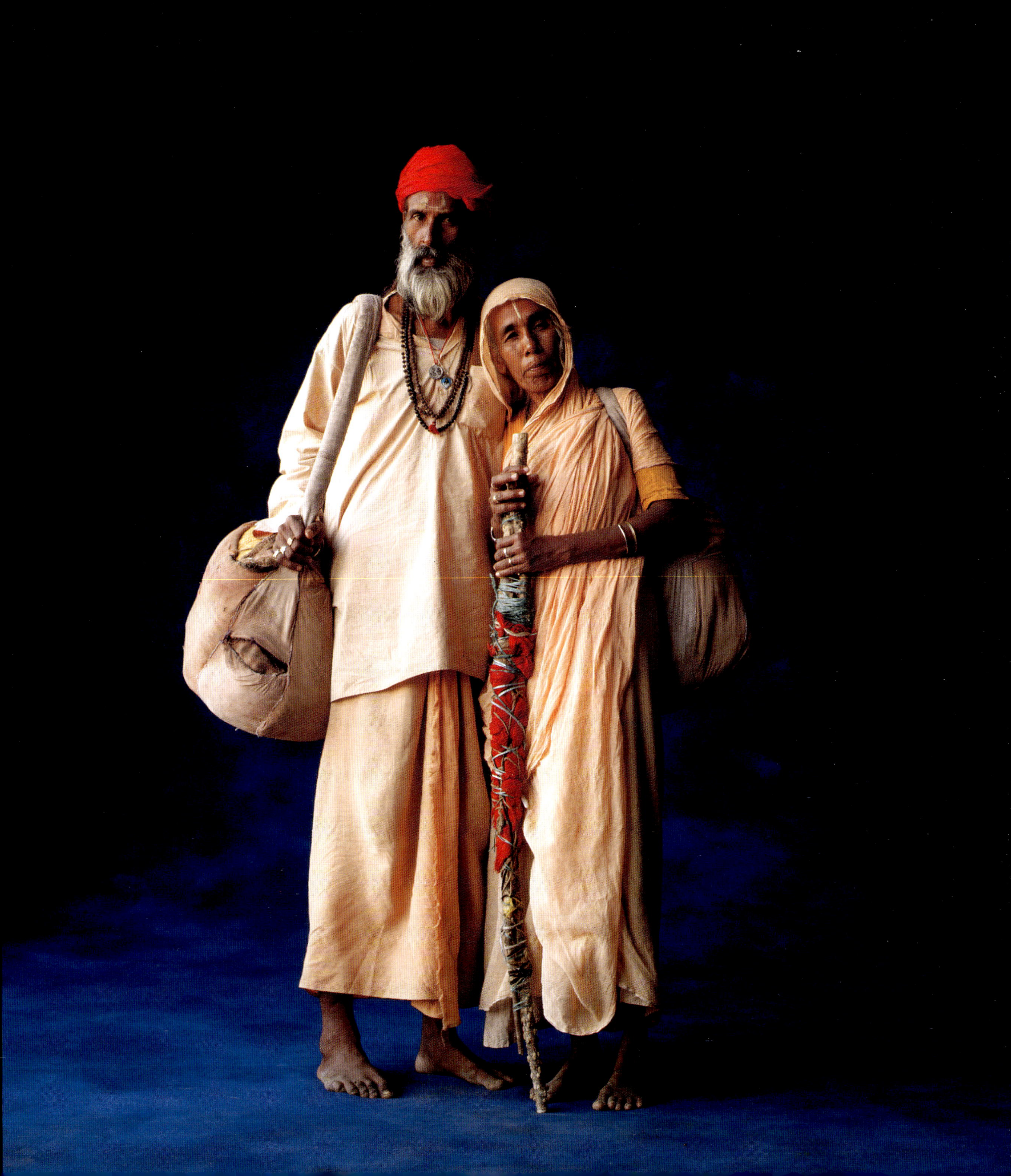

BRINDA BAN, FIFTY-FOUR, AND BIMOL SAM, FIFTY. PUSHKAR, RAJASTHAN

DESERT FLOWERS

SADHUS AND HERDERS OF THE INDIAN DESERT

It became clear that we could not complete our project without working in India. That is where people have been, longer than anywhere else, concerned with ontological concepts—with the search for the essence of being. The land and its people are marked by this search. In Myanmar we had been confronted with dignity in a political, human rights context. In East Africa we experienced it in the grounded, thoroughly down to earth attitudes of the people. In India we hoped to see the dignity that arises from an awareness in a religious and philosophical dimension.

After all, it was in North India that the Buddha initiated the first nonviolent revolution, striving to end the humiliations perpetrated by a caste-ridden society. Later it was the Muslim Sufi saints who offered a new outlook on equality for the downtrodden, and only recently it was Mahatma Gandhi who ended colonialism in a dignified, nonviolent manner. If true dignity differs from pride, then India is the place where it flourishes.

There was another reason we traveled to northwest India—the desert. Our experience in East Africa had shown us how the desert defines people in a unique way. It allows no room for what is extraneous and transforms people by demanding and fostering their finest qualities. Therefore we planned to continue into the Thar Desert of Gujarat after photographing at the Muslim and Hindu festivals in Rajasthan.

Back in 1984 we had been in Rajasthan during the turmoil that spread across northern India after Indira Gandhi's assassination. Delhi, Uttar Pradesh, and Haryana were on the brink of civil war, and even though Rajasthan was as peaceful as ever, it was not the appropriate moment to pursue what had captivated us. We promised ourselves we would return and take a closer look at these fascinating people whose dignity rests quietly behind their moustachioed pride and golden earrings and nose rings. In 1984 we did not know it would be another fourteen years before this would happen.

Two important festivals were scheduled in Pushkar and Ajmer in November 1998: the annual Pushkar Camel Fair and the Ajmer Urs of the Sufi saint, each of which attracts a million or more pilgrims. It was a rare coincidence that would simultaneously bring a wide spectrum of Muslim and Hindu believers to areas just seven and a half miles from each other. While Ajmer is the most sacred of all Muslim places of pilgrimage in India, Pushkar is one of the holiest Hindu places and has, perhaps, the only existing temple dedicated to Lord Brahma.

Months before the events, we went to Pushkar to make arrangements. With the help of the Chairman of the Municipal Corporation, we selected a location for the studio close to the Kapalishwara Temple in the heart of the grazing grounds for sixteen thousand camels. What we had seen as parched, empty grassland became the center of a makeshift town for tens of thousands of visitors at the full moon of Kartika (November). Our square, black studio marked the main intersection and was visible from every knoll in the fair ground.

Like many years before at the Manao Festival in Myitkyina, the people of the Indian desert showed up at the studio eager to be

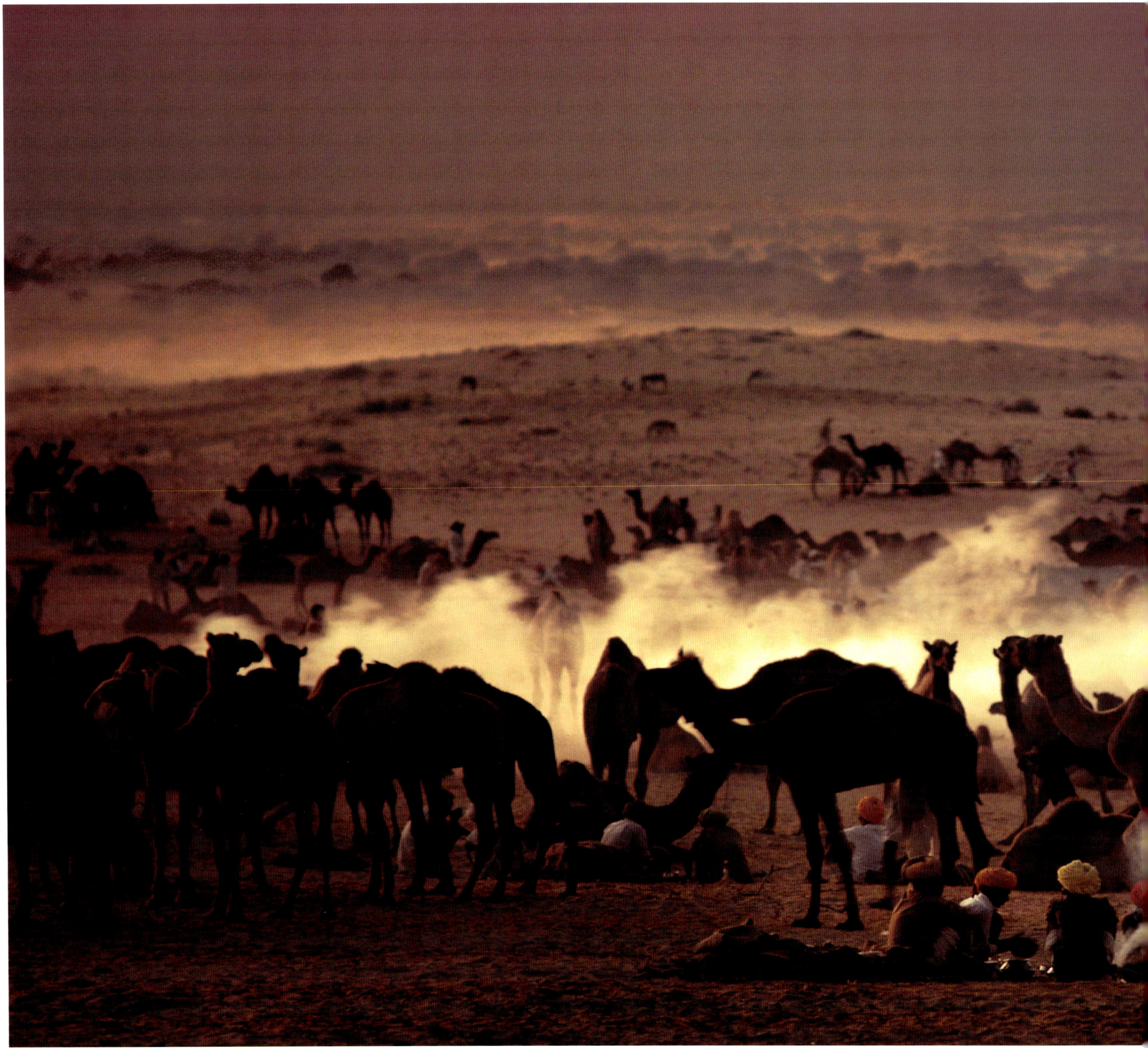

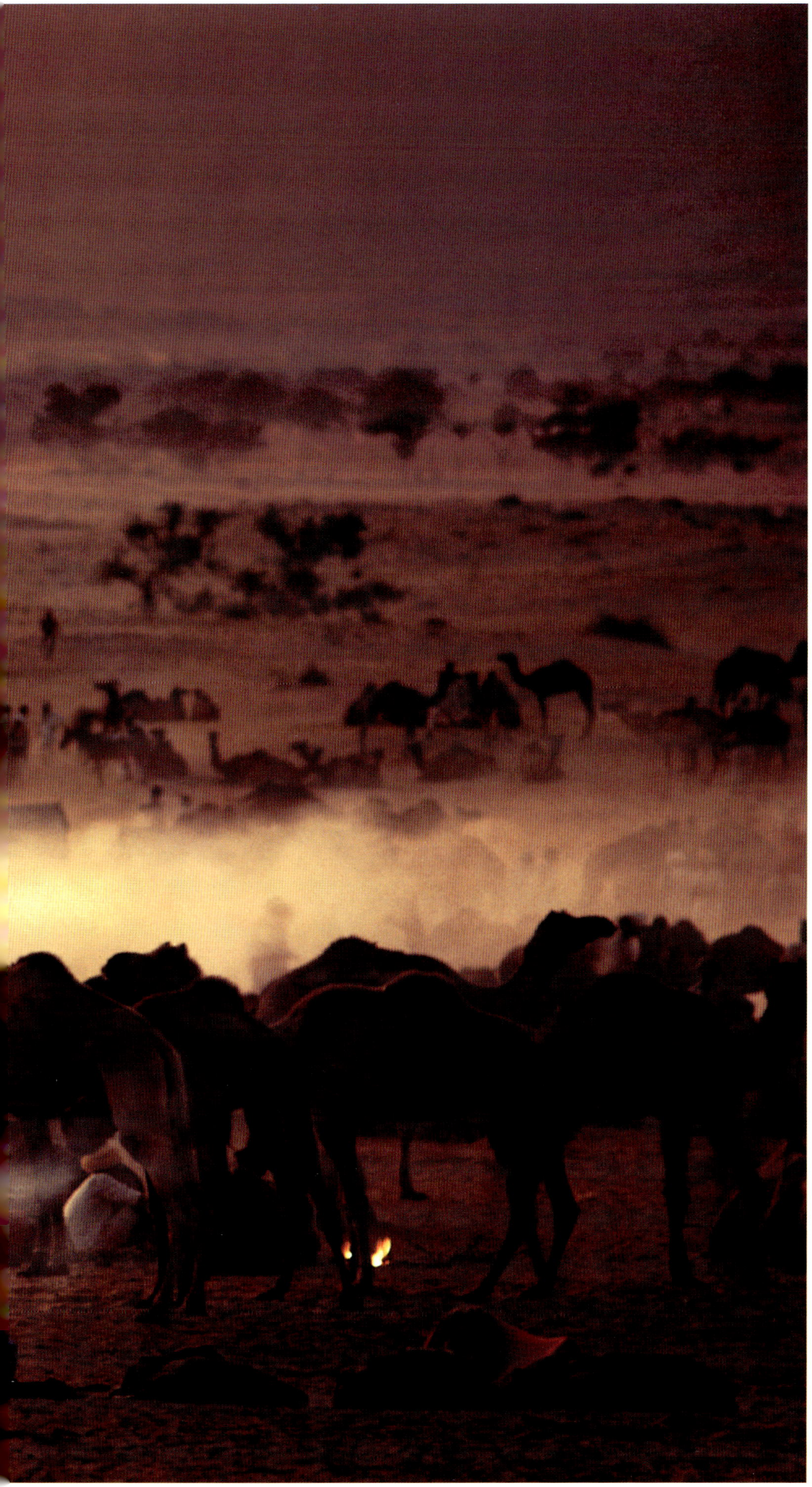

photographed. Our problem was not in finding the right people, but in selecting from amongst so many who were so appropriate. Saveras (page 61 and 63), Gujars (pages 64 and 75), snake charmers (page 65 and 74), and dancers (page 60), besieged our camp and we had to hire two authoritative camel herders as watchmen to be able to work.

The trading of animals, which begins almost ten days before the full moon, is as essential to the fair as its religious tradition of bathing at one of the fifty-two *ghats* of the Pushkar lake. A dip in its shallow waters on *Kartika Purnima* (full moon night) is supposed to rid believers of all their sins—even capital ones. In addition to devout couples (page 54), who came from as far as Calcutta and Madras, the town was overflowing with Brahmans (page 91), and renunciates—swamis, sadhus (page 68 and 69), *sanyassins* and yogis (page 70). They are known by many names, but are all on a path they believe will lead towards *moksha*, the liberation from all bondage.

It was neither religion nor the trading of animals that brought another group of participants to the fair. This group was comprised of people who move from one religious gathering to the next imitating holy men and begging where people attach virtue to almsgiving. Hermaphrodites, whose presence is considered auspicious at certain occasions, and cripples, who became sadhus to survive and feed their families (page 73), were only some of the many people attracted by the opportunities.

At the same time, a different mood prevailed in Ajmer at the Urs festival that celebrates the reunification of the saint with God. Nearly as many people came to the Urs as to the Pushkar Fair, just seven and a half miles away at the Dargah of Khwaja Moinuddin Chisti, the tomb of the twelfth-century Sufi saint. This saint is deeply revered by Muslims, Hindus, and Sikhs alike. Sufism, the mystical aspect of Islam, has little in common with the creed, as interpreted by Near Eastern Muslim revolutionaries.

Sufi saints were often poets, mystics whose poetry stemmed from the same divine ecstasy as that of the Hindu Bhakti saints. Some of what they wrote is so similar it is nearly indistinguishable. When Khwaja

CAMELS AT THE PUSHKAR MELA, RAJASTAN, INDIA.

Moinuddin Chisti wrote at the beginning of the thirteenth century that, "it is incumbent on the follower of the path of 'Tariqat' [the path leading to Divinity] that he must first divorce or renounce the physical world, and then the second world thereafter and ultimately his own 'self' [Nafs], when alone he can pursue his right path, failing which he should abandon the enterprise of Sufism," his message was very similar to that of the Hindu saints. And in saying, "Verily he is an Aarif who is clothed with three qualities—firstly, piety; secondly, conduct eliciting respect; and thirdly, modesty," he has given us a description of dignity that could not be more fitting.

This kind of Islam was not foreign to us—we had experienced it in Pakistan and at the Nizamuddin shrine in Delhi—and so we were sure that during the Ajmer Urs we would find examples of intense piety and devotion. Our problem was finding a place to set up our studio in a city of narrow lanes through which thousands of people move in a solid mass towards the Dargah. After many discussions we finally were able to assemble it on the first story roof of a cloth shop at the Dargah Bazaar, just opposite the entrance to the shrine. And while our black "Ka'bah"shaped studio attracted the fancy of the crowd, we were overwhelmed by the sheer numbers of people. On the last Friday of the Urs, when the Qul ceremony took place, some eight hundred thousand praying, chanting, and singing pilgrims passed our studio. Developing a sense of trust was not as easy as it was in Pushkar. On their way to the shrine, people were absorbed in devotional fervor. On their return they were joyous and open-minded. Some of them had traveled long distances—from Andra Pradesh, Bangalore, and Punjab. What was surprising was that there were so many non-Muslims who came to pay tribute to a Muslim saint. Particularly in view of communal strife—the hatred that so often flares up in North Indian cities—Ajmer during the Urs, though charged with religious feelings, was an example of communal tolerance and understanding.

We were only halfway through our India assignment. We left Rajasthan behind and drove with our two Sumo Jeeps to Bhuj, our base in northern Gujarat. Our plan was to photograph the people of the wasteland along the border between Pakistan and India—the legendary battlefields of the last Indo-Pakistan war. There, far away from mainstream India, the subcontinent's last nomadic tribes are still herding their animals as they have done since times immemorial. Reaching them is not easy; the border region is a national security zone and visiting permits are issued on a case-by-case basis. The permits allow you to travel only along prescribed routes and visit well-developed villages along the road, places where nomads don't normally linger. While we were waiting for our permit to go north into the border area we set up our studio at Tundawandh, a roundhouse "*bhunga*" village of settled Rabaris. The women of the village, like Chassibe (page 84), had already taken a huge step into the twentieth century—by sending their traditional embroidered cloths to Bhuj. None of them could read or write, but children like Sango (page 78), were attending primary school, while their fathers (pages 86 and 87), were still traditional camel herders. The people of Tundawandh were already taking the second step after getting settled. While they still follow their *Bhopa's* (priest's) command to the word, they are slowly adapting to the rules of mainstream Indian society.

As we had expected, it was our locally hired liaison Mangar Sumar, himself a Ghadavi who has lived for decades in the Banni region, who knew how to find the true nomads—the Kachchi Rabaris (who do not want to have anything to do with the Rajasthani Rabaris) and the Jaths, a Muslim buffalo-herding tribe (not to be confused with the Hindu Jats of Rajasthan). They are two of the many small nomadic or seminomadic groups that live in the Banni area of northern Gujarat, close to the salt marshes of the Great Rann of Kutch. While driving north along the wide, tarred, tank-worthy highway towards the border, Mangar knew where we could sneak off into the wilderness.

We searched for two days before we finally found a clan of nomadic Dhebaria Rabaris some nineteen miles east of Bharandiala. They are basically shepherds with a few camels and live off the land and their sheep. It took some time, and Mangar's fluency in the Rabari language, until this small clan of not more than twenty members was willing to let us stay and move with them.

Once, while they moved on, we drove to a camp of Muslim Danetha Jaths who stayed with their buffalos in a swamp not far from the Pakistan border. Putting up our studio in their camp and photographing the Jath women was much more difficult than photographing the Rabaris. The Jaths are Muslims, speaking the same language and dressed as their peers across the border in Sindh. As a result of the belligerent mood at the border, they are reticent and try to avoid any contact with strangers. Like the Rabaris, they too live off what little the land provides, and the *ghee* (clarified butter) and *mawa* (milk cake) from their buffalos. But while the Rabaris sleep under the open sky, the Jaths set up tents and stay for prolonged periods wherever they stop. Women like Hirambai and Bachambai (page 80), do not practice purdah, though they are proud of their huge golden nose rings which even young girls seem to wear with pleasure.

Returning to the Rabaris was like coming home. It was then that we realized we were in danger. Over the days we had seen Indian tanks moving along the horizon, and driving across the desert we hit upon many of their tracks. That very night when we returned to the Rabaris on the fringe of the saltpans and were sitting around the campfire, a platoon of battle-dressed Indian soldiers appeared from out of the dark of the night. As their Delhi-born officer told us, they were on night reconnaissance and had lost their way. It was part of the dry season manoeuvres that had just started. Since we were able to direct them to the nearest army camp, which we had passed on the way in, they never asked about our huge studio or what we were doing there in the middle of their highly classified war games.

For two days we stayed with the Rabaris, photographing the entire clan whose members see themselves neither as Pakistanis nor Indians. Theirs is a world that is flat and without boundaries. When we explained to one of the elders that we had been traveling for years and had seen the earth to be round, he answered "I have been walking this land for over seventy years and it has always been flat. It is I, if anyone, who can prove with my life's experience that the world is flat."

Before we left India we set up our studio once more on the roof of the Gurdwara Sis Ganj in the center of Old Delhi's Chandni Chowk. After the Golden Temple in Amritsar, this is the Sikhs' most venerated place of worship. For a month we had photographed Hindus, Muslims, and nomads who still worship the Mother Goddess in her original form. At the Delhi Gurdwara we were now photographing Sikhs, who form a robust part of the Indian religious establishment. After two days, Narungen Singh (page 94), a Sikh farmer from Punjab, and Harpreet Kaur (page 93), an eighteen-year-old Sikh student who spoke about studying in America, were the last of a few hundred people we photographed in our "search." While the photography might have ended there, the search had not.

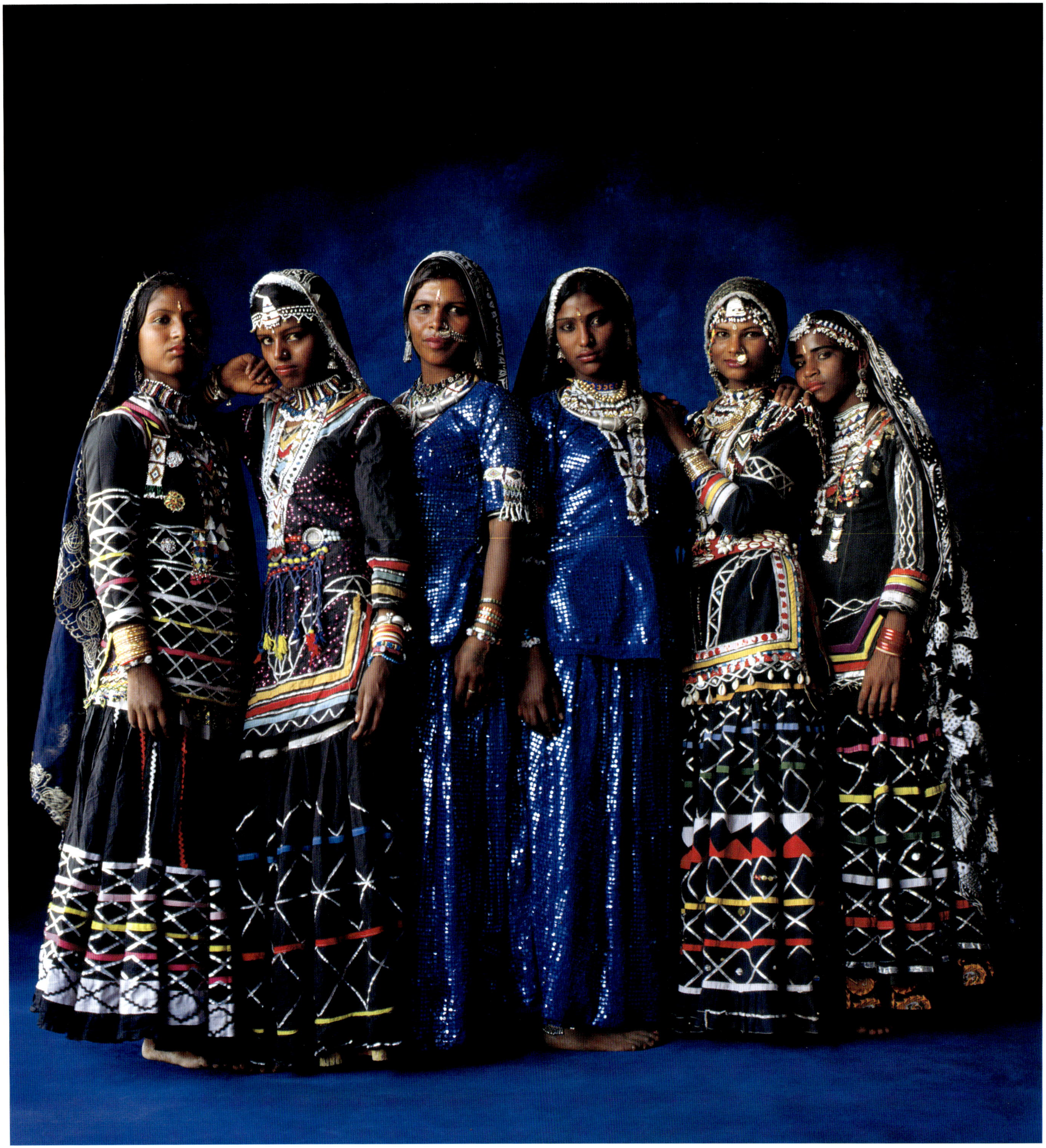

LEFT TO RIGHT: MENA, TWENTY-TWO; SEVA, TWENTY; RAJULI, FIFTEEN; SINDIKI, TWENTY; SUNNITA, TWENTY; AND REKA, TWENTY-FIVE; DANCERS, SAVERA. PUSHKAR, RAJASTHAN.

Mena, Seva, Rajuli, Sindiki, Sunnita, and Reka belong to a Savera dance troupe that comes to the Pushkar mela (religious festival) to entertain the many traders and visitors who camp out in the desert. In November the nights are pleasant, and the festival coincides with the full moon.

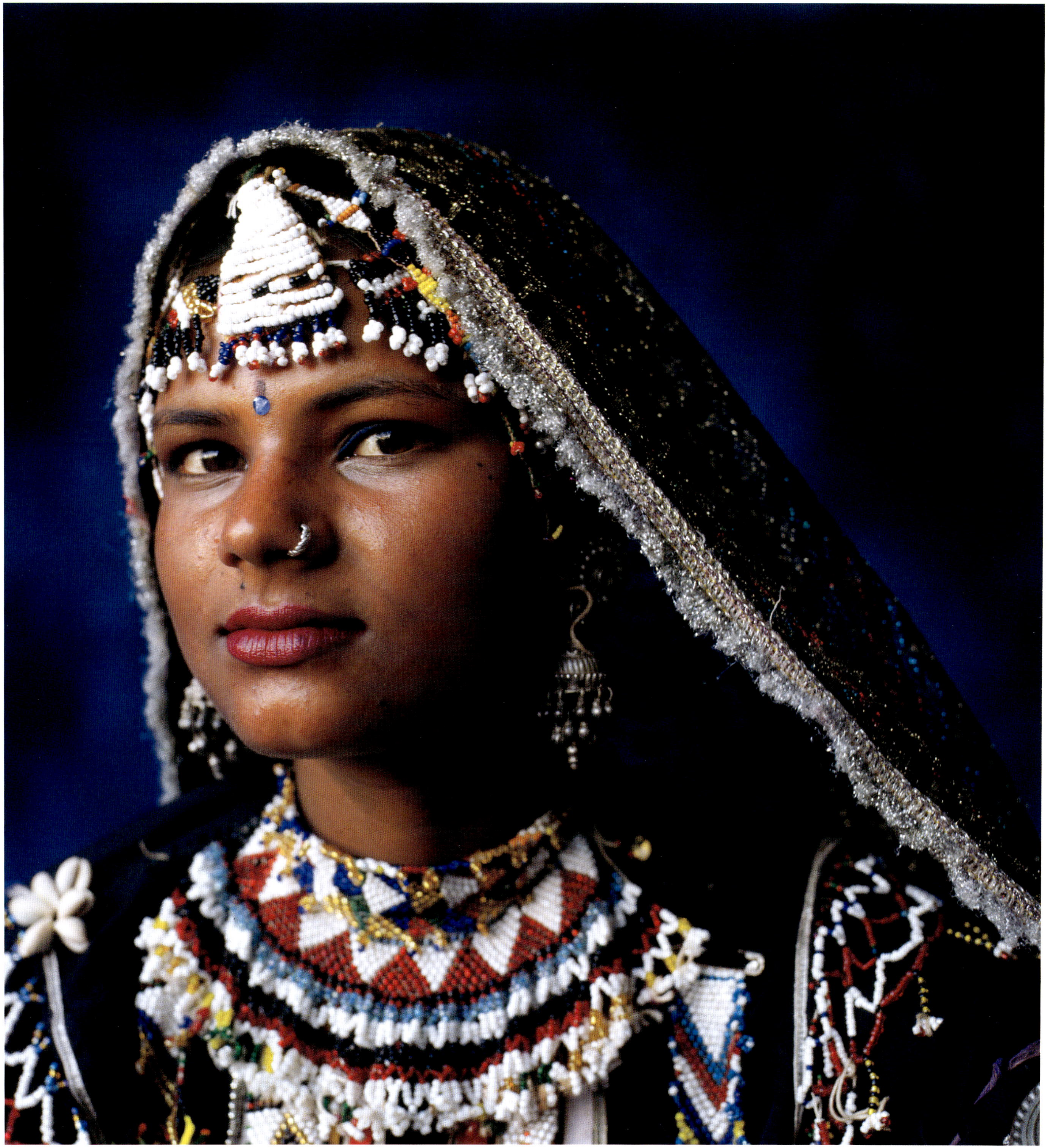

SUNNITA, TWENTY,
DANCER, SAVERA.
PUSHKAR, RAJASTHAN.

Sunnita came with her clan from Jaisalmer to Pushkar. Although they have a permanent home, they travel most of the time. There is a large demand for entertainment around the festival campfires. The men are musicians, and the women, dancers.

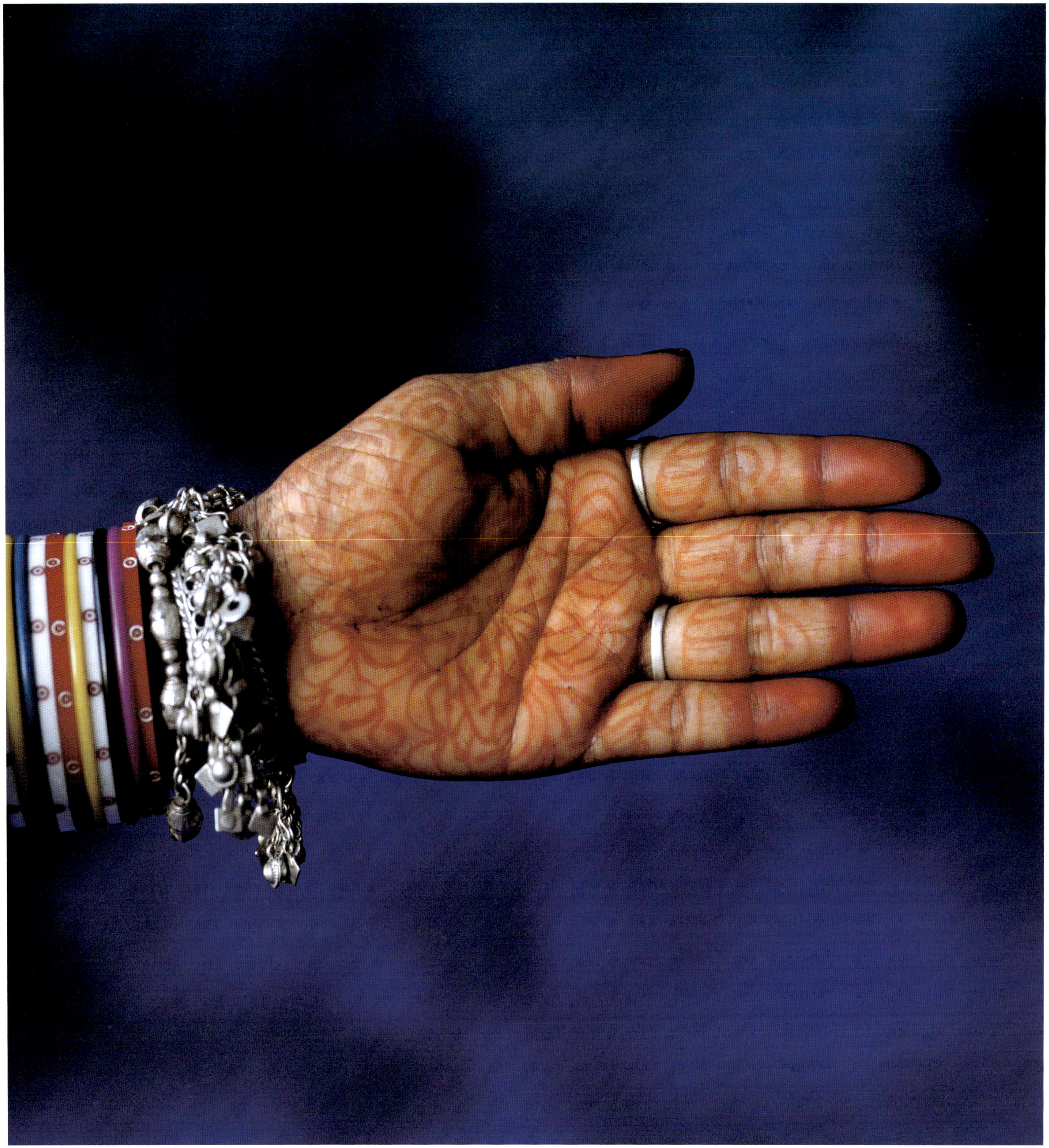

HENNA-PAINTED HAND OF CAMELLA, TWENTY-FIVE, DANCER, SAVERA. PUSHKAR, RAJASTHAN.

An intricate henna design graces the hand of Camella, a Savera dancer from Jaisalmer. Savera women only dance in the evening, spending the day painting the hands of female visitors to the fair. Their own hands serve as examples of their skill.

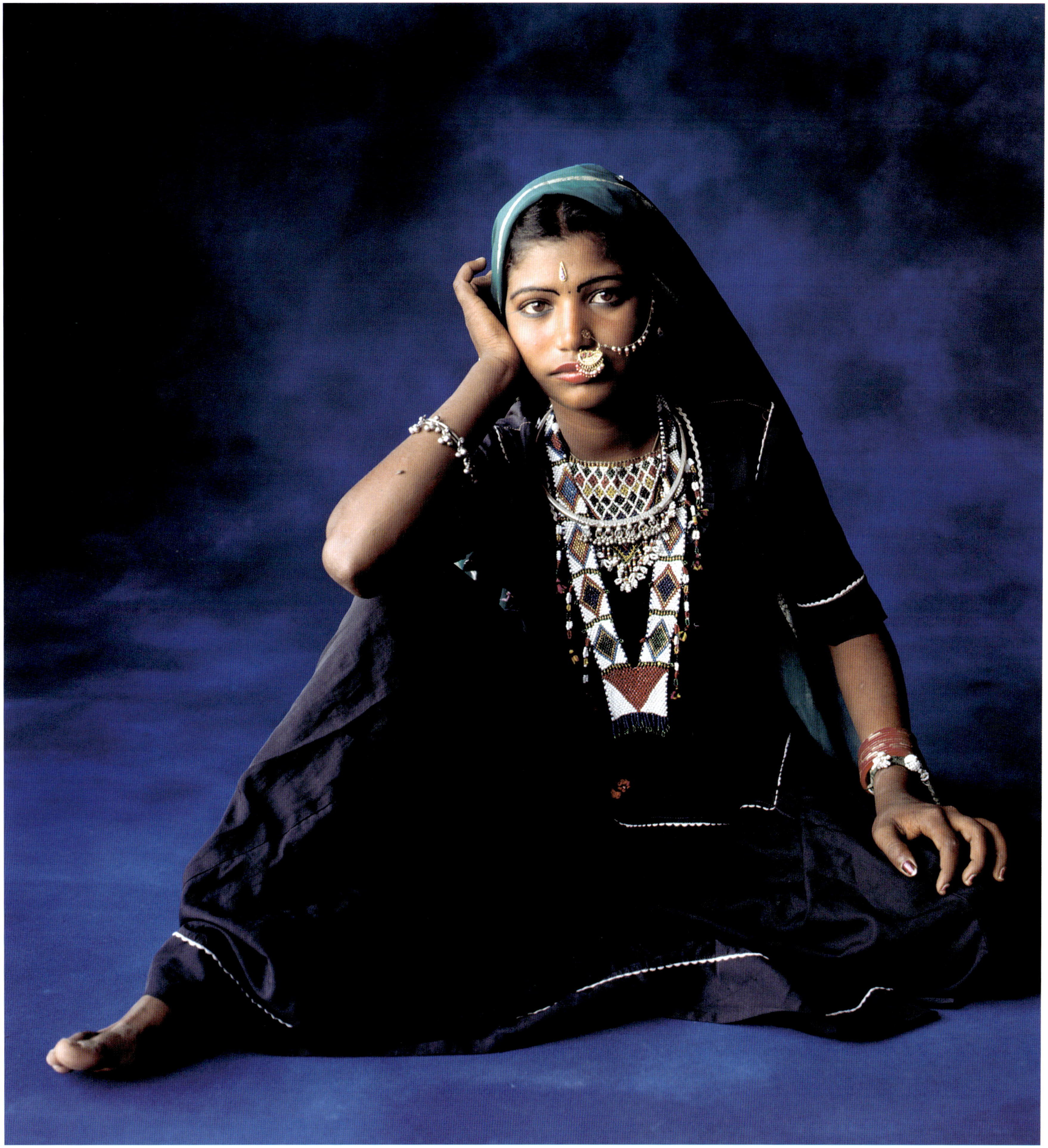

REKO, TWENTY-ONE,
DANCER, SAVERA.
PUSHKAR, RAJASTHAN.

Reko dances in a troupe of Saveras who come to perform during the mela. In Rajasthan, highly esteemed female performers dance to traditional folk music. Although some Rajasthani women subscribe to the system of purdah, the Saveras do not wear the veil.

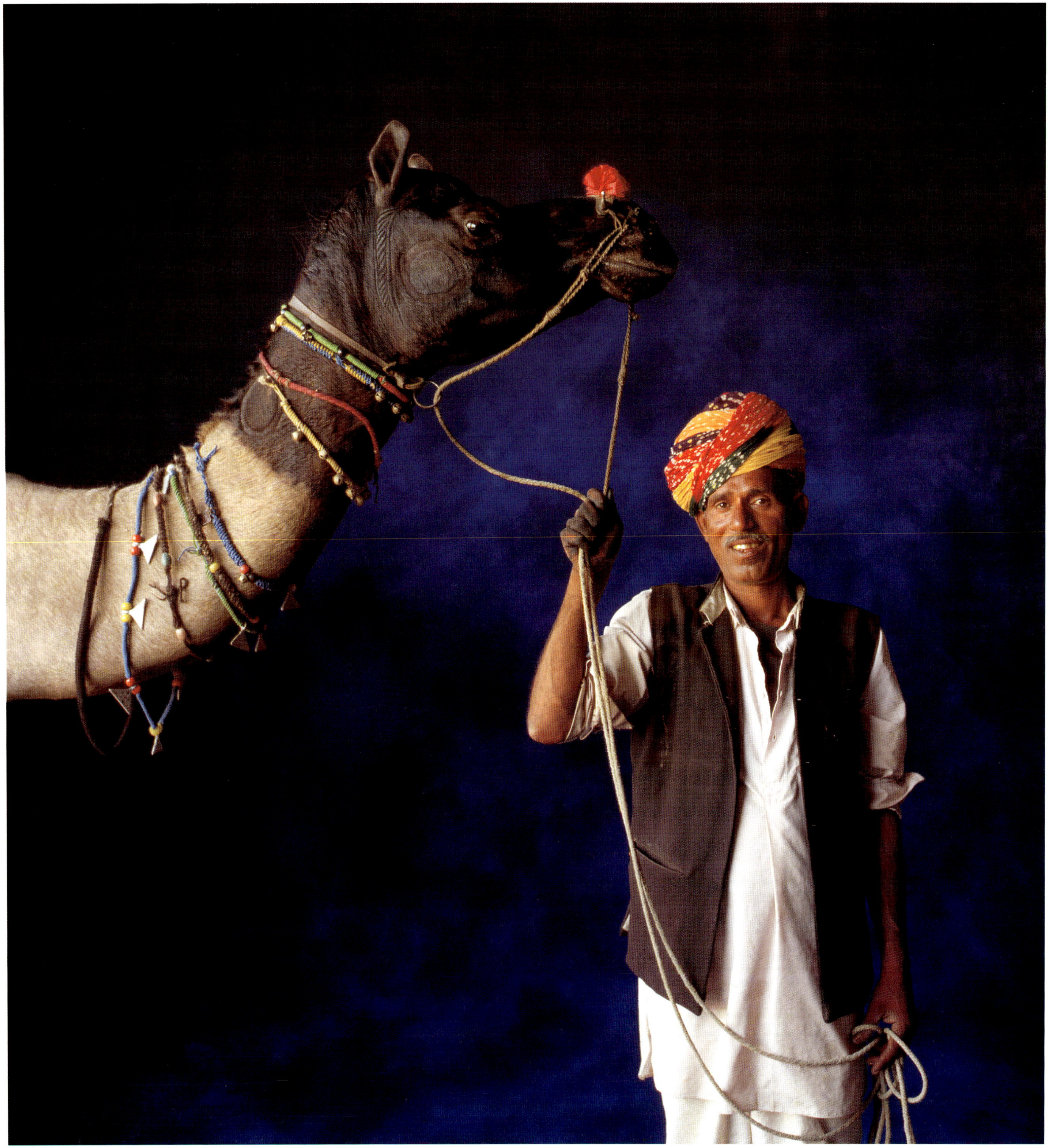

NANU RAM, FORTY, FARMER AND CAMEL BREEDER, GUJAR. PUSHKAR, RAJASTHAN.

Nanu Ram came to Pushkar to sell two camels and buy two new ones. This beautifully dressed young camel was called Raja, and was considered very special. Nanu Ram wanted to sell Raja for 35,000 rupees ($900). Camels can live up to thirty-five years of age.

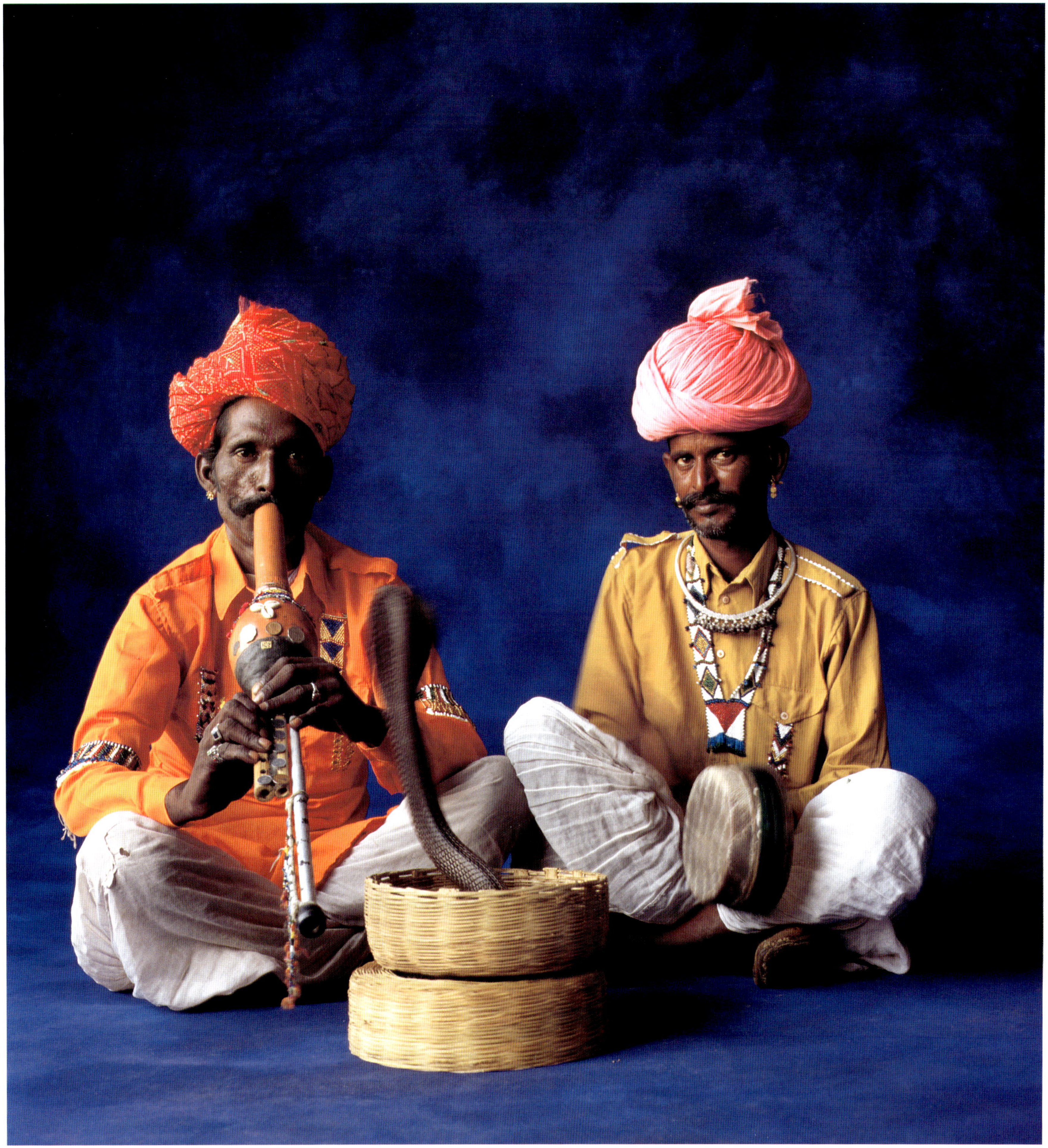

BARSNAT, THIRTY-FIVE, AND MOUNAT, THIRTY, SNAKE CHARMERS, SAVERA. PUSHKAR, RAJASTHAN.

Barsnat and Mounat came with their entire clan of dancers and musicians. They have been touring the major north Indian fairs for over ten years. Their snakes are not poisonous since the fangs have been removed.

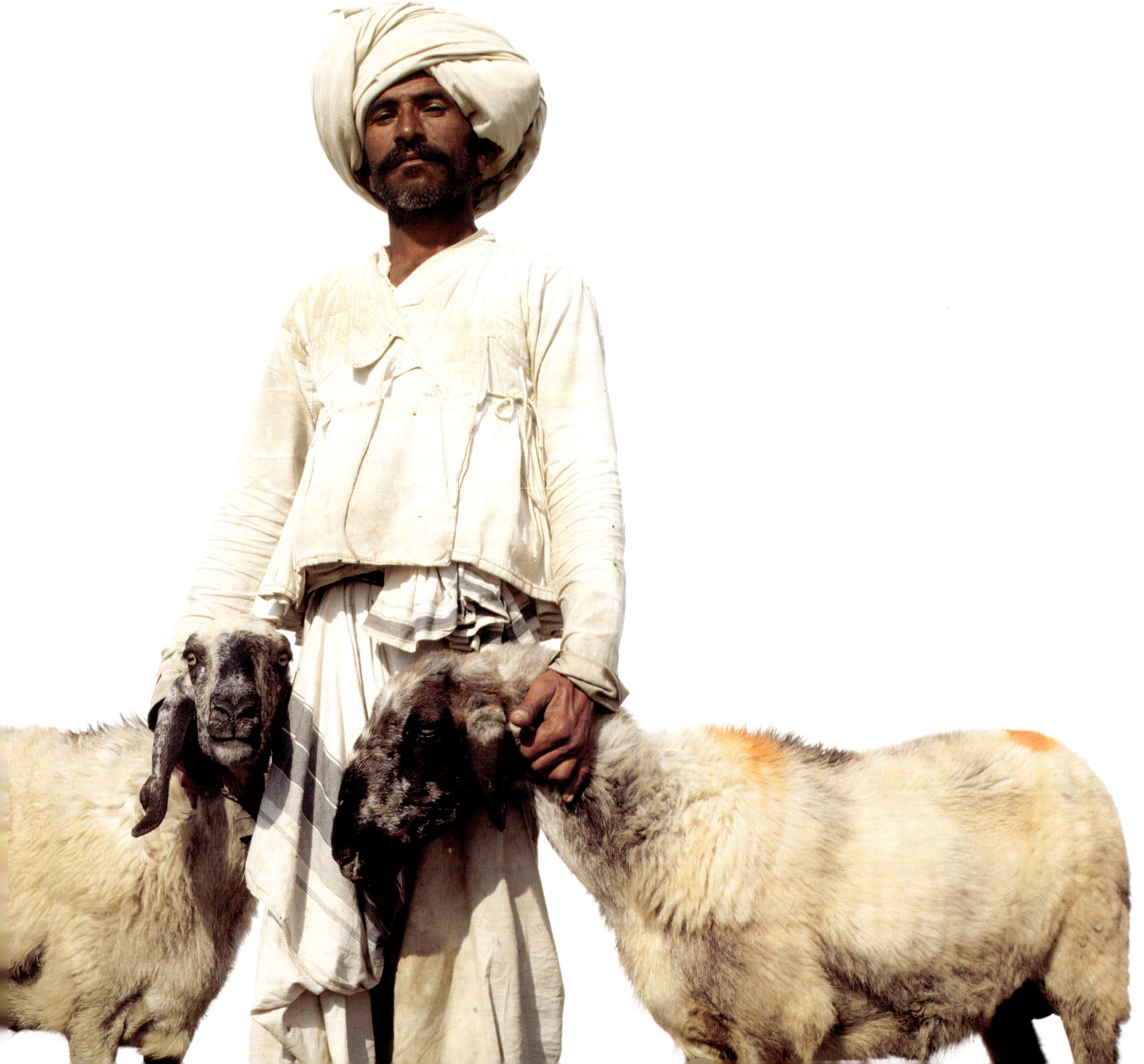

OPPOSITE: SARGARA, THIRTY, SHEPHERD, RABARI. GREAT RANN OF KUTCH, GUJARAT.

Sargara is a nomadic Rabari shepherd. For ten months of every year his clan moves along well-established grazing routes at the fringe of the salt pans of the Great Rann of Kutch. During the rainy season they build simple lean-tos. The rest of the year they live a nomadic lifestyle.

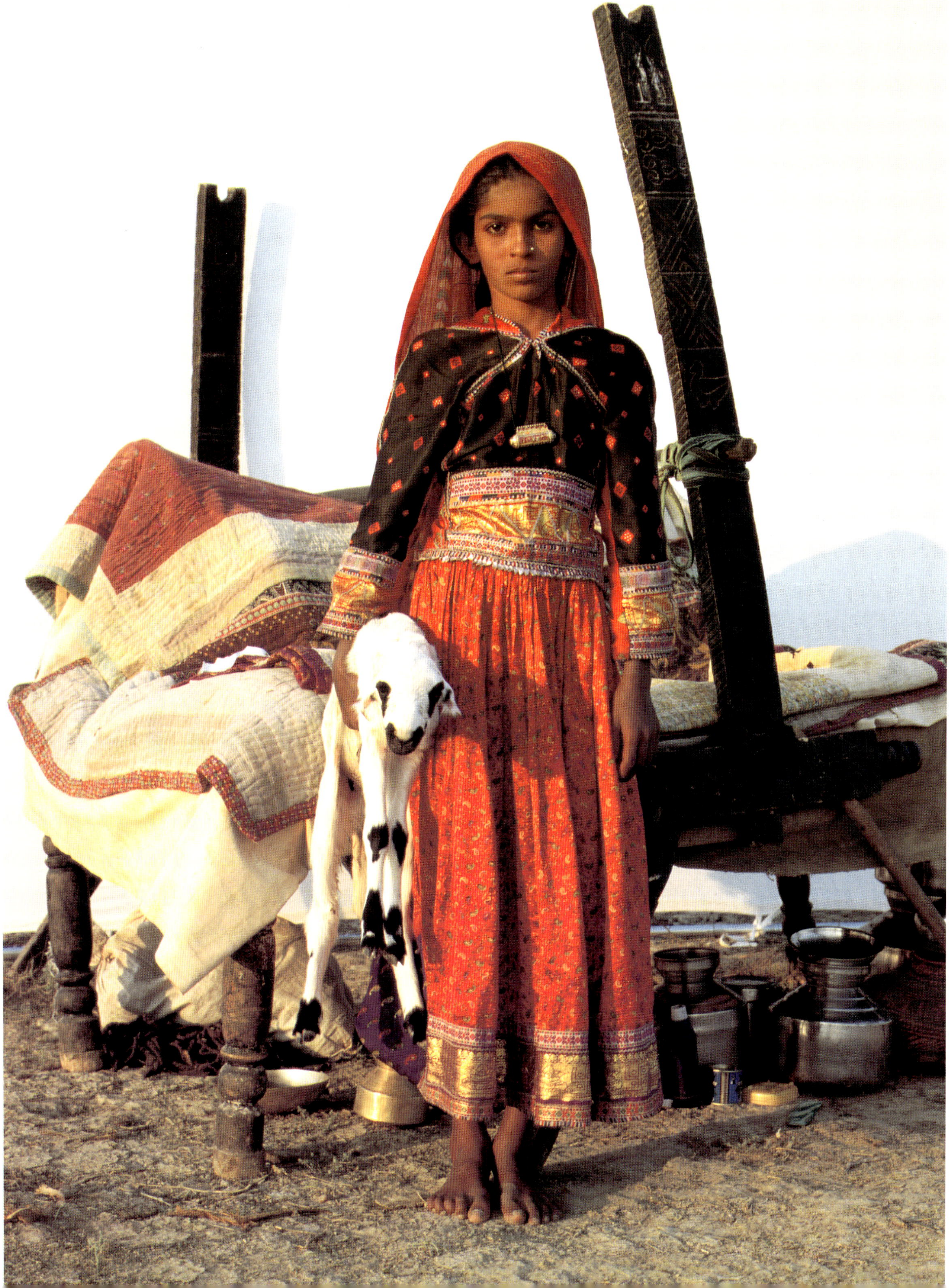

SHASHIBEN, ELEVEN, RABARI. GREAT RANN OF KUTCH, GUJARAT.

Shashiben has never attended school because her clan is always on the move, following age-old grazing routes with their flock of goats and sheep. Shashiben will soon be proficient at turning wool into handwoven materials. She milks the sheep and goats and carries heavy brass water containers on her head from distant waterholes.

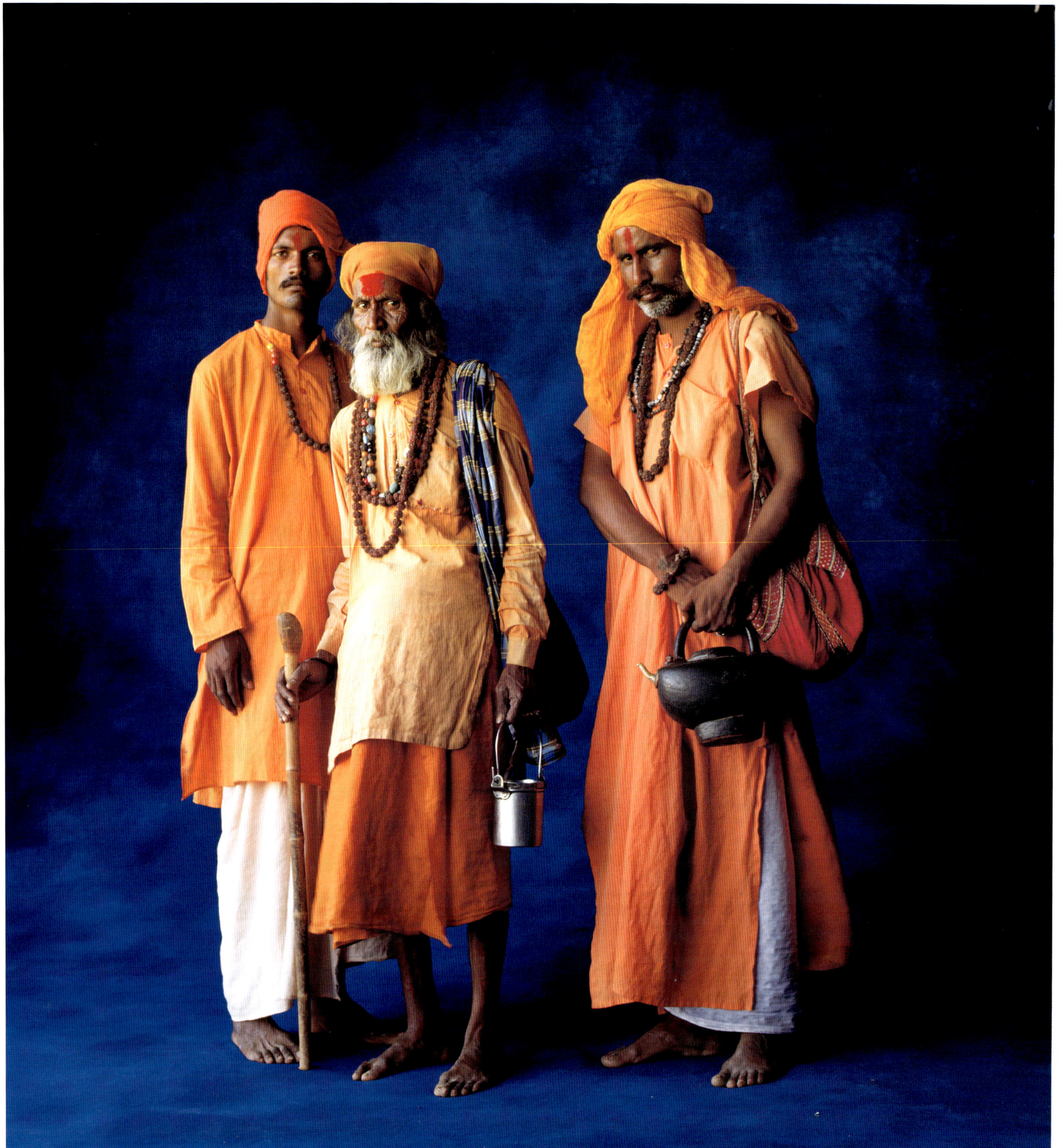

LEFT TO RIGHT: PRIMNATH, TWENTY-FOUR; RAM NARAYAN, FIFTY; AND JAGDISH, THIRTY; SADHUS. PUSHKAR, RAJASTHAN.

Primnath has been following a religious path for eight years, Ram Narayan for twenty, and Jagdish for ten. They wander from one religious festival to the next. Although they live off the alms they receive, they are not thought of as beggars, but rather as deeply religious men who have renounced all worldly goods.

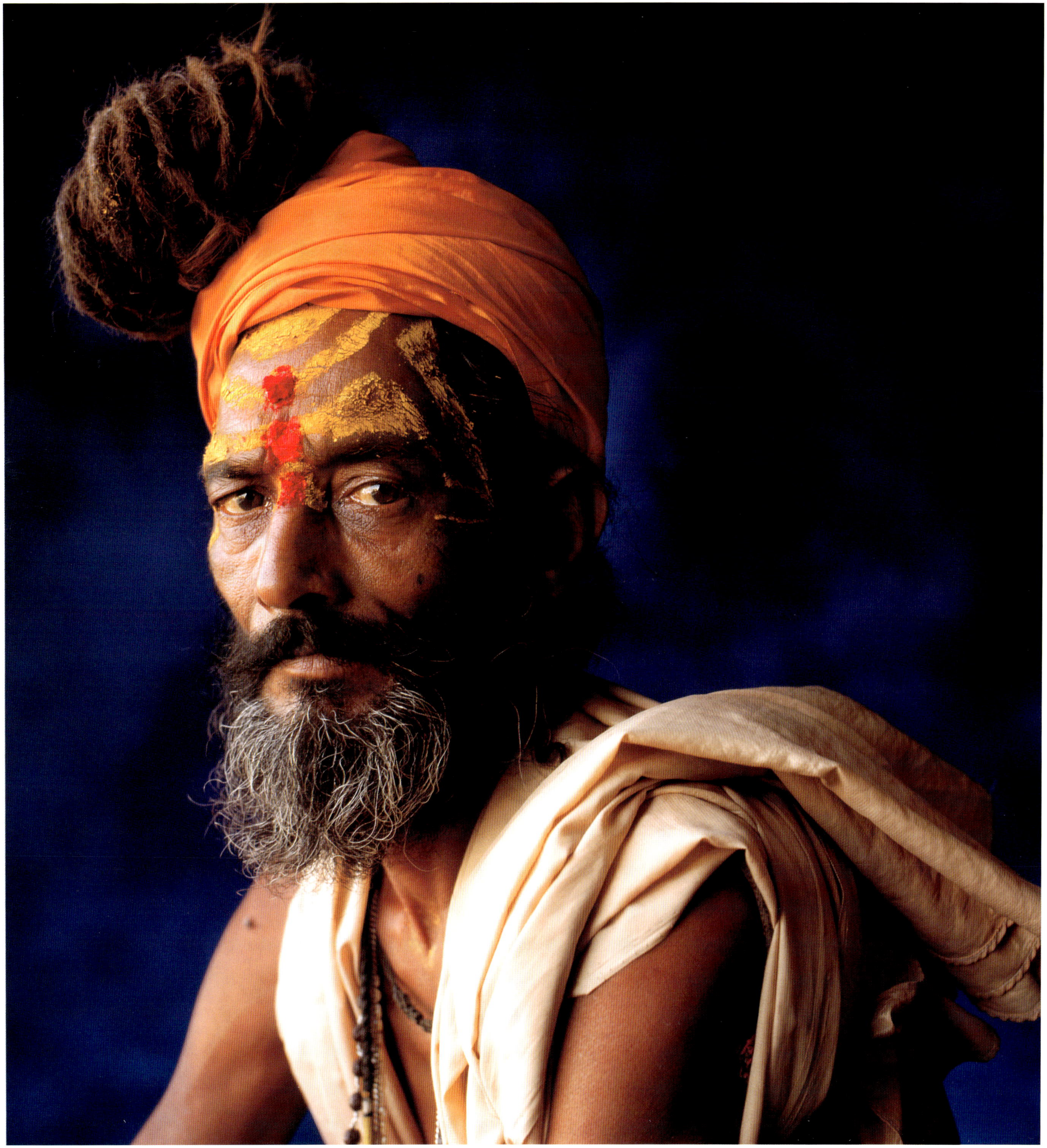

NAGA BABA,
FORTY-FIVE, SADHU.
PUSHKAR, RAJASTHAN.

Naga Baba, as a registered sadhu, has permission to smoke ganja in public. He grew up in an ashram in Sojad City and now lives in Jodhpur.

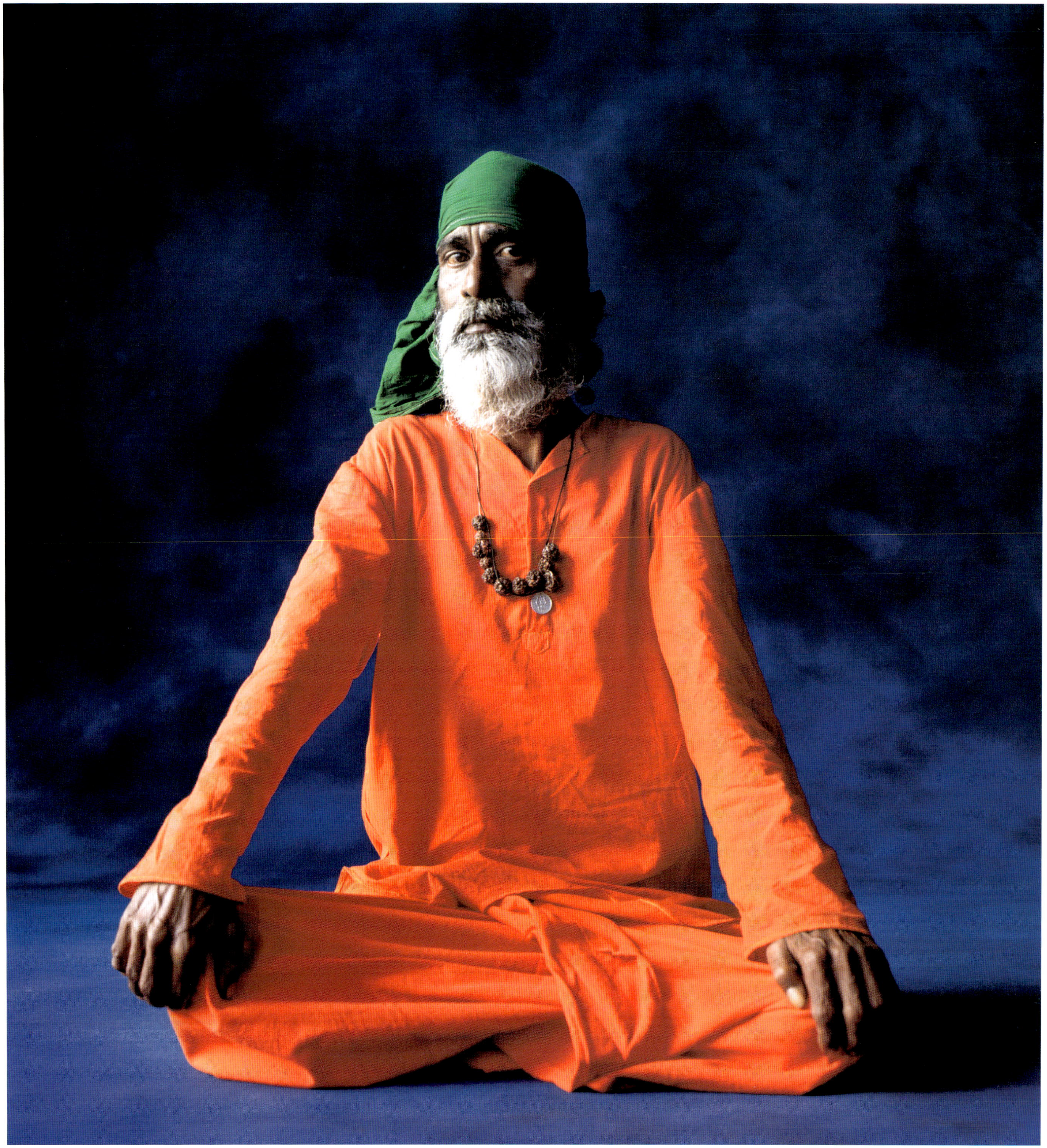

MADAN BARKA,
FIFTY-TWO, YOGI.
AJMER, RAJASTHAN.

Madan Barka has been a railway servant for twenty-five years. He left his wife and three children in Nagpur to become a Hindu yogi (a reflective or mystical person). Madan Barka's religious beliefs cross customary boundaries, as demonstrated by his participation in Ajmer's great Sufi festival.

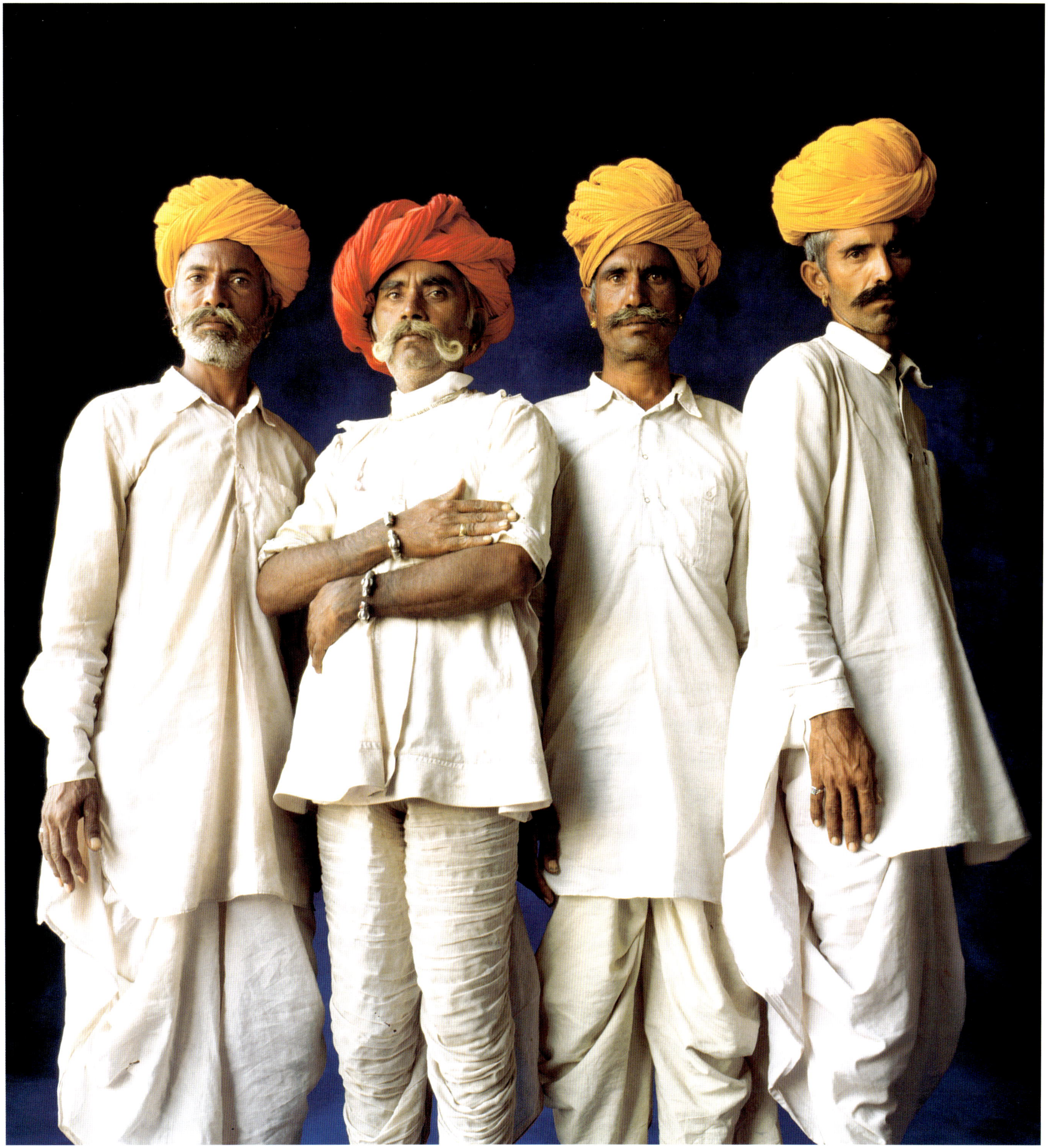

LEFT TO RIGHT: CHOTURAM, THIRTY-FIVE, FARMER; PUNARAM, FIFTY, GOATHERD; DUNGARAM, THIRTY-TWO, CAMEL TRADER; AND SARWAN SINGH, FIFTY, NIGHT WATCHMAN; RAJASTHANI. PUSHKAR, RAJASTHAN.

These four men are typical of visitors to the Pushkar camel and cattle fair. Most of the traders arrive five days before the full moon so they can finish their trading before the start of the mela.

THE POVERTY OF OUR CENTURY IS UNLIKE THAT OF ANY OTHER. IT IS NOT, AS POVERTY WAS BEFORE, THE RESULT OF NATURAL SCARCITY, BUT OF A SET OF PRIORITIES IMPOSED UPON THE REST OF THE WORLD BY THE RICH. CONSEQUENTLY, THE MODERN POOR ARE NOT PITIED—BUT WRITTEN OFF AS TRASH. THE TWENTIETH-CENTURY CONSUMER ECONOMY HAS PRODUCED THE FIRST CULTURE FOR WHICH A BEGGAR IS A REMINDER OF NOTHING.

—JOHN BERGER

HUNAMANTA, THIRTY-FIVE,
AND KRISHANA, TWENTY-TWO,
BEGGARS. PUSHKAR, RAJASTHAN.

Hunamanta and Krishana are crippled beggars who have coated themselves with ashes in the manner of sadhus. Hunamanta has traveled from Calcutta, and Krishana from Karnataka. Because of the many compassionate pilgrims who attend fairs like the Pushkar mela, beggars are attracted from all over India.

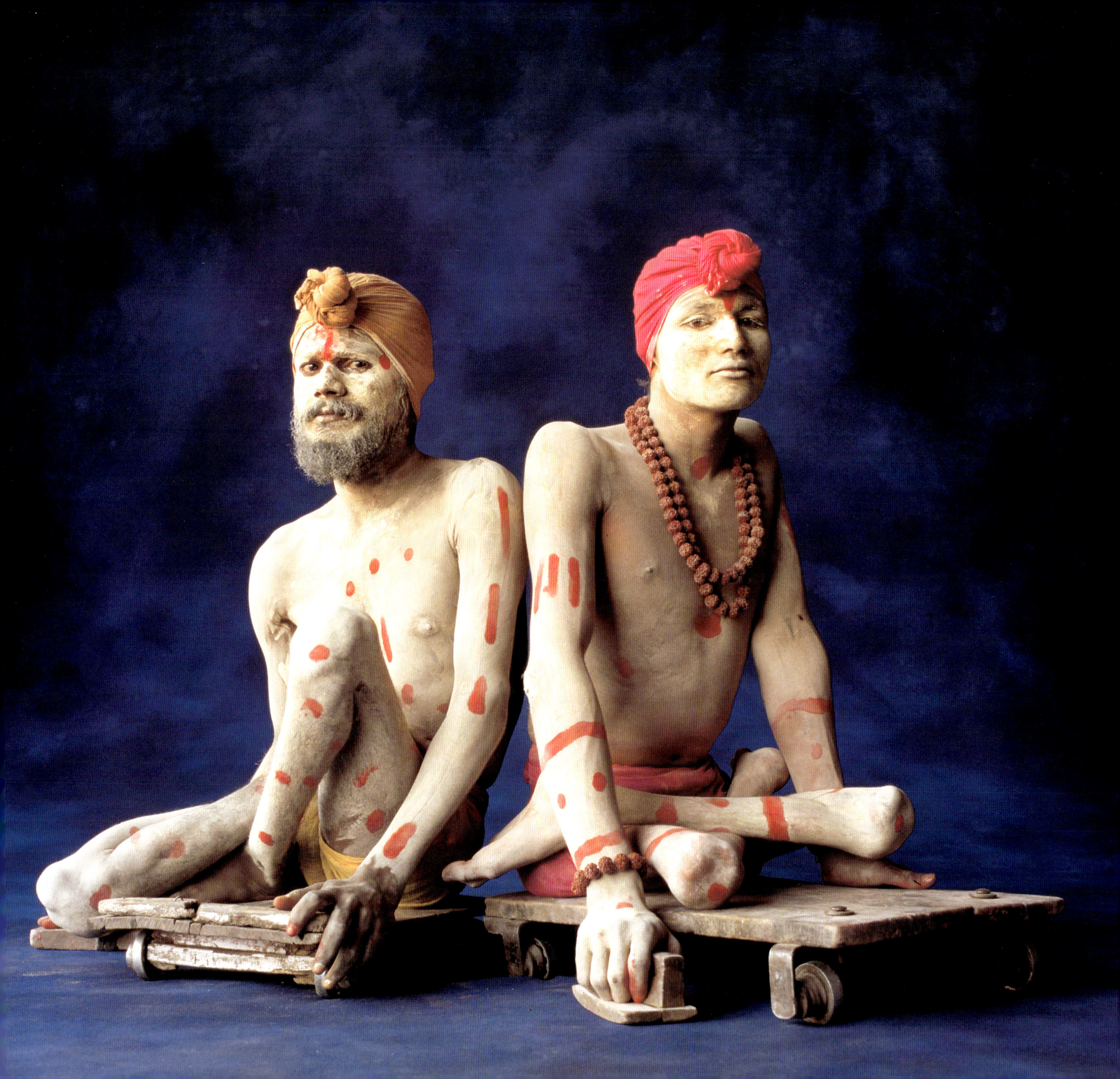

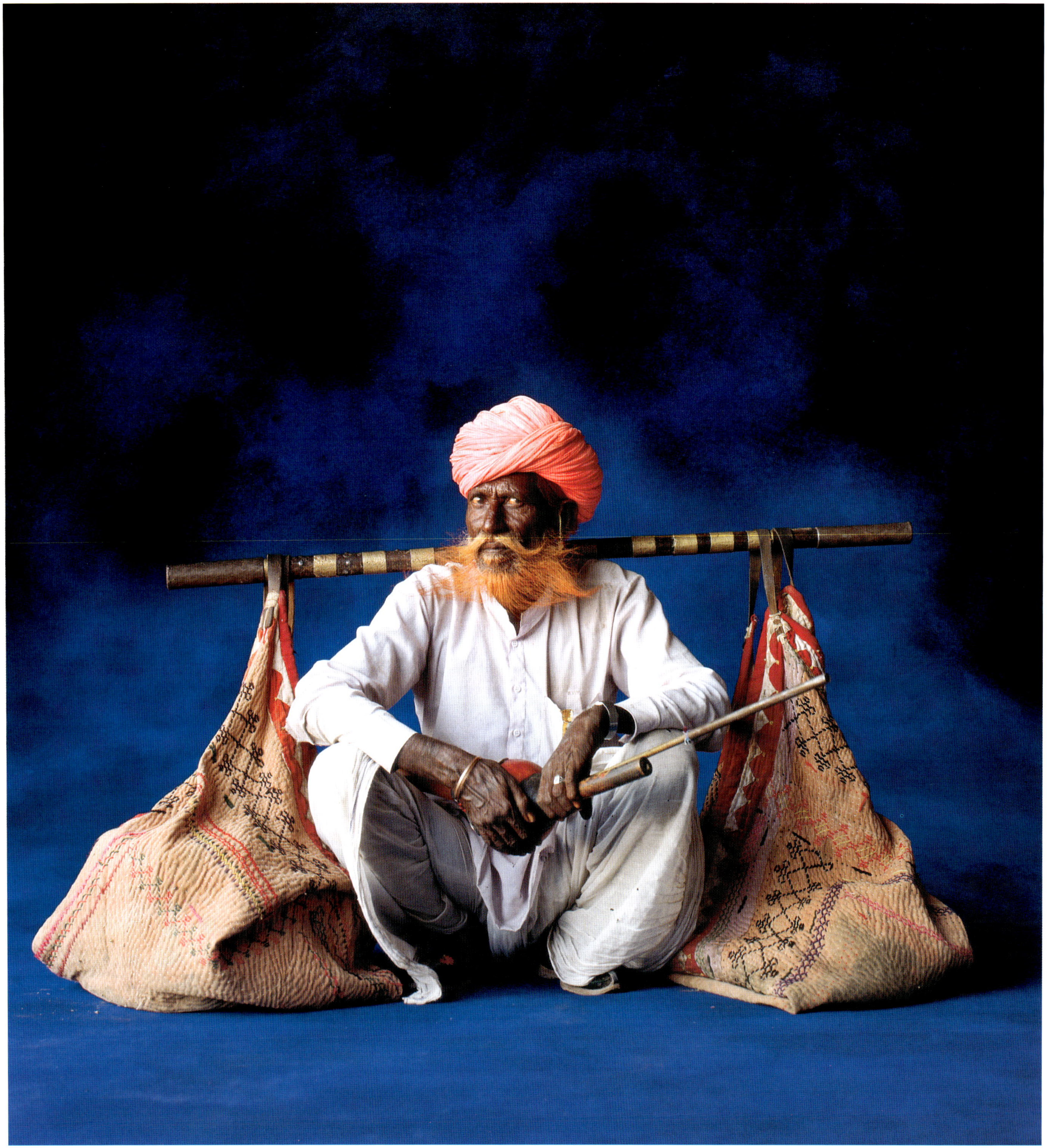

SONATH, EIGHTY,
SNAKE CHARMER,
SAVERA. PUSHKAR,
RAJASTHAN.

Sonath carries his king cobras in two bags across his shoulders. As a snake charmer, he has traveled the width and breadth of northwest India most of his life. There is usually a mela going on somewhere, yet even in the periods between festivals he simply has to open his sacks on a street corner to attract patrons.

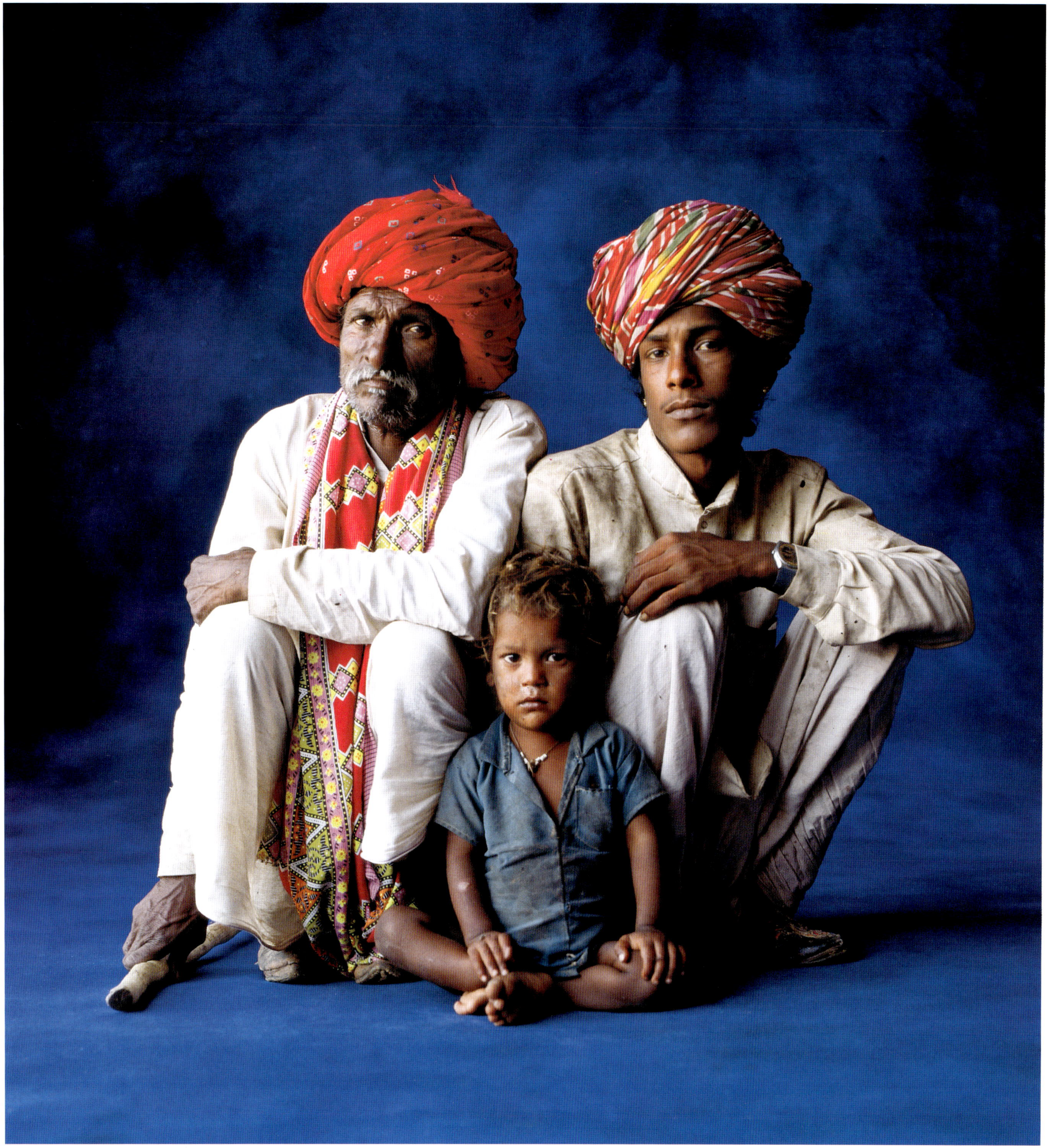

LEFT TO RIGHT:
MANGER, SIXTY; BARJO, TWENTY-ONE, AND HIS SON RAMES, THREE; CAMEL BREEDERS AND FARMERS, GUJAR. PUSHKAR, RAJASTHAN.

Manger came to Pushkar to sell seven camels. Barjo has his own small farm and one camel. He and his son traveled one and a half days by cart to reach the fair, sixty miles from his farm.

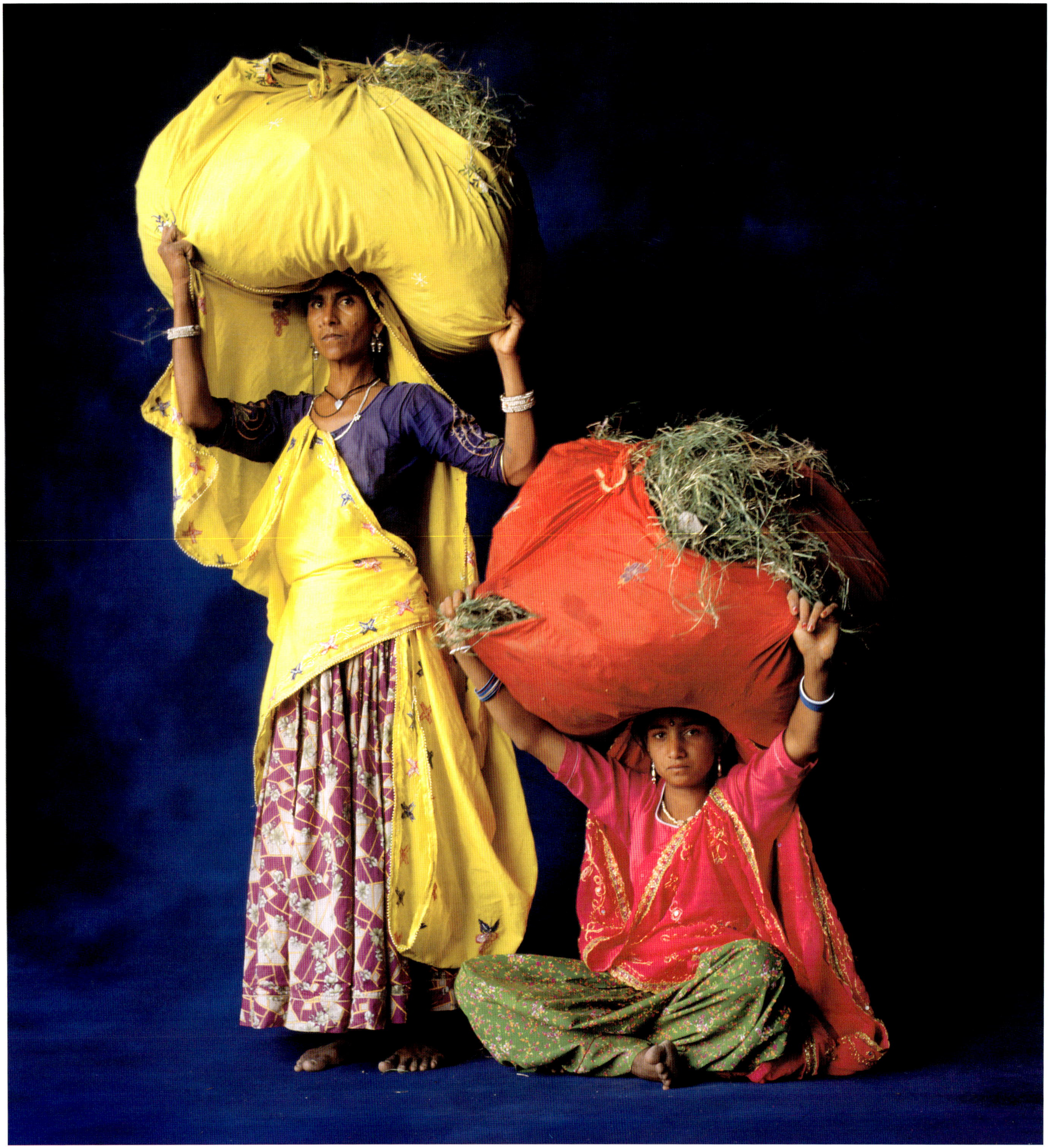

SUKA, THIRTY, AND BIMLA, EIGHTEEN, RAJASTHANI. PUSHKAR, RAJASTHAN.

Suka and Bimla sell fodder to the camel and cattle traders. Both live in Kaneida, a village not far from Pushkar. The mela provides them with additional income. With sixteen thousand camels to be fed over several days, the farmers of Pushkar have a high demand to meet.

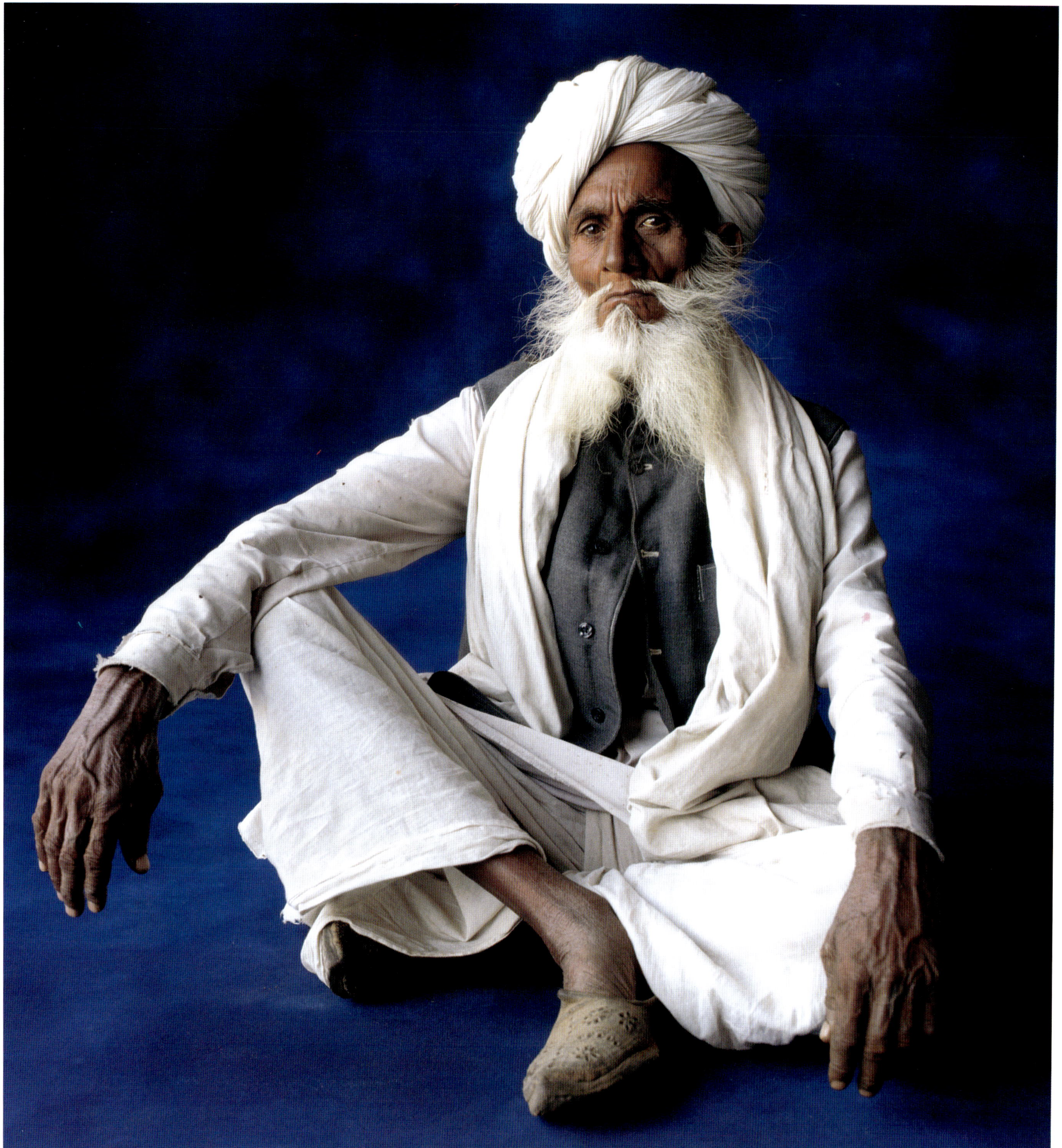

BHAWARLAL, SIXTY, CAMEL HERDER, RAJASTHANI. PUSHKAR, RAJASTHAN.

As is common with Rajasthani men, Bhawarlal values his mustache and beard. As a rule, elderly men from rural Rajasthan groom their beards in a highly individual fashion.

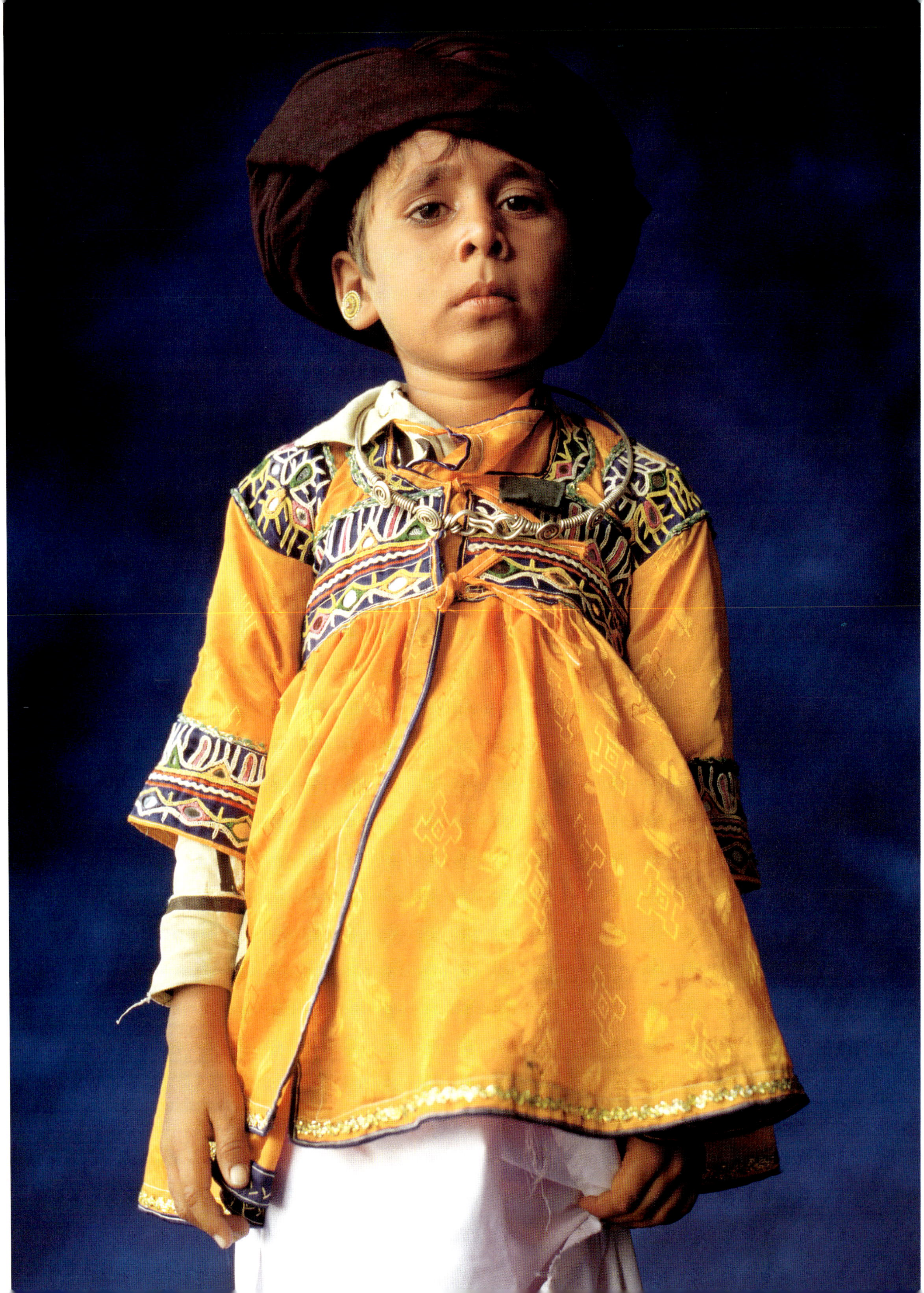

SANGO, FOUR, RABARI.
TUNDAWANDH, GUJARAT.

Sango's mother made the intricately embroidered shirt he wears here. His father, Manda, herds camels, and after completing the five grades of Tundawandh's elementary school, Sango too will most likely become a camel herder.

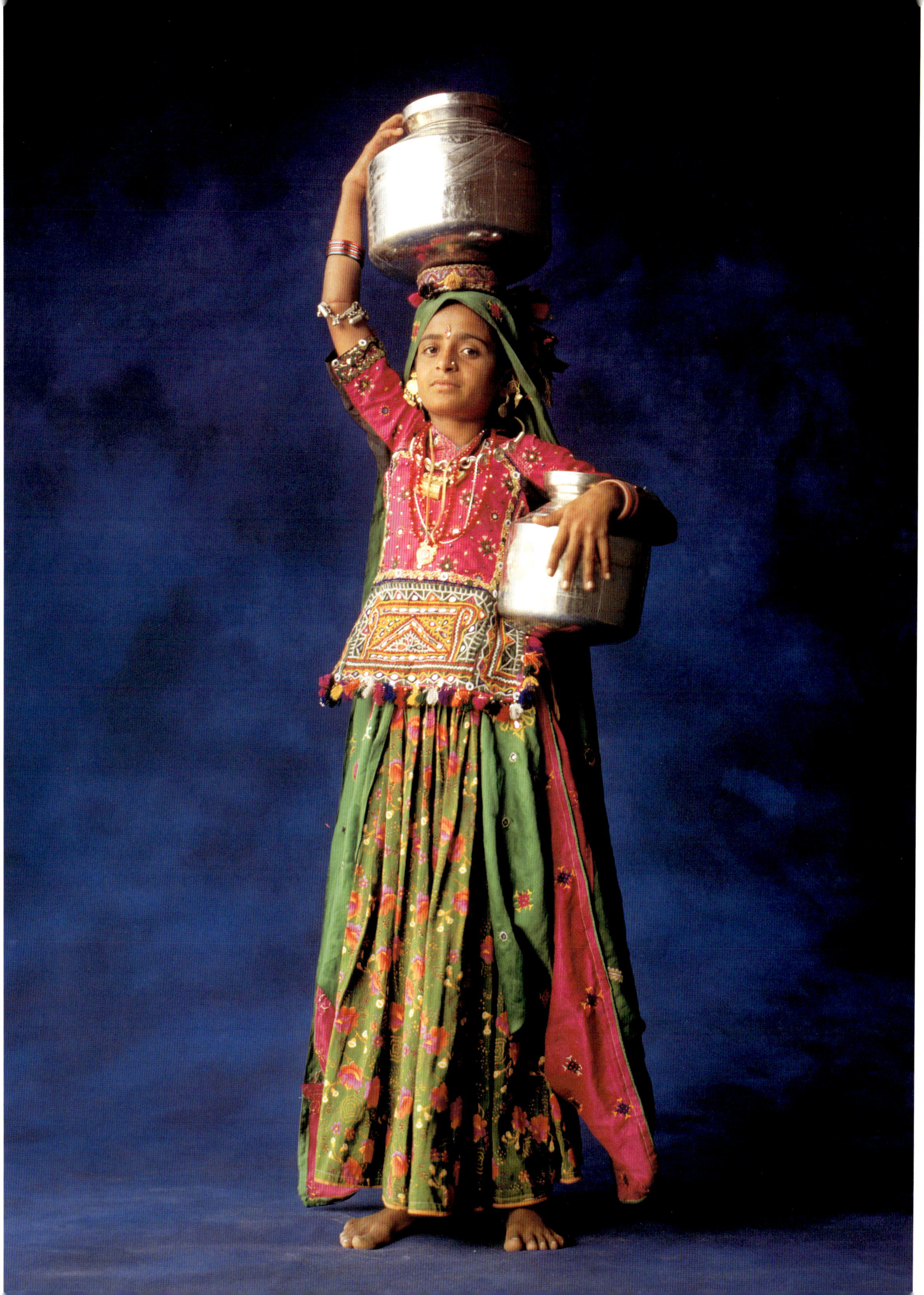

KAUBEN, FIFTEEN, RABARI.
TUNDAWANDH, GUJARAT.

Kauben is in school. While the children of the nomadic Rabaris do not attend school, a new age has begun for the youngsters of Tundawandh. Their fathers are shepherds and camel herders while their mothers earn their living making embroideries; it is common that the older generations can neither read nor write.

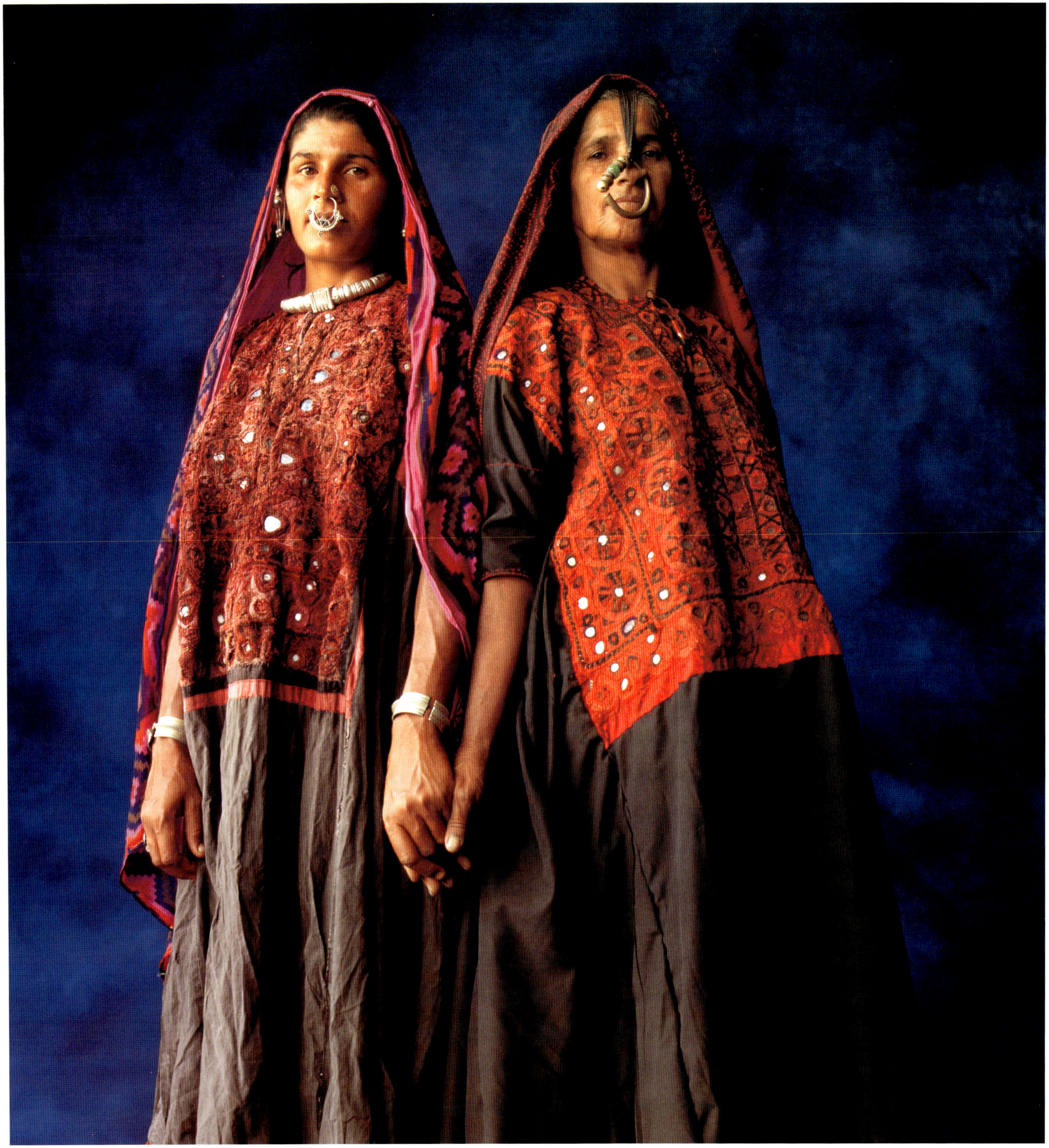

HIRAMBAI,
TWENTY-FIVE, AND
BACHAMBAI, THIRTY,
DANETHA JATHS.
GANDHA, GUJARAT.

Hirambai and Bachambai live in the marshes of the Banni area of northern Gujarat, a region reserved for cattle and buffalo herders. Buffalo toss and turn in the mud before going out to graze.

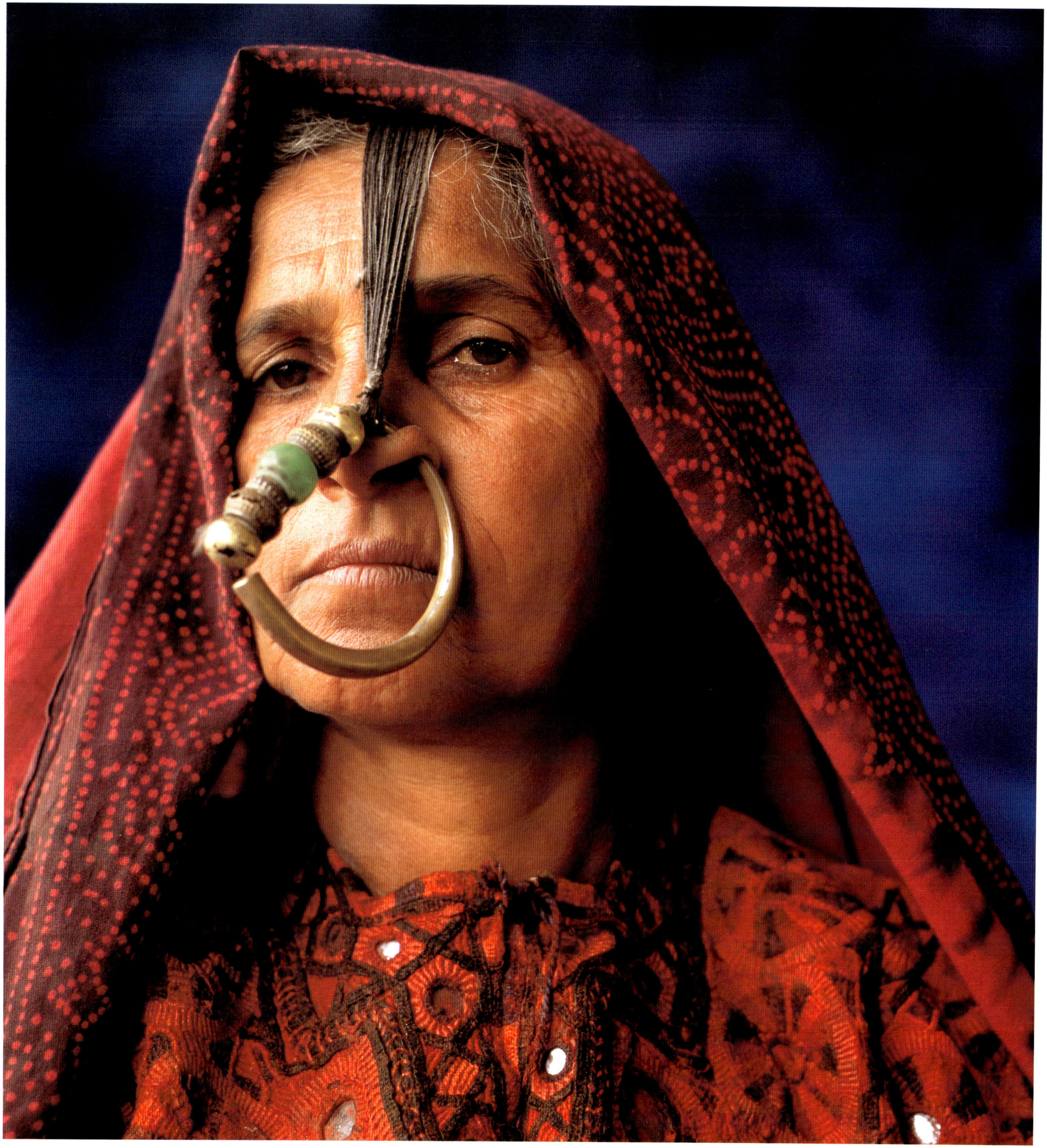

BACHAMBAI, THIRTY, DANETHA JATH, PASTORALIST. GANDHA, GUJARAT.

Bachambai is a Muslim Danetha Jath woman. The Jaths are a poor buffalo-herding tribe. The women tend to be very shy and keep out of sight of strangers. Many Jath women pride themselves on their huge gold nose rings.

CHASSIBE, THIRTY, RABARI.
TUNDAWANDH, GUJARAT.

Chassibe earns her living producing exquisite embroideries. Groups of women chat in the shade of their verandas as they embroider blouses and jackets.

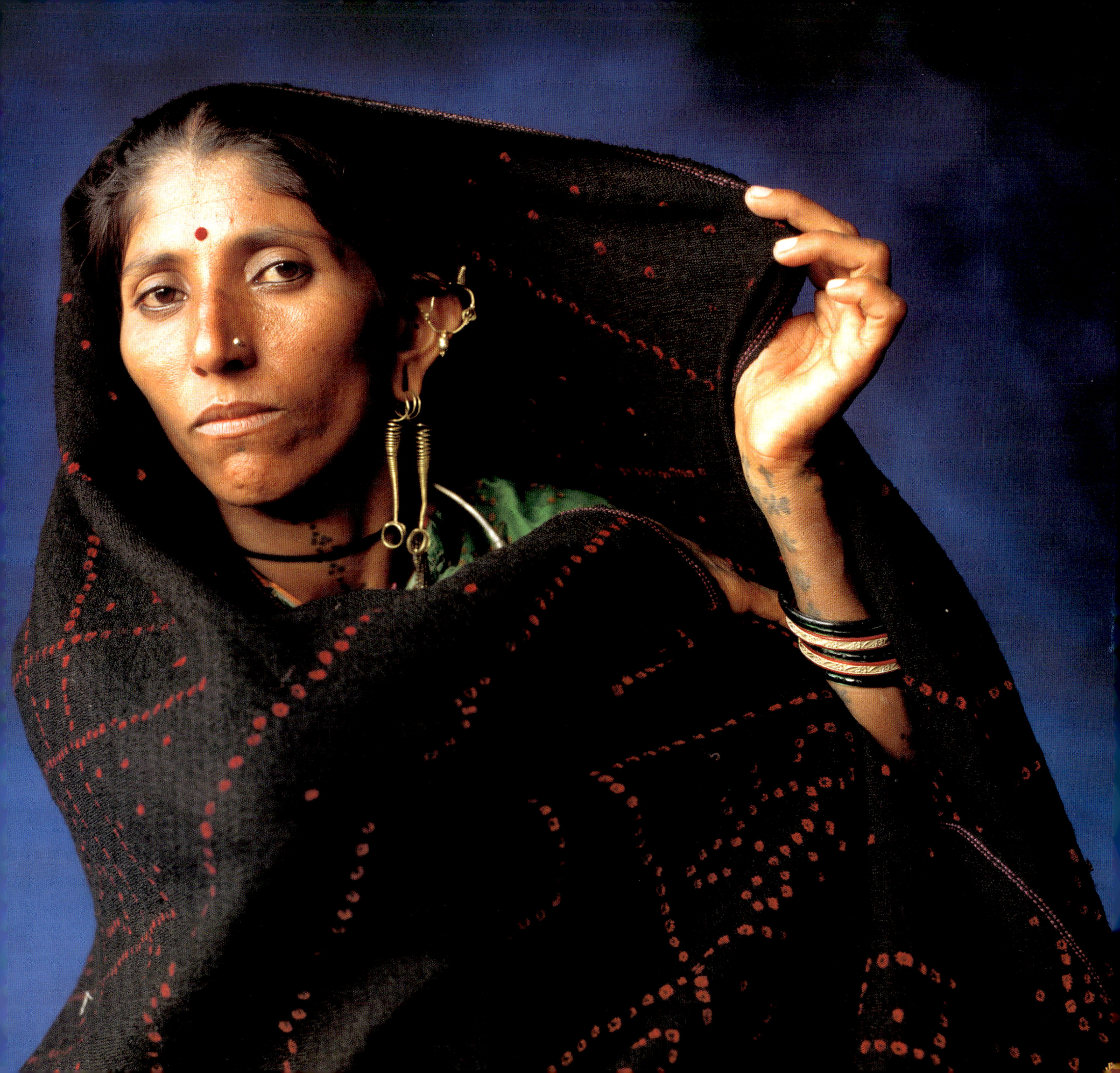

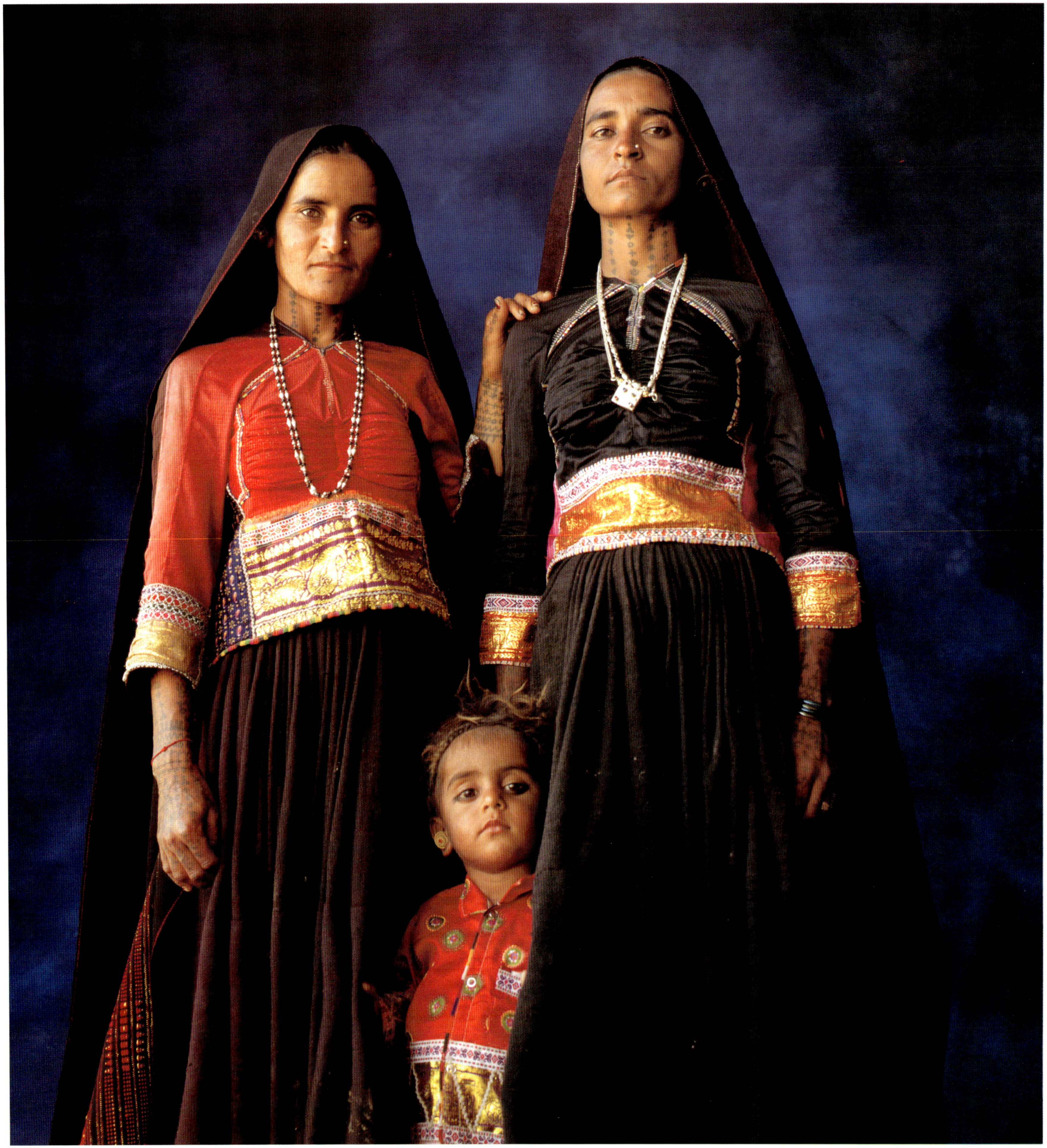

LEFT TO RIGHT: SAHE, NINETEEN; SAHE'S DAUGHTER BAHMU, FOUR; HABE, NINETEEN; DHEBARIA RABARI. GREAT RANN OF KUTCH, GUJARAT.

While the men are out tending the goats and sheep, Dhebaria women keep the camp in order. They walk long distances to fetch water, cook on small open fires, care for the children, and weave and embroider.

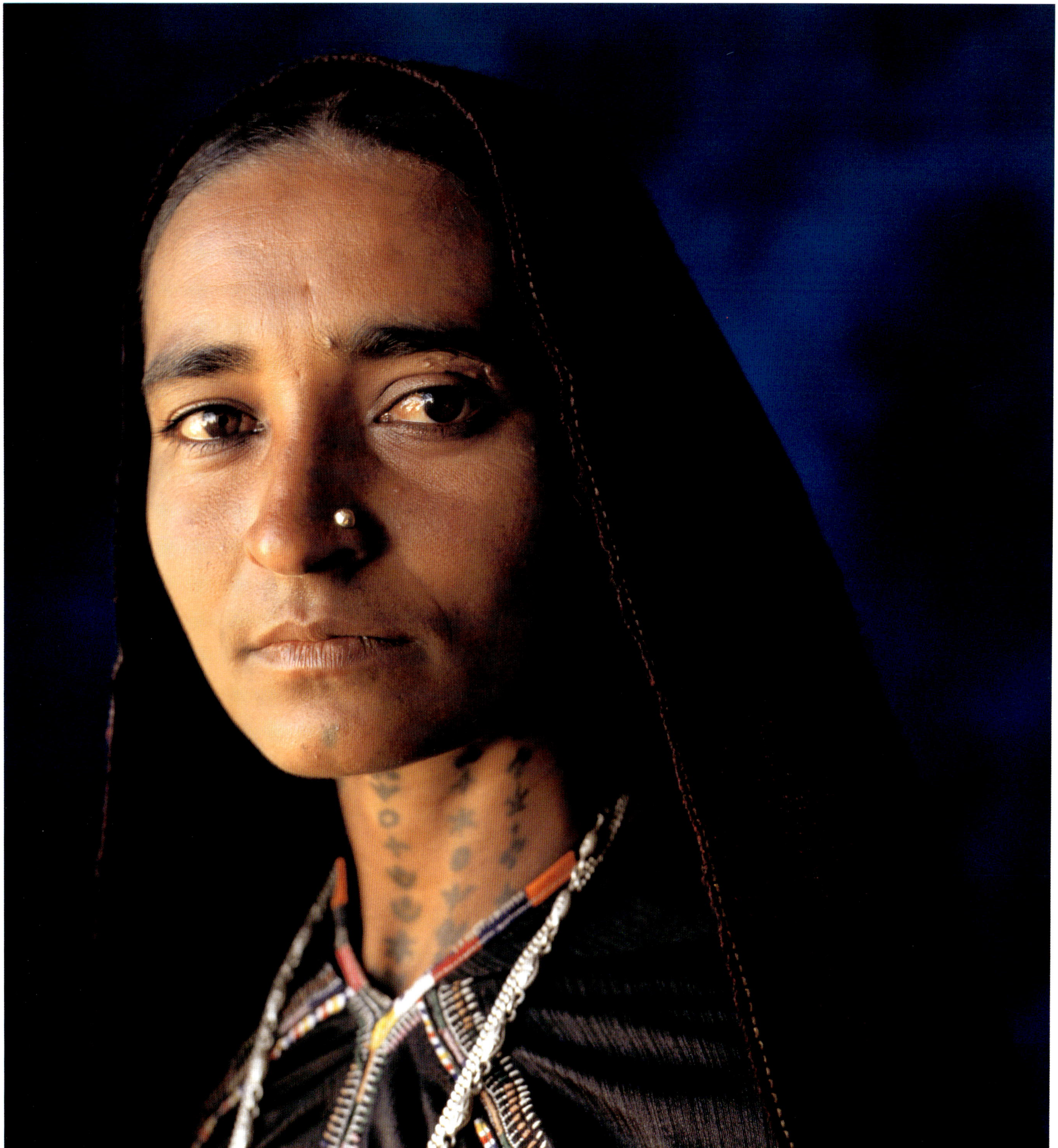

HABE, NINETEEN,
DHEBARIA RABARI.
GREAT RANN OF KUTCH,
GUJARAT.

Among the nomadic Dhebaria Rabari, the men wear white while the women wear black. Black wool is seen as wastage, and cannot be sold on the market. Although black is a color of mourning, the Rabaris often elaborately embroider their dresses.

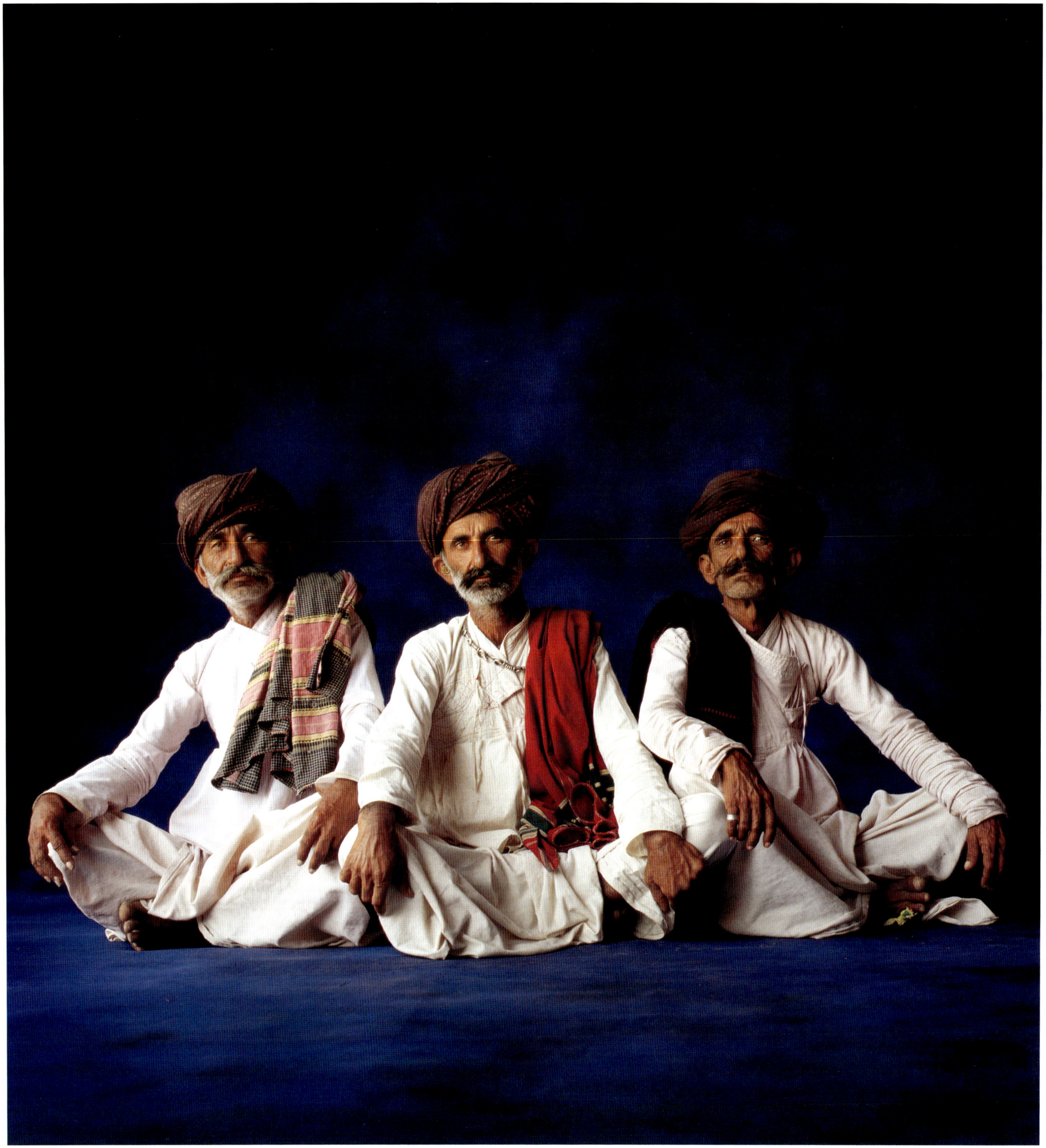

LEFT TO RIGHT:
SAGEN, FIFTY-FIVE;
HIRA, SIXTY; AND
LAKA, FORTY; CAMEL
HERDERS, RABARI.
TUNDAWANDH, GUJARAT.

Sagen, Hira, and Laka are settled Rabari camel herders. They are brothers, and together they own thirty camels. They live in simple but beautifully decorated round houses. They leave their village every morning and return again at sunset.

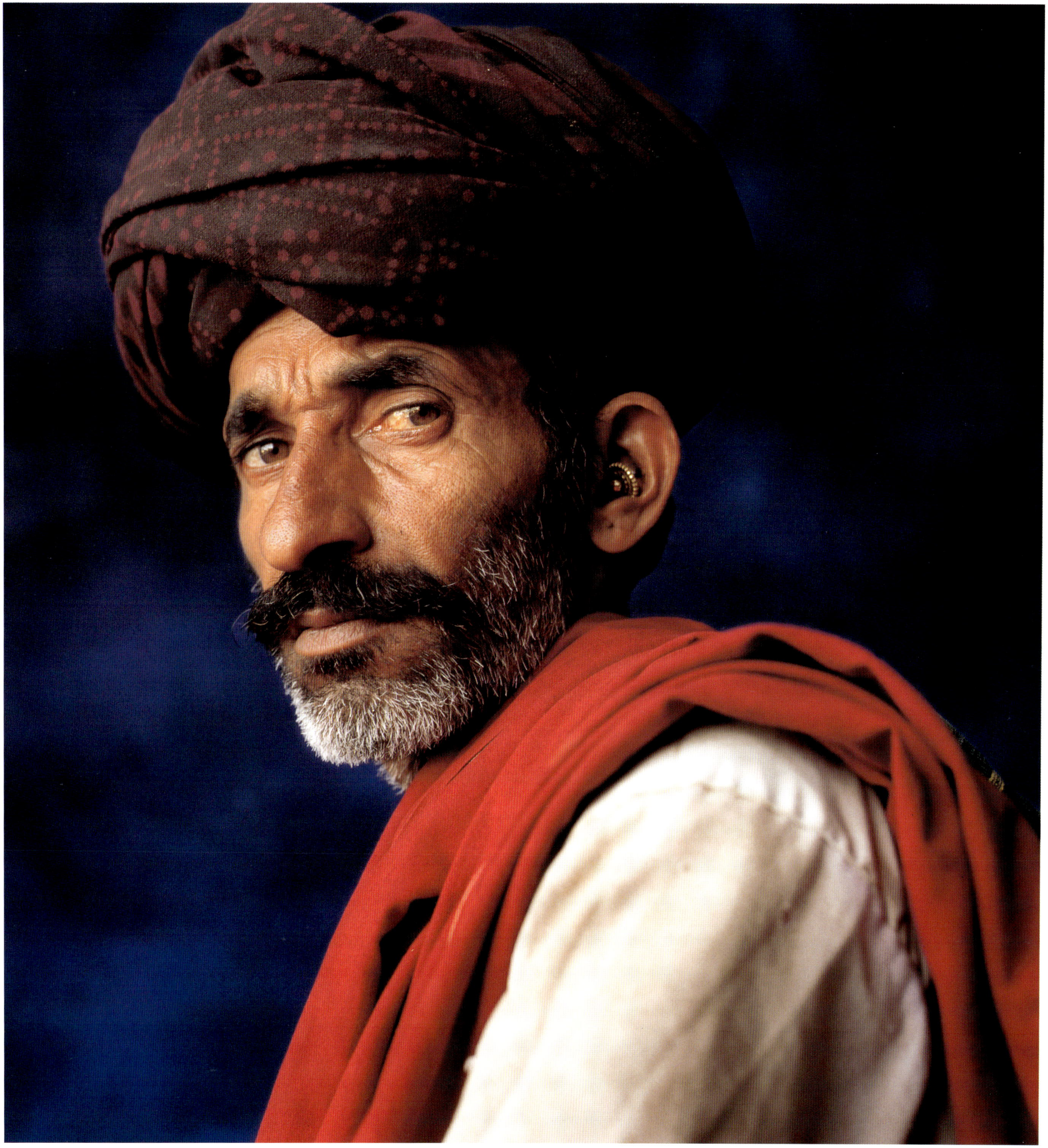

MANDA, THIRTY-TWO, RABARI. TUNDAWANDH, GUJARAT.

Manda lives in the village of Tundawandh, south of the regional capital of Bhuj. He accompanies his thirty camels daily on their grazing route. His children attend the village school. Their lives are much more comfortable than those of their nomadic cousins.

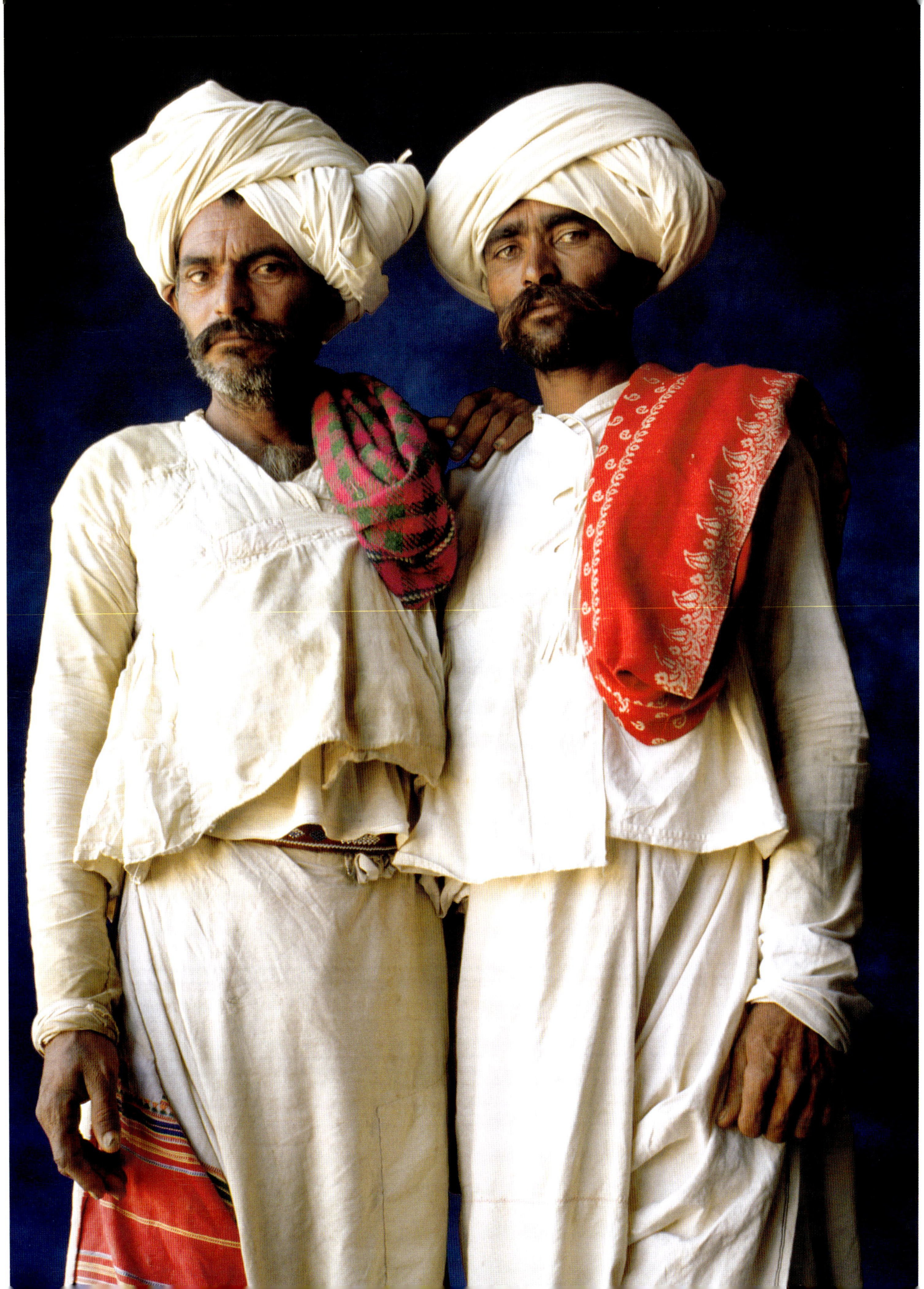

BURA, TWENTY-FIVE, AND PALO, TWENTY-FIVE, DHEBARIA RABARIS, SHEPHERDS. GREAT RANN OF KUTCH, GUJARAT.

Except for the two months of incessant rainfall each year, when the land is inundated and impassable, Dhebaria Rabari shepherds are always on the move. Their endurance, living as they do at the border of the salt pans of the Great Rann of Kutch, is proverbial.

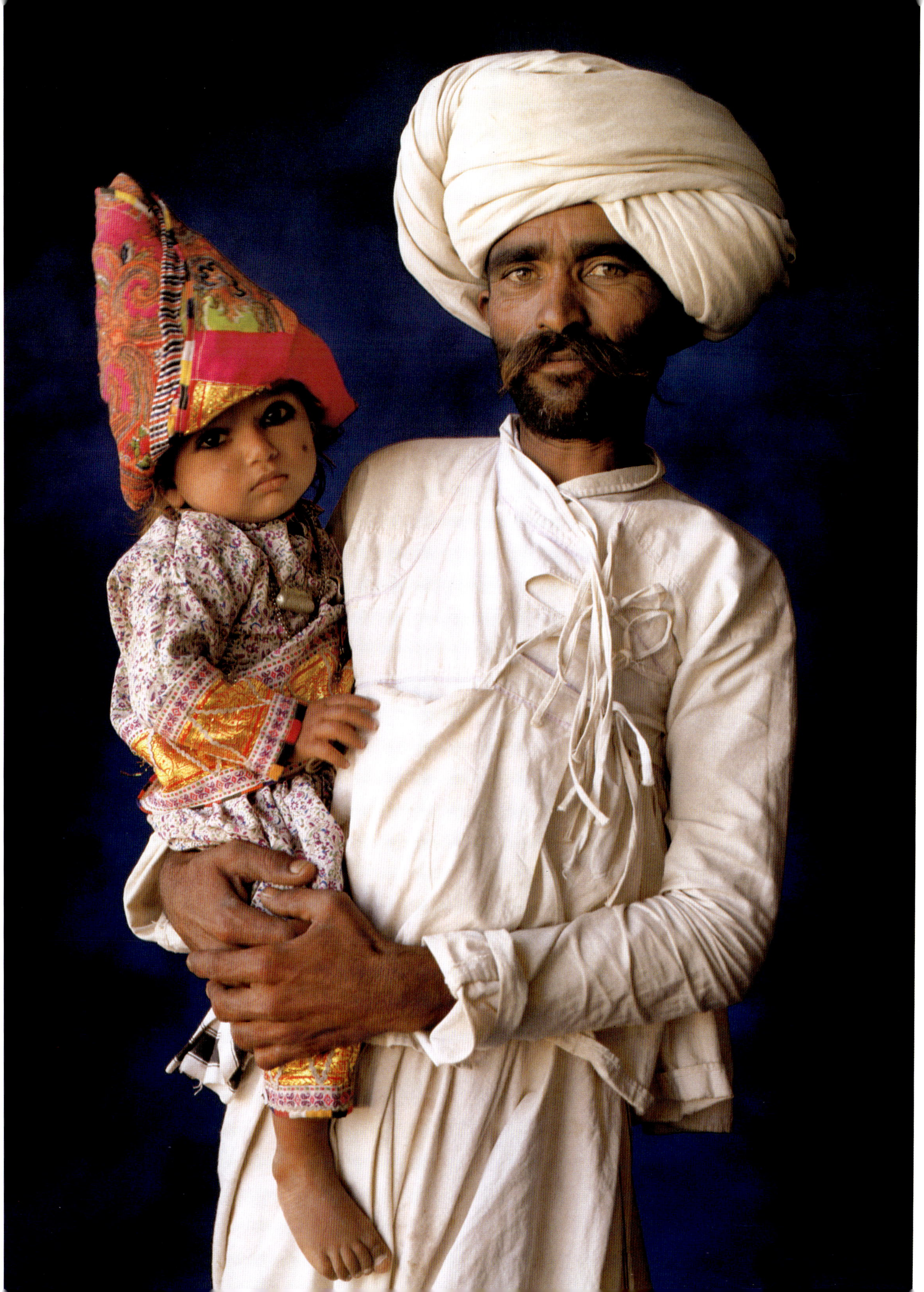

PALO, TWENTY-FIVE, AND HIS DAUGHTER, ROWO; SHEPHERD, DHEBARIA RABARI. GREAT RANN OF KUTCH, GUJARAT.

Every morning, shortly after sunrise, Palo leaves camp with the other men and their flocks of goats and sheep. The women then pack their belongings onto the family camels and move to the next site, where at sunset they will be joined by the men and their flocks.

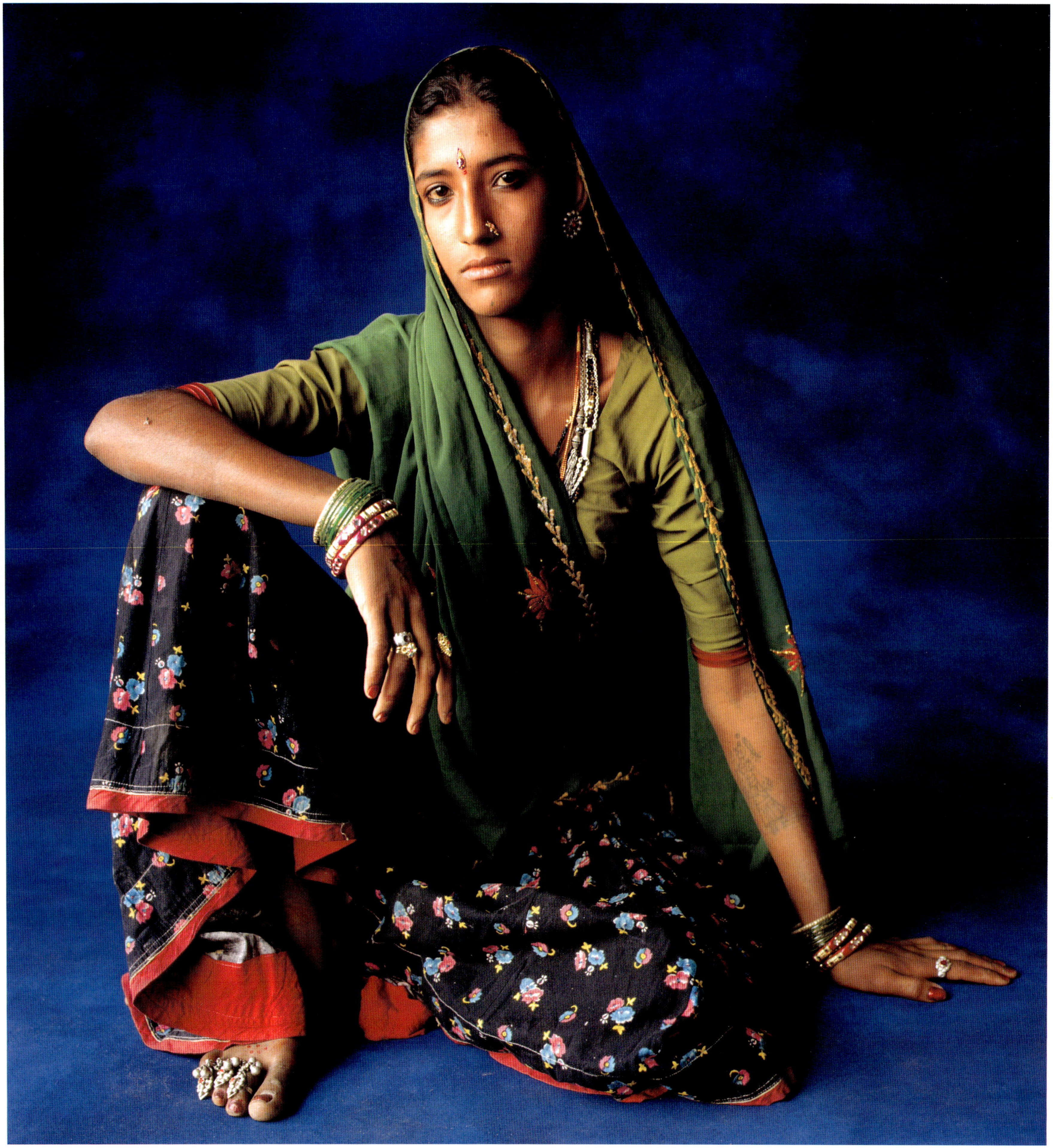

RASSIA, TWENTY-TWO, RAJASTHANI. PUSHKAR, RAJASTHAN.

Rassia, from the village of Naduara, is married to a Rajasthani farmer. She and her husband come every year to the Pushkar mela. She believes that participating in a puja (a religious ceremony), during the auspicious time of the *Kartik Purnima* (full moon) will cleanse her of her sins.

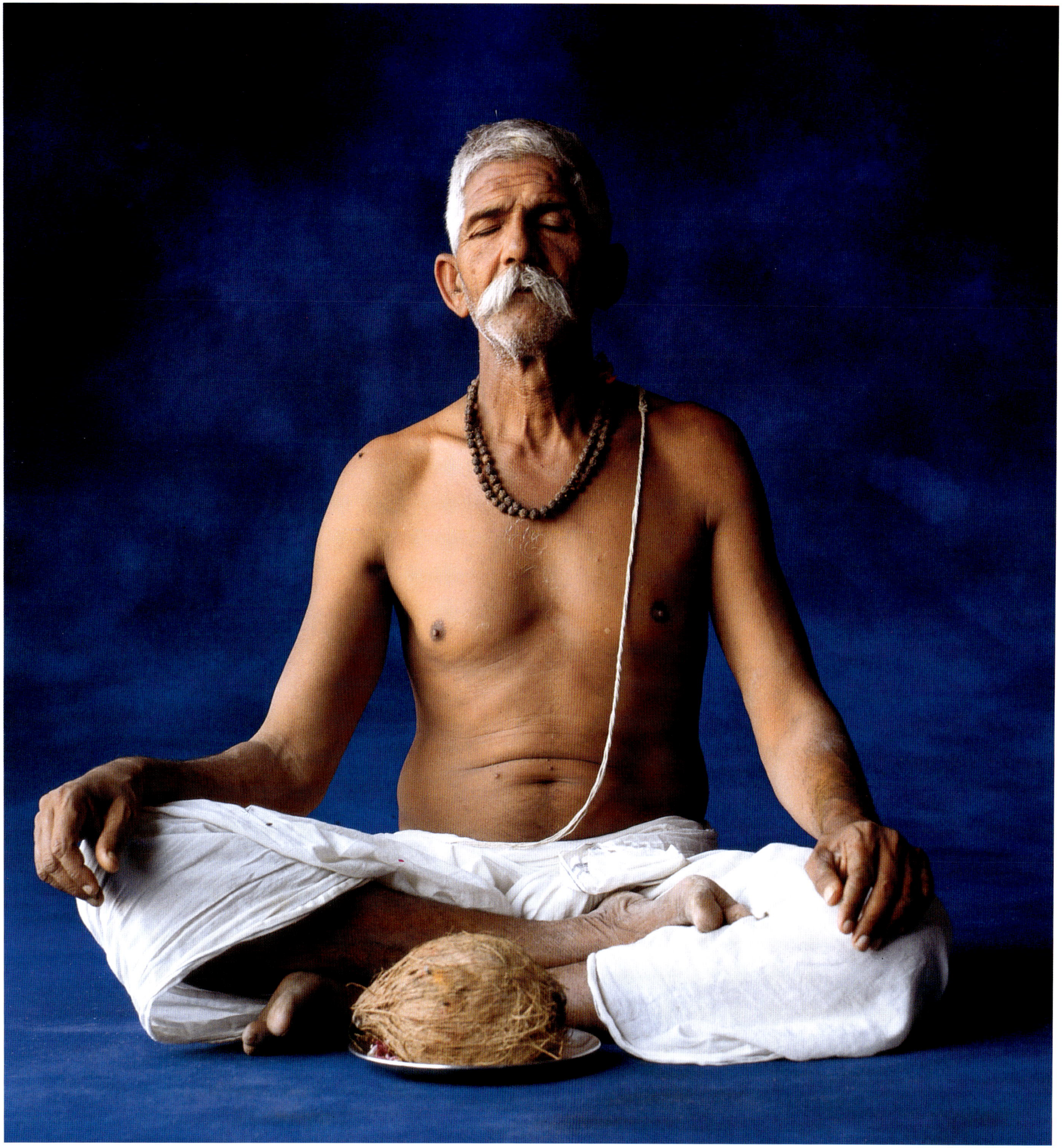

SAT NARAN GI, FIFTY-SIX. PUSHKAR, RAJASTAN.

Sat Naran Gi, a Hindu Brahman priest, performs ritual *pujas* five times a day at a ghat (stepped embankment) by Lake Sarovar, the sacred lake of Pushkar. The first *puja* takes place at 4 A.M., then Sat Naran Gi bathes in the sacred water.

HARPREET KAUR, EIGHTEEN, STUDENT, PUNJABI. SIS GANJ SAHIB, OLD DELHI.

Harpreet Kaur, a Sikh woman, studies fashion design and would like to go to America one day. She came with her parents from Ghaziabad to pray at the Sis Ganj Sahib, one of the Sikhs' most important temples.

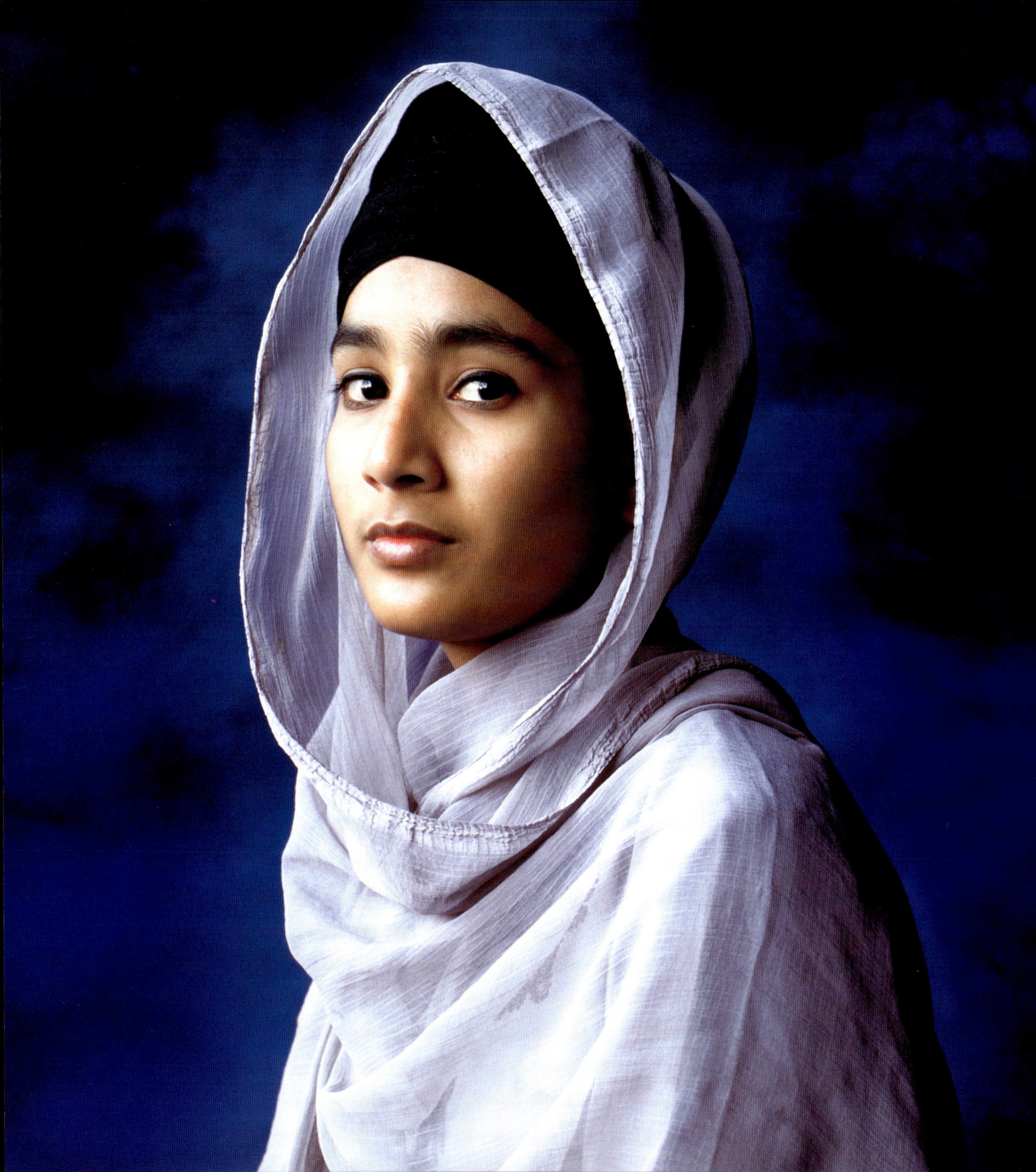

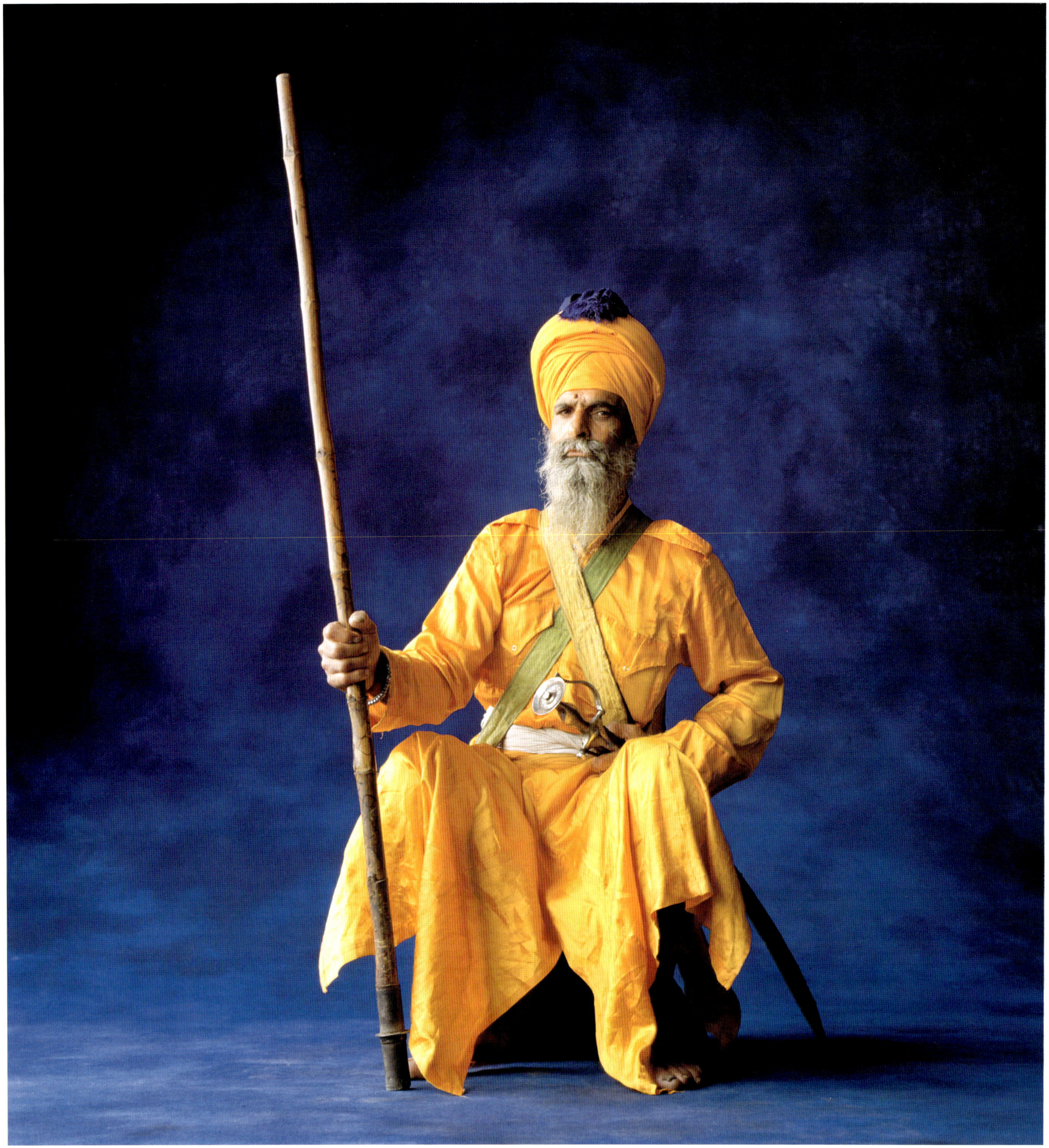

NARUNGEN SINGH, FIFTY, PUNJABI. SIS GANJ SAHIB, OLD DELHI.

Narungen Singh, a Sikh, was once a farmer in Punjab and is now a *yakrawath* (traveling holy man). Dedicating one's life to spritual practices is common for older people across Indian religions. Five characteristics identify members of the Sikh religion: they do not cut their hair, they carry a comb, and they wear wear a steel bracelet, a *kirpan* (sword), and traditional loose undergarments.

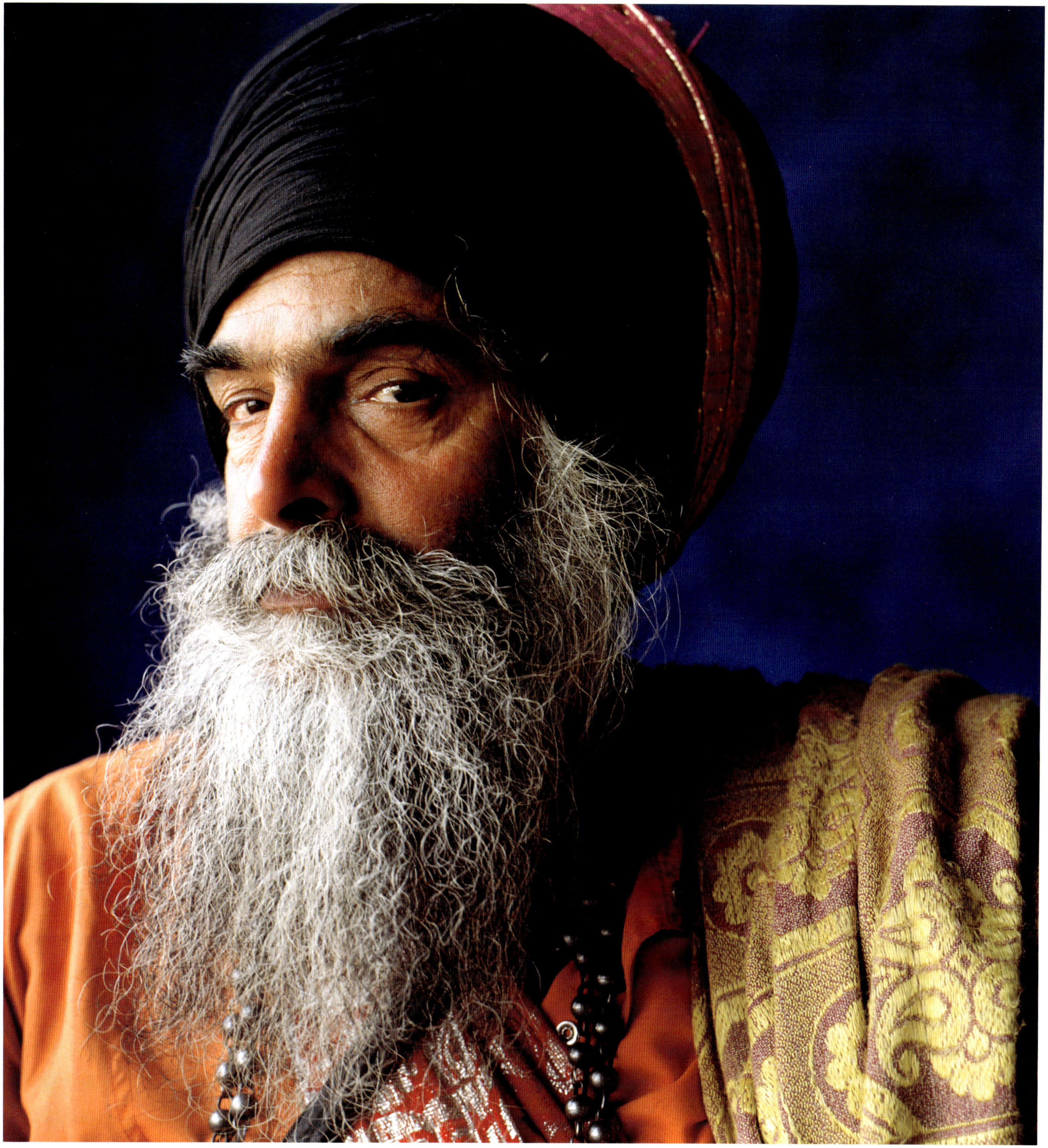

PARKA SINGH, FIFTY-TWO, FARMER, PUNJABI. SIS GANJ SAHIB, OLD DELHI.

Parka Singh, a Sikh from Punjab, wears his best outfit to show respect when visiting the temple. To pray at the Sis Ganj Sahib in Old Delhi is expected of every devout Sikh when he comes to the capital.

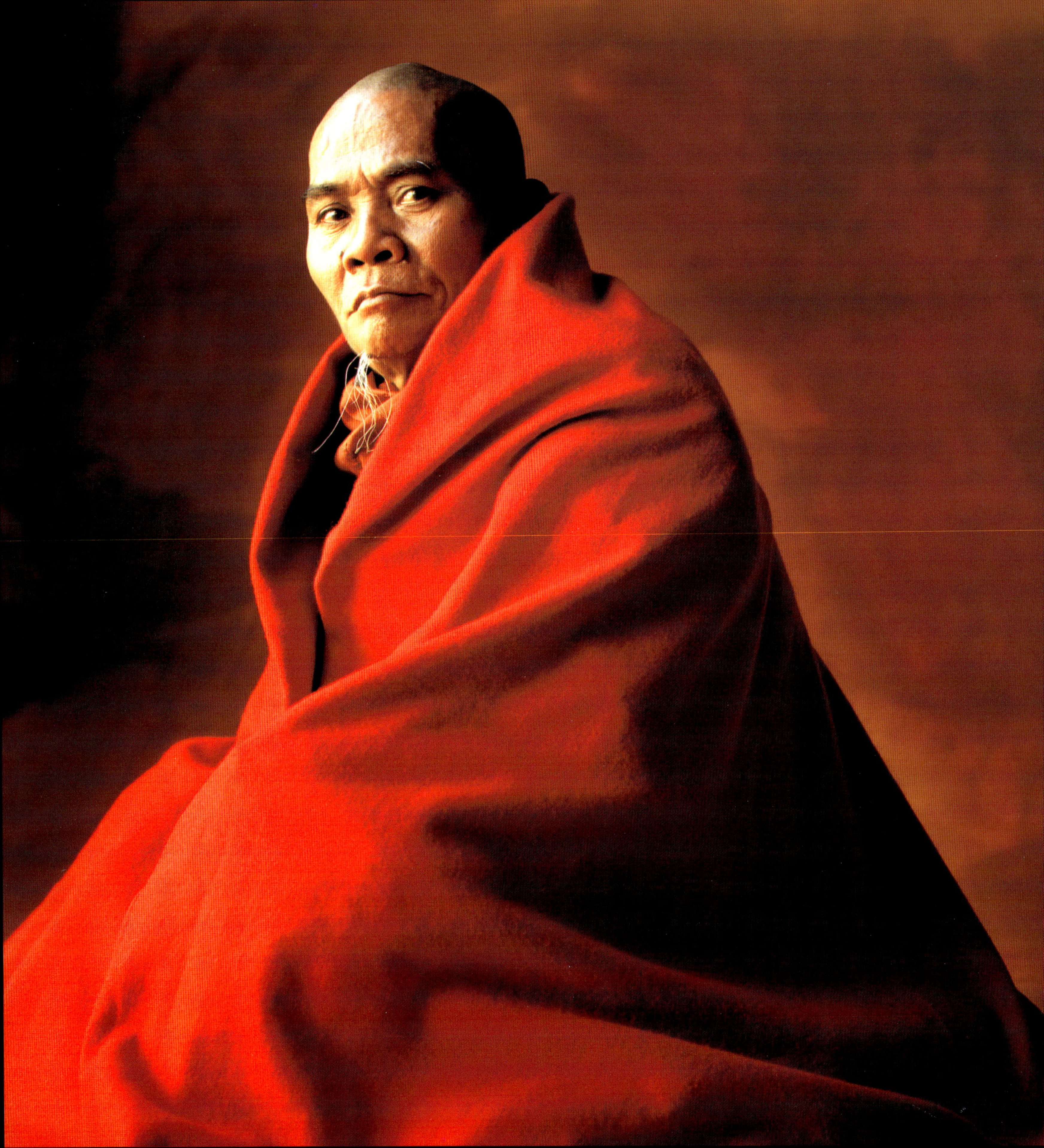

U THEI THILA, FIFTY-EIGHT, ABBOT, BAMAR. SAGAING, MYANMAR.

YIELD OF THE HILLS

PEASANTS AND CENOBITES OF THE GOLDEN TRIANGLE

Today's Myanmar, the Burma of the past, has gone through a terrible century. After the degradation of being colonized, Burma became the stage for some of the most brutal battles of the Second World War. Westerners have read about the heroism and suffering of European, American, Canadian, and Australian soldiers, but few know about the agony and grief of the Burmese people during these years. When independence was finally achieved, it brought decades of civil war instead of peace and democracy, and since the 1960s, a military government that has not relinquished power to this day. For half a century the people of the northeast, especially those along the Chinese border, had little or no contact with the outside world.

It was this Burma, with a rich past, that had become one of Asia's most "backward" nations. Burma's many contradictions had captivated Pfanni's and my imagination back in the 1980s. Over the years we had visited most of the country, except those regions that were out of reach even for government officials. In 1993 we finally saw a light at the end of the tunnel. The Burmese Communist Party and its armed units had disbanded, and most of the other rebellious groups were willing to end the civil war. Once hostilities had ceased, Pfanni and I were the first foreigners to receive permission to visit Kachin State.

Our portable studio was ready, and conveniently the animistic Manao Festival, the meeting of the Kachin tribes, was to happen again in January 1994 for the first time in decades. Had things gone as planned, we would have missed it. It was supposed to start on the tenth of January, the Kachin National Day. On that day we were still negotiating with the reticent authorities in Yangon. However, Providence was on our side. On the tenth, when the festival should have taken place, an earthquake (6.4 on the Richter scale) occurred. The Kachin elders, perceiving this to be a bad omen, postponed the festival to the twenty-first. This was enough time for us to cut through the red tape in Yangon, fly to Myitkyina, and prepare for our first "outdoor studio" shooting.

The Manao Ground outside Myitkyina was a good test for our studio. At times the gusts of wind were so strong that they would have blown the studio away had we not secured it with huge bamboo poles and arranged for the side panels to be opened with an emergency cord whenever the wind became threatening. But these were mere technicalities. What we experienced during the days of the festival was unique.

There are 135 different groups or tribes in Myanmar, each with their own language or dialect. Most of them live in the Golden Triangle, and a dozen of them in Kachin State. Some tribes live in such remote hills along the Chinese border that they have not been visited by outsiders since the 1930s, and even then very little was known about their original lifestyle.

All of these tribes sent representatives in ceremonial dress to the festival. The Kachin tribes were celebrating their reunion after decades of war, insecurity, and uncertainty. For two days the drums did not stop beating, and group after group sang their "hora, hora" while they danced around the huge totem poles that were set up to commemorate the importance of the occasion. A Sioux dance of the 1860s in the South Dakota Badlands could not have been much different.

The Kachin elders had given us permission to set up our studio in the center of the festival ground. Because of its shape and color and the thousands of people around it, we called our studio the "Ka'bah of Myitkyina." Many tribes were represented, including the Chingpaws,

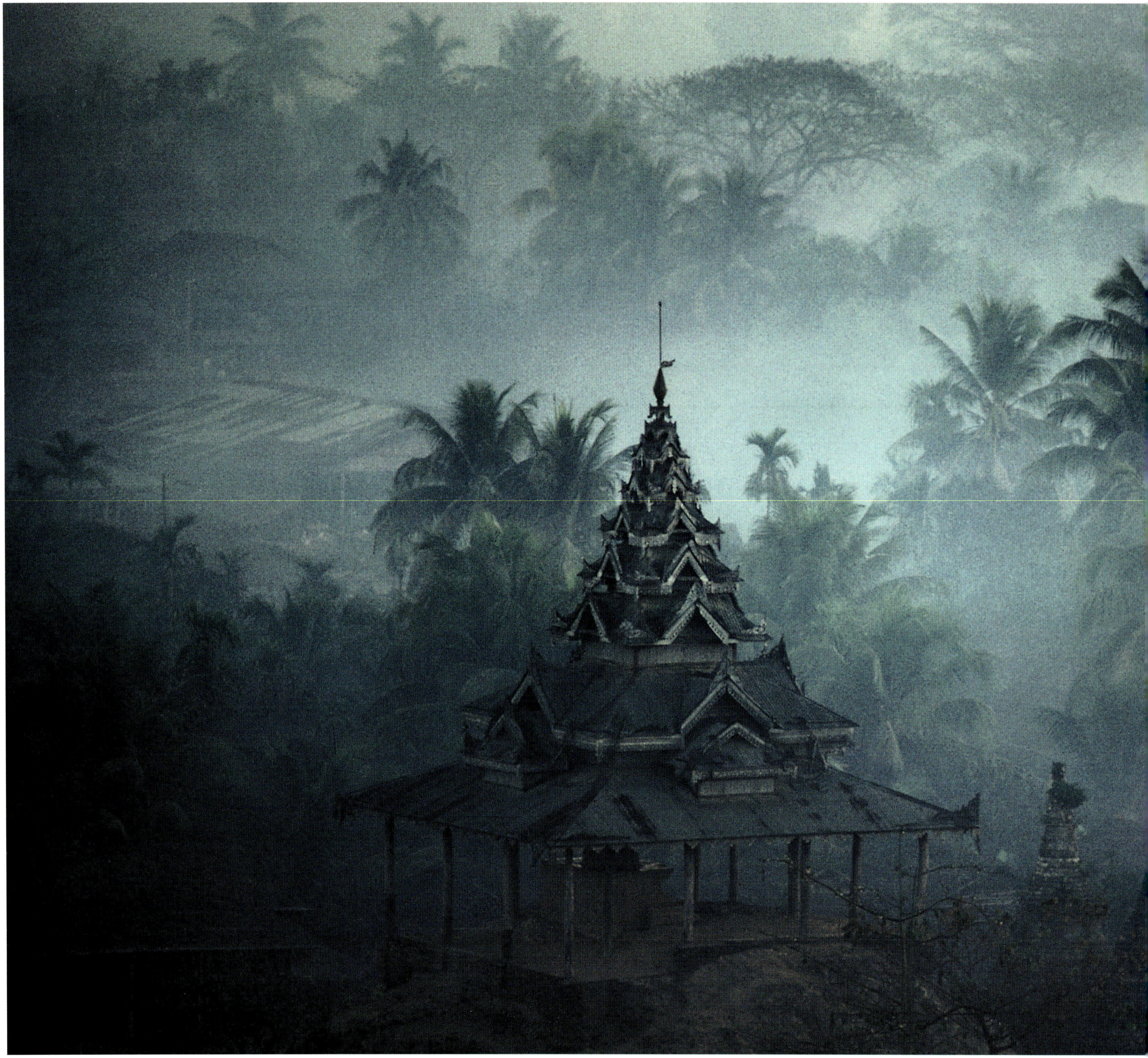

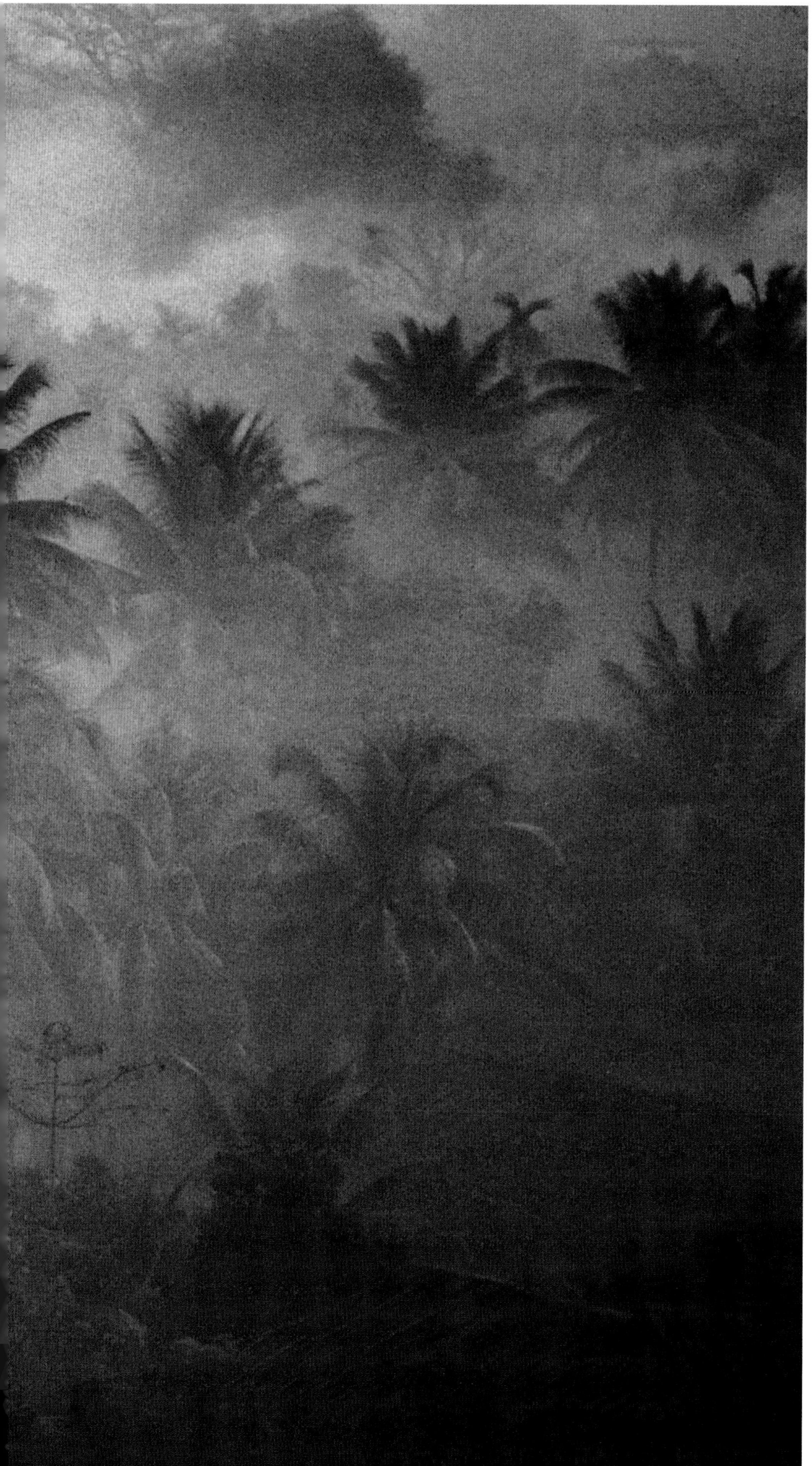

Lisus, Marus, Kakus, Lachiks, Rawangs, and Zaiwas, all of them in their ceremonial costumes. There were the delicate Lisu maidens (page 127), the Rawang chief Hkan Jawhkin (page 104), and the Chingpaw dance leader Nawlai (page 105), figures from a real-life operetta. In view of the Kachins's recent history, these people were visual proof of the resilience that helps people survive hardship and privation. We were mesmerized by their natural charm—and we were romanticizing. Only when we left, released from the spell of their enchanting appearance, were we able to see the encounter from a sociopolitical perspective. Had the Manao not been celebrated, we would never have reached all these people in their villages. Luckily we managed to set up our studio in at least one of the villages near the confluence of the Maika and the Malika. This is the very place where the Ayeyarwady (Irrawaddy) River, the lifeline that holds the nation together, is born. One of the women we photographed there was Hkaung Nan, a 120 year old Maru. She didn't know when she was born, but the age of her sister, who was ten years younger and had recently died at the age of 110, had been officially approved. We realized that there were few adult men in the village. As we found out later, the missing men were among the thousands of Kachins who went to the mines at Hpakant to make their fortune digging for jade.

After the fantasia at the Manao, we soon caught up with reality. We had flown into Myitkyina, but we wanted to leave either along the river or by a land route. Neither of these options appealed to the authorities, who wanted us out as quickly and easily as we had entered. We balked, and finally one morning we packed our equipment into an old and battered Toyota pickup to drive 155 miles south to Katha on the Ayeyarwady. In spite of the peace accord signed by the Kachin leader, there were still opposing fractions of the KIA (Kachin Indepedent Army) operating in the field. Crossing KIA territory anonymously, swiftly, and without an armed escort in an aged pickup was seen as the safest method of getting us out of Kachin State. The idea was good, and after several breakdowns we made it safely to Katha.

For the return trip we reserved all of the first-class cabins ($1.50 per berth) on the MS *Padone*, one of the slow boats that travels from Katha to Mandalay three times a week. These battered boats, first utilized back in 1948, are the lifeline of the Upper Ayeyarwady. They stop at every village, so they require between two and three days for the journey—exactly what

MORNING MIST ENVELOPS A MONASTERY, MYANMAR.

we wanted. With slight alterations we were able to set up the studio in the huge lounge at the bow. Cruising due south we had a reliable source of light, and with hundreds of multi-ethnic passengers idling their hours away, we also had an ideal selection of people to photograph. It seemed that this was the only floating studio the Ayeyarwady had ever seen, and rarely had a trip on a riverboat been more enjoyable. Mandalay was welcoming us back to civilization. In the past, while photographing with our 35mm cameras, the city had often been our base. Now, with our larger cameras and portable studio, we were here to do what we had dreamed of doing ten years earlier.

Sagaing is the most enchanting little village in Burma. The valleys and hills of Sagaing, not far from Mandalay on the opposite side of the Ayeyarwady, are home to six hundred monasteries. We followed some old leads, and soon our studio stood in the Tadana Weima Sin Pyu Shin La, a delightfully secluded nunnery where young women from diverse tribes study the Buddhist scriptures. These nunneries are normally off-limits for men, but the *Sayadiy* (abbess) made an exception and gave us the chance to take pictures like those of Ma Ega (page 131), visual documents of a life lived with a unique perspective of one's existence. It was the same, a few days later, when we set up our studio at Myanmar's largest monastery, the Maha Ghanda. Twelve hundred resident monks, most of them young men, live in an atmosphere of joyous piety. They helped us to set up and dismantle the studio, and for once we could leave our equipment overnight within their premises without fearing that it would be stolen. At the Maha Ghanda monastery we met and photographed some outstanding *pongyis* (monks) and *sayadaws* (elder monks). The most impressive of them were U Gusala (page 135), who could sit for hours without moving so much as a finger or his facial expression, and Ashin U Kosala (page 132), who reminded us of some of the most inspiring images of the Enlightened One.

Since the studio had been set up under huge trees, the light was different. We needed to use much longer exposures than usual, but with the *pongyis* who were used to sitting motionless for hours, this was no problem at all.

Before breaking camp and leaving Myanmar we drove further north to Natkhayain village. It is inhabited by a nondescript Bamar rice-growing community. Since it was harvesting season, this was the ideal time and location to find Bamar peasants. Peasants make up the majority of the people of Myanmar, and they had as little in common with the military junta in Yangon as any of the persecuted tribals along the border. Photographs such as those of Maung Hla and Maung Minay (page 119), or of Ma Aye Ngwe (page 118), reveal the strength of these people. They are descendents of an immigrant tribe, as are the tribals further to the north. Their culture, the way they interact with nature and their metaphysical requirements are in perfect equilibrium. The basics of human existence become graspable when watching them follow their daily routine.

We knew that we had to come back, and in January 1995 we were again in the north. This time we started in the Shan hills, photographing Lisus and Palaungs at Pain Pyit, a village north of Mogok. The inhabitants were similar to the festive people we had seen the year before at the Myitkyina Manao. This time we photographed them in their natural environment. Even though the Lisus were Christians and the Palaungs were Buddhists, there was a sense of trust between them. Saw Po Sha, our invaluable liaison and translator during these Myanmar trips, himself a Karen Christian, helped us understand the situation through his own example. The junta persecuted his people, but he bore no ill will toward them. In true Christian spirit, he was forgiving and positive, and so were most of the Buddhists we met and talked to. As we saw it, the problem in Myanmar was not of the people; they were, like the Palaungs and the Lisus of Pain Pyit, able to solve their differences without the use of force.

The situation was different in Mogok, the ruby capital of the world. Here local power brokers, coupled with government interests from Yangon, produced a tense atmosphere. This tension can be seen in some of the photographs of ruby miners (page 115), and ruby traders. The photographs we took in Mogok were the only ones of people belonging to a semi-industrial society.

After crossing the Ayeyarwady on a ferry, we continued to Moksobo in Sagaing province. This is the heartland of the Bamar people, and as in Natkhayain the year before, we set up our studio on a threshing field at the height of the harvesting season. We were looking for that dignified bearing that is fast vanishing amidst the stresses and strains of industrial society. Daw Mya Aye and Daw The Tin (page 112), struck us as having that potential, as well as Moe Kaing (page 113), and U Tum Shaw (page 116).

Crossing Sagaing province was a dust-laden experience, but one we would not have wanted to miss. We had to cross two more rivers, the Mu and the Chindwin, on fragile ferries to reach the Chin Hills, our final destination. Like the Lisus and many Kachins, most Chins are Christians, and they are perhaps the most secluded of the Myanmar border tribes. Their country is spectacularly beautiful. They live one step beneath the sky, or as they say, one step beneath heaven.

The path back into civilization brought us once more into the valley of Sagaing, to the Kani monastery and a Shin Pyu, the initiation ceremony of young boys.

We had documented the north of Myanmar, but some of the tribes that live east of the Salween were not accessible from the Myanmar side. Our next trip therefore brought us into the hills of northern Thailand. For four weeks we used any available means of transportation to reach the villages of the White and Red Karen, the Akha, the Yao, the Mizu, the Padaung, the Palaung, and the Lahu. By now we were more comfortable with approaching the people we wanted to photograph. We knew successful photographs depended on a photographer-subject relationship based on trust. Sometimes we stayed with people without photographing until that feeling of mutual respect emerged. All of the photographs were taken at times when there was a genuine sense of trust.

In northern Thailand, Khun Thawach, or Khun Ti as he prefers to be called, was our local liaison. He arranged for the elephants that brought us to the White Karen, organized the mules that transported our gear to the Akha, and got us the longtail boats that sped us to the "giraffe" women. When left with no other option, he arranged for local porters. Without his help, we never could have accomplished what we did.

For centuries the tribes of the Golden Triangle have been on the move—a slow movement that took a generation for a step further south. Now it has come to a sudden halt, and with it the heaven that spans their world comes crashing down, burying forever their identity and original life-style.

Most of the tribes we visited had only moved into northern Thailand during the last century. They don't see themselves as nationals of either Myanmar or Thailand. They are still part of a culture in which people are constantly on the move and accountable only to their clan and their spirits. Many of them still grow poppy and thus they have come within the ambit of global consciousness.

In the not-too-distant future all this will come to a halt. Once four-wheel drive vehicles and motorbikes reach their villages, the younger generations will get absorbed into the national culture. Tribal life will end with only the elderly remaining in the remote uphill villages. In Thailand we saw what will soon happen to the people of northern Myanmar, who still belong to a culture that harks back to a blurred past somewhere in prehistoric China.

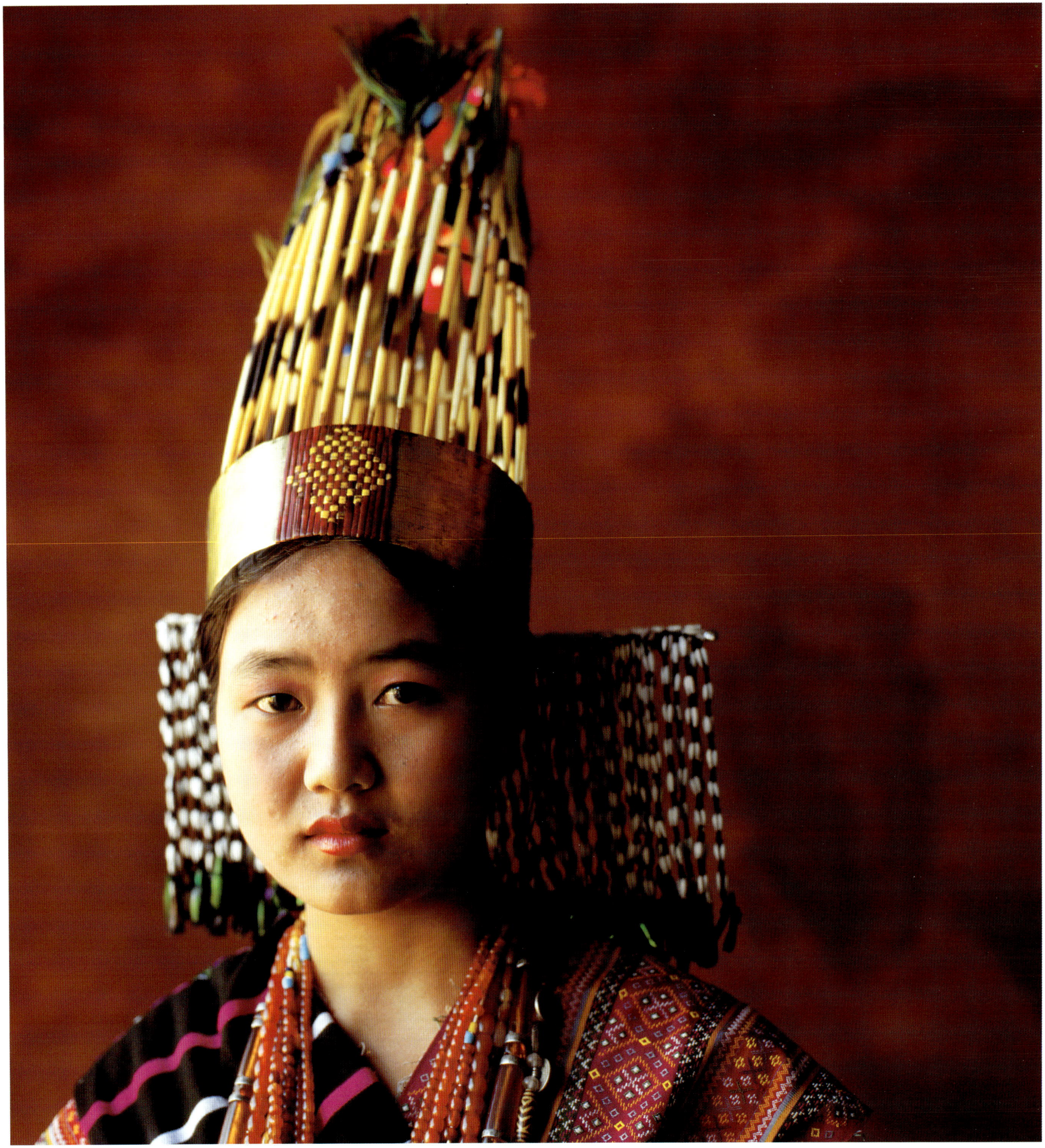

NI HLIR CIN, SIXTEEN, STUDENT, ZAHAN CHIN. TLAU HUMUM, MYANMAR.

For the weekly market day in Falam, Ni Hlir Cin is dressed in her best clothing. Together with her mother she walked three hours from her village to reach the regional capital.

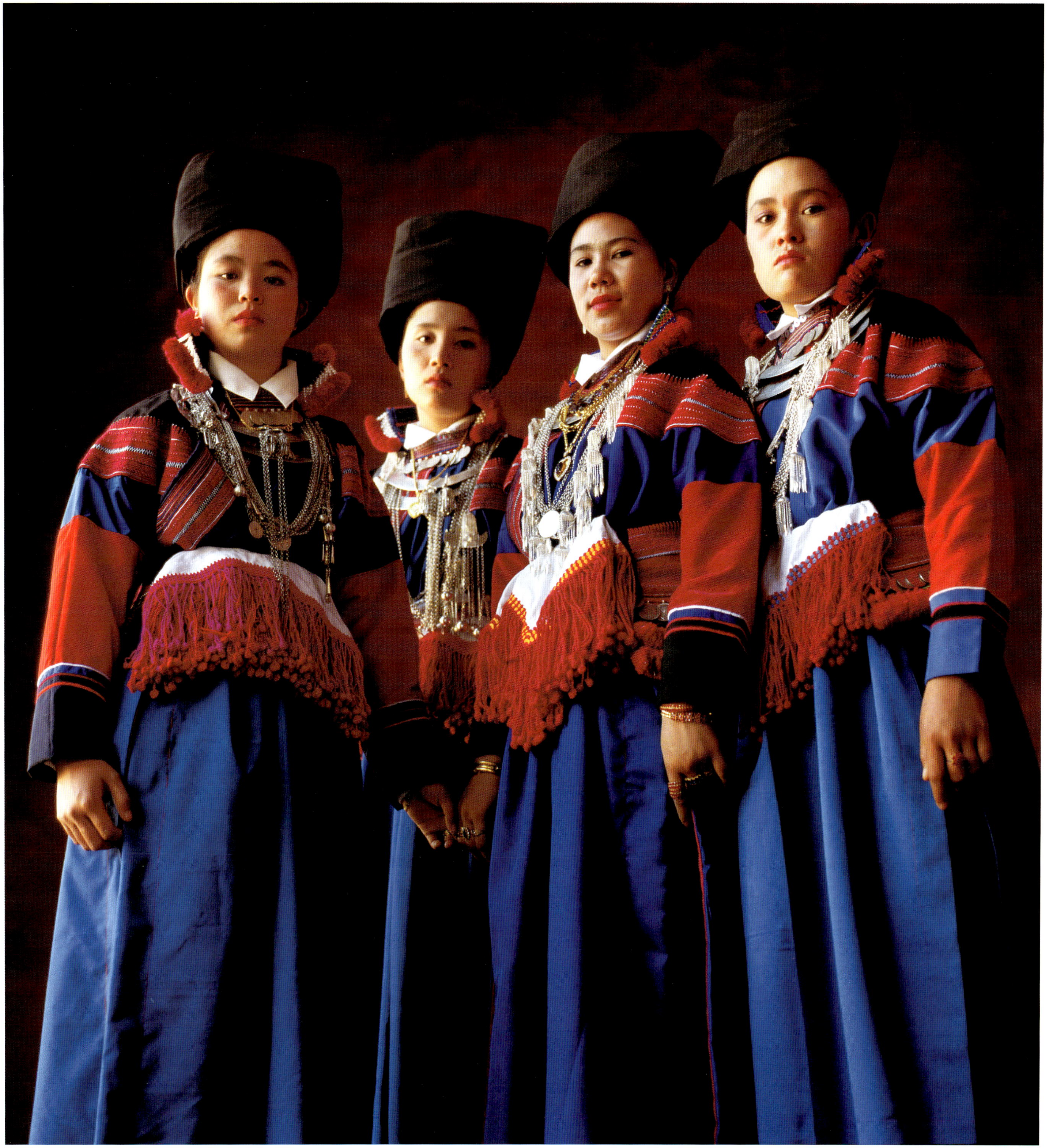

FOUR LISU STUDENTS.
MOGOK, MYANMAR.

During market days in Mogok, the Lisus come in great numbers from their villages in the hills. The market days are an important social event for which people dress in their best clothes.

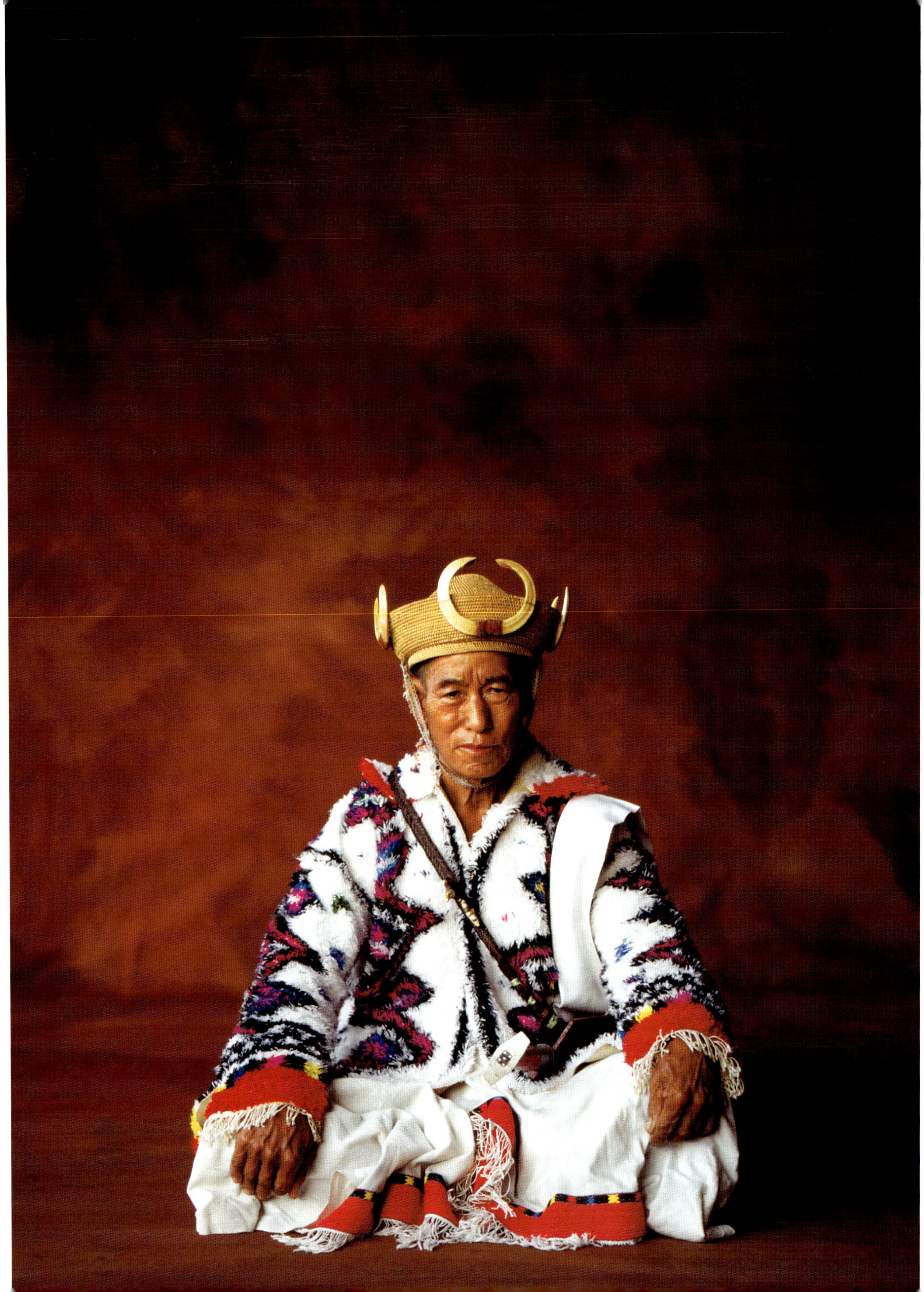

HKAN JAWHKIN, SIXTY-FIVE, HEADMAN, RAWANG. MYITKYINA, MYANMAR.

Hkan Jawhkin is the headman of his Rawang village in northern Kachin State. He came to the Manao Festival in the full dress of an animistic necromancer. His hat is decorated with the tusks of wild boars.

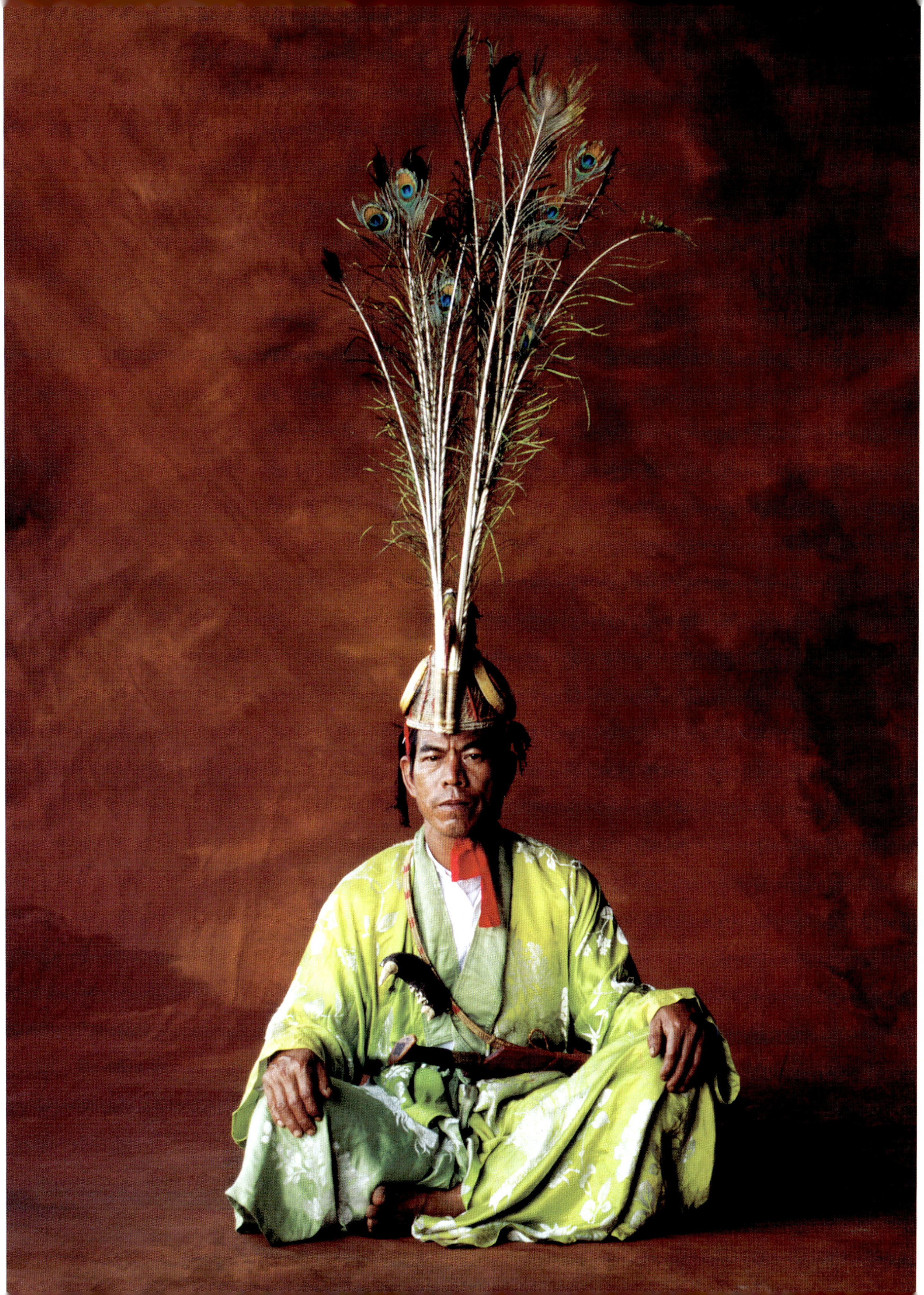

NAWLAI, FORTY-ONE,
DANCE LEADER, CHINGPAW.
MYITKYINA, MYANMAR.

Nawlai is a member of the largest ethnic group in Kachin State. He acted as dance leader during the two days of continuous dancing and chanting. Most of the different tribes of Kachin State were participating for the first time in more than thirty years, during which the festival could not take place due to the imposition of martial law.

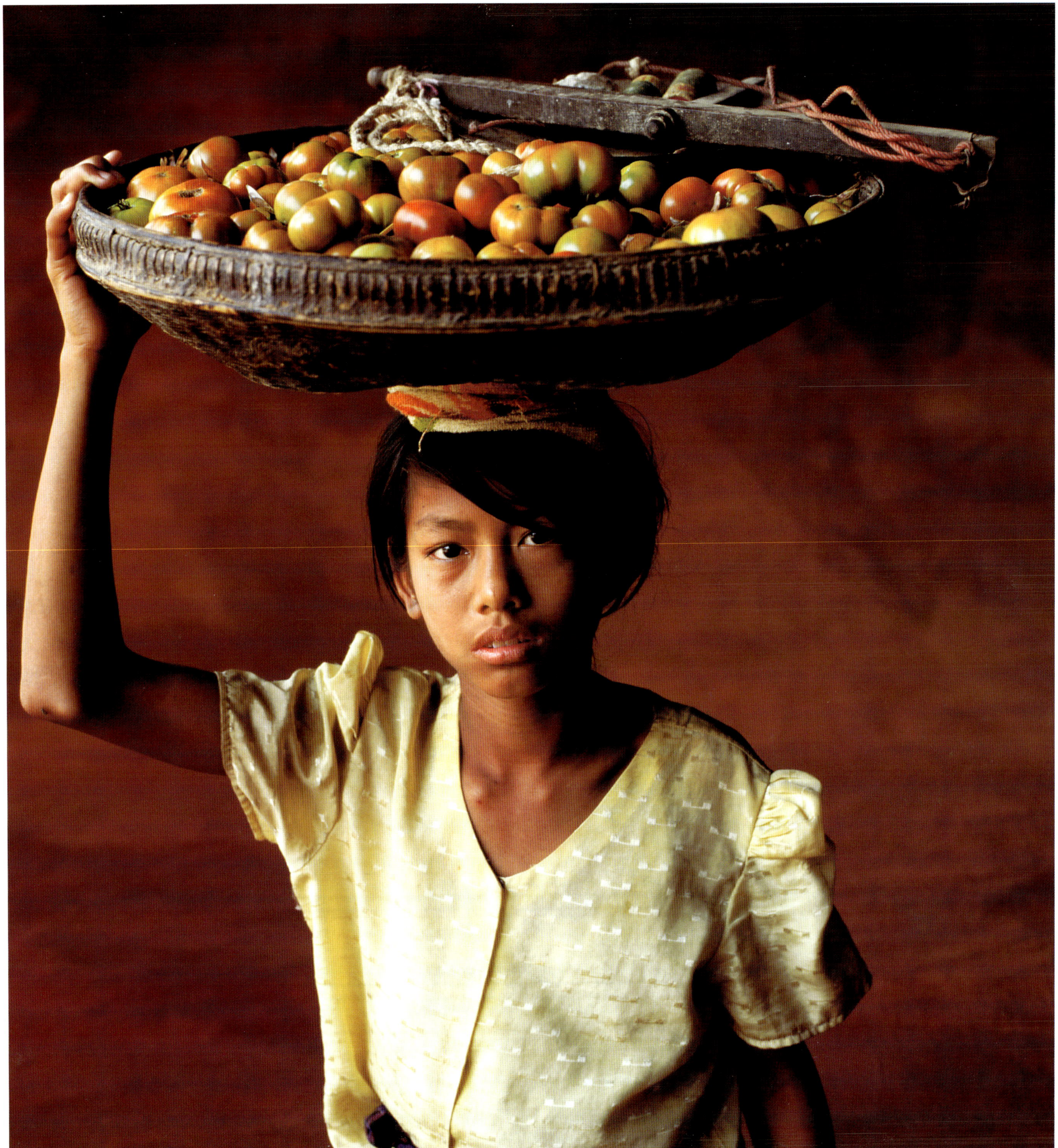

MA KETHEWG KAING, TWELVE, STUDENT, BAMAR. NATKHAYAIN, MYANMAR.

At twelve, Ma Kethewg Kaing is already contributing to the family income. She was on her way to the nearest town to sell vegetables from her family's small garden.

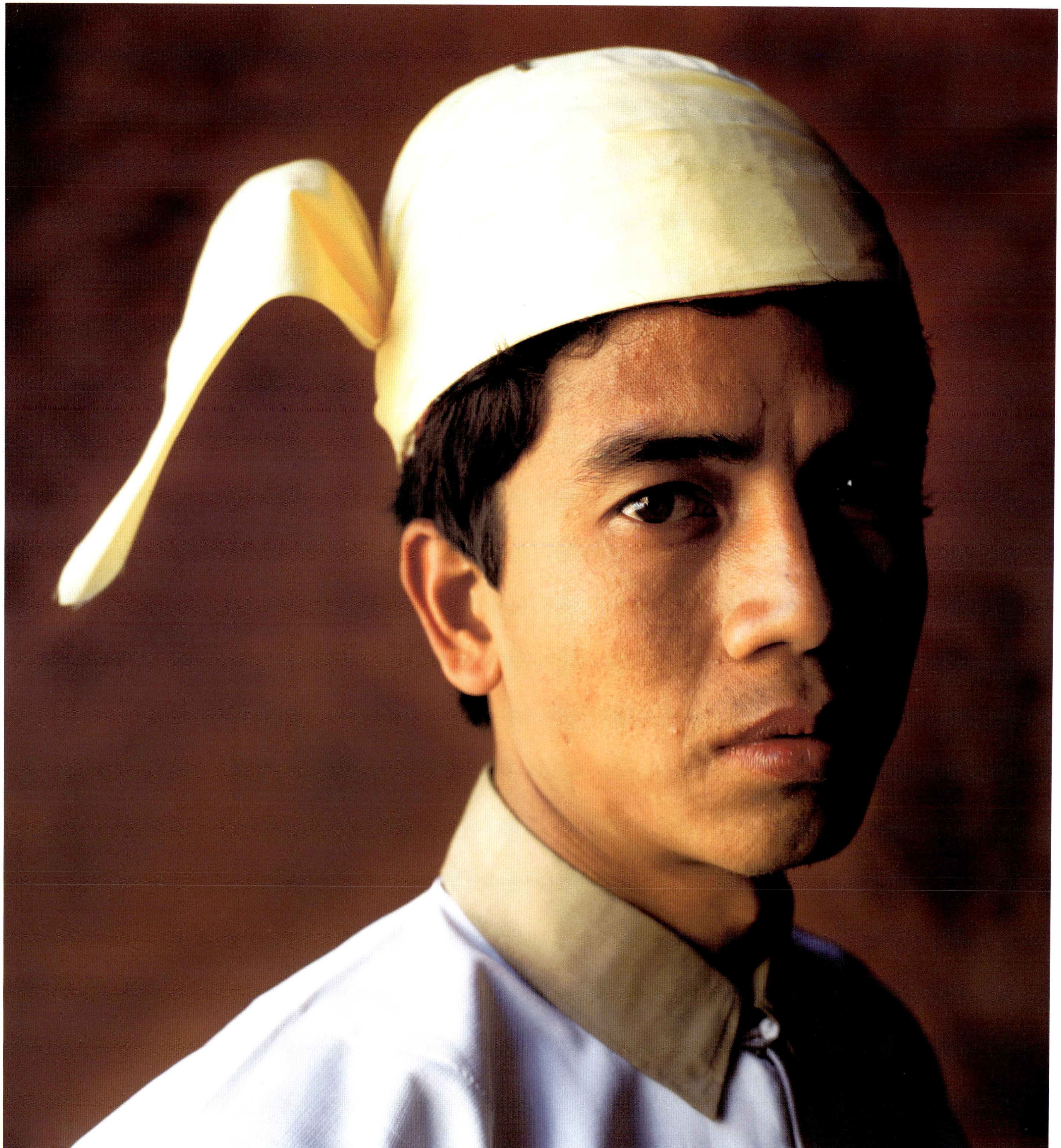

TIN TUN, THIRTY-ONE, PHOTOGRAPHER, BAMAR. SAGAING, MYANMAR.

Tin Tun has a photography studio in Sagaing. He was taking photographs at a Buddhist initiation ceremony, dressed for the occasion in the traditional *gaung baung* headdress, which is rarely seen in public these days.

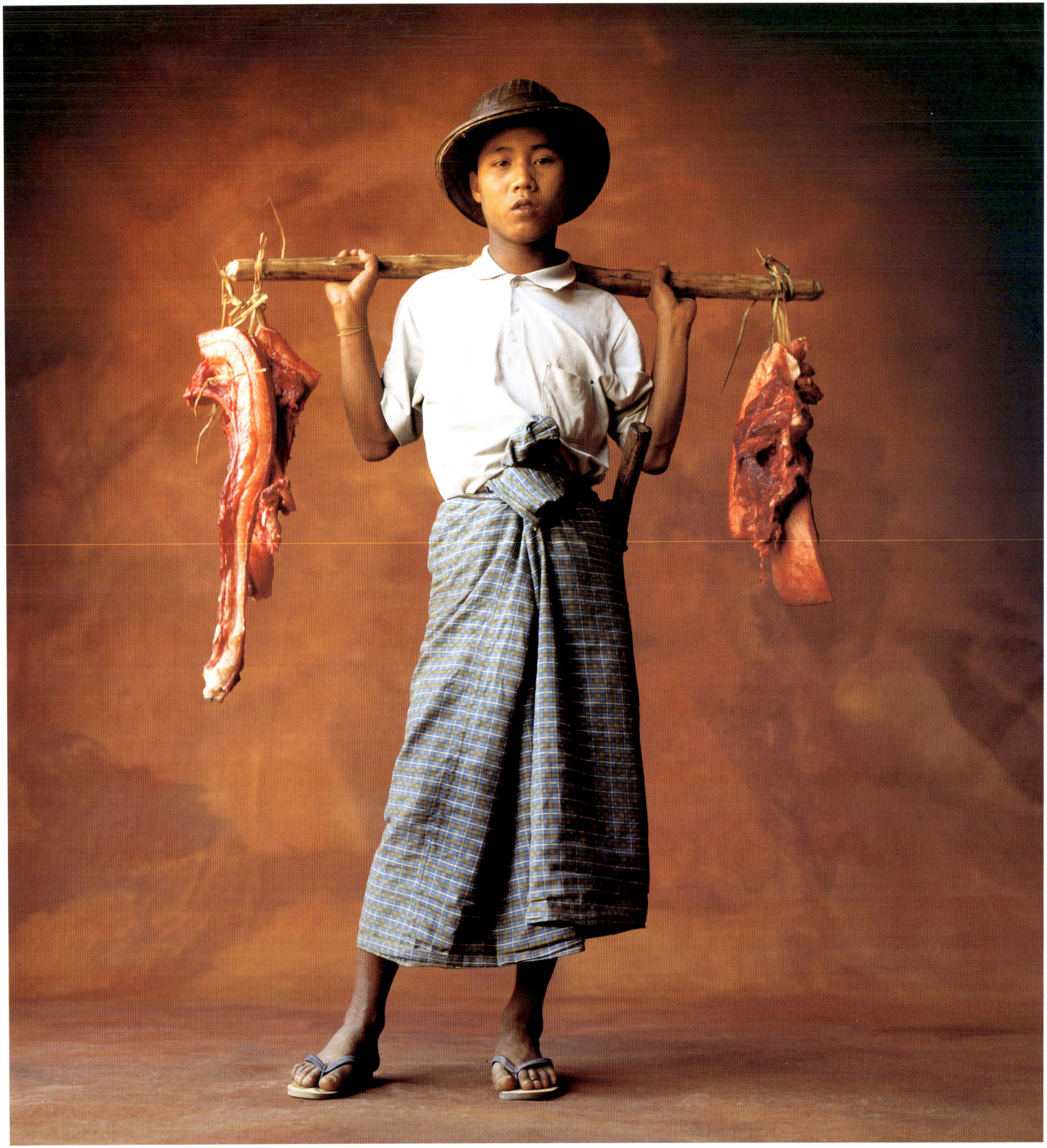

BYAR SAR, TWENTY, LISU.
PAIN PYIT, MYANMAR.

Byar Sar still lives with his family. They had slaughtered an ox and he was carrying meat to the house of a neighbor. Most Lisus are Christians and, unlike their Buddhist neighbors, have no prohibition against the slaughtering of animals.

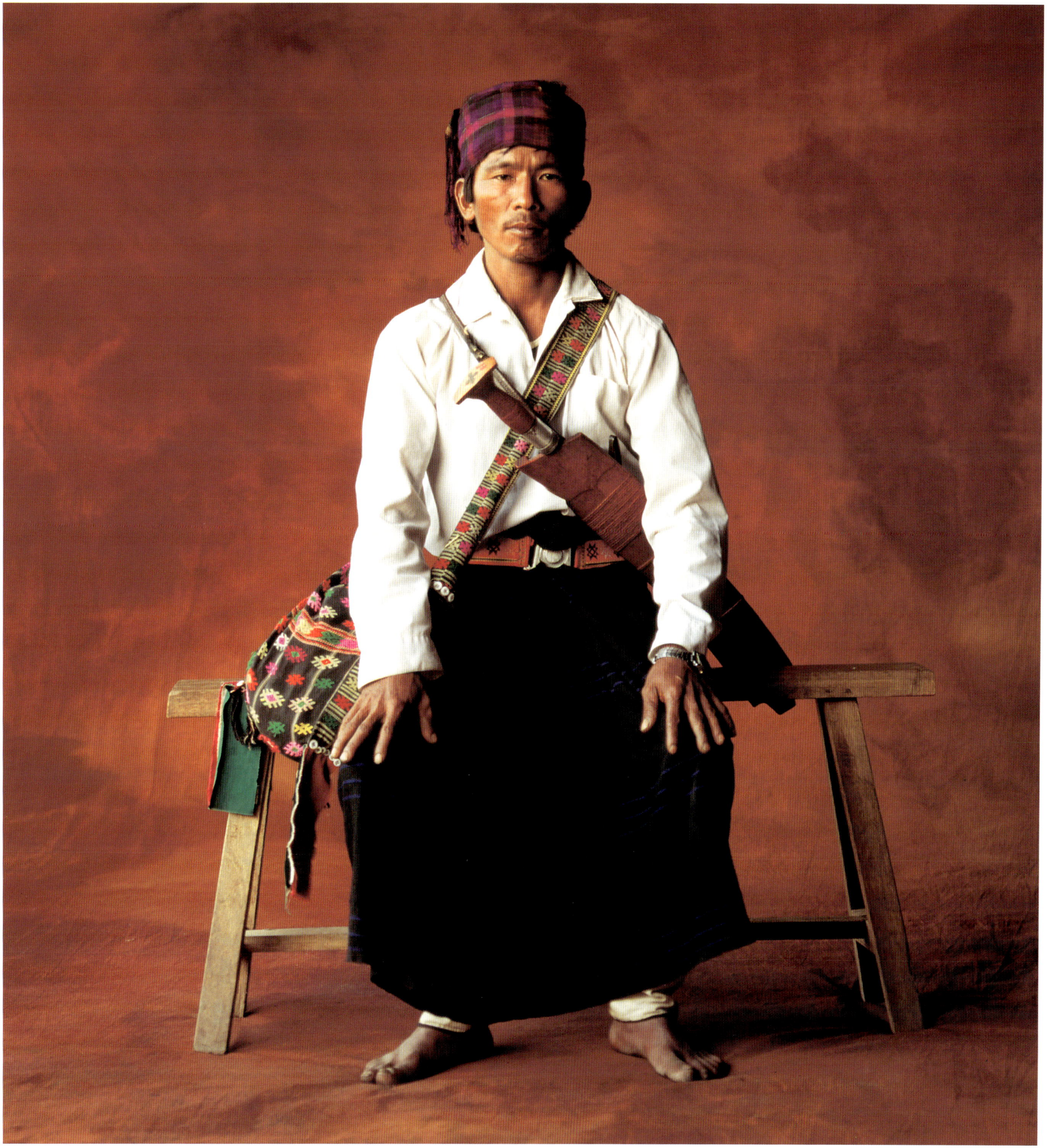

LUM ZE, THIRTY-EIGHT, MARU. MYITKYINA, MYANMAR.

Lum Ze is from the far northeast of Myanmar. The Marus live a self-sufficient lifestyle in hilltop villages. Because they are so isolated, a visit to Myitkyina exposes the Marus to a very different lifestyle.

THEIR CULTURE, THE WAY THEY INTERACT WITH NATURE AND THEIR METAPHYSICAL REQUIREMENTS ARE IN PERFECT EQUILIBRIUM. THE BASICS OF HUMAN EXISTENCE BECOME GRASPABLE WHEN WATCHING THEM FOLLOW THEIR DAILY ROUTINE.

LEFT TO RIGHT: MA YIN NEW, SIXTEEN; MA NWAY MOE, FOURTEEN; NI KARAY, SIXTEEN; AND MA NYUNT YEE, SIXTEEN; BAMAR. MOKSOBO, MYANMAR.

Ma Yin New, Ma Nway Moe, Ni Karay, and Ma Nyunt Yee carry the paddy from the threshing ground to the village's storage room. Moksobo, in Sagaing State (where the last dynasty of the Burmese royal house came from), is considered the home of the Bamar race.

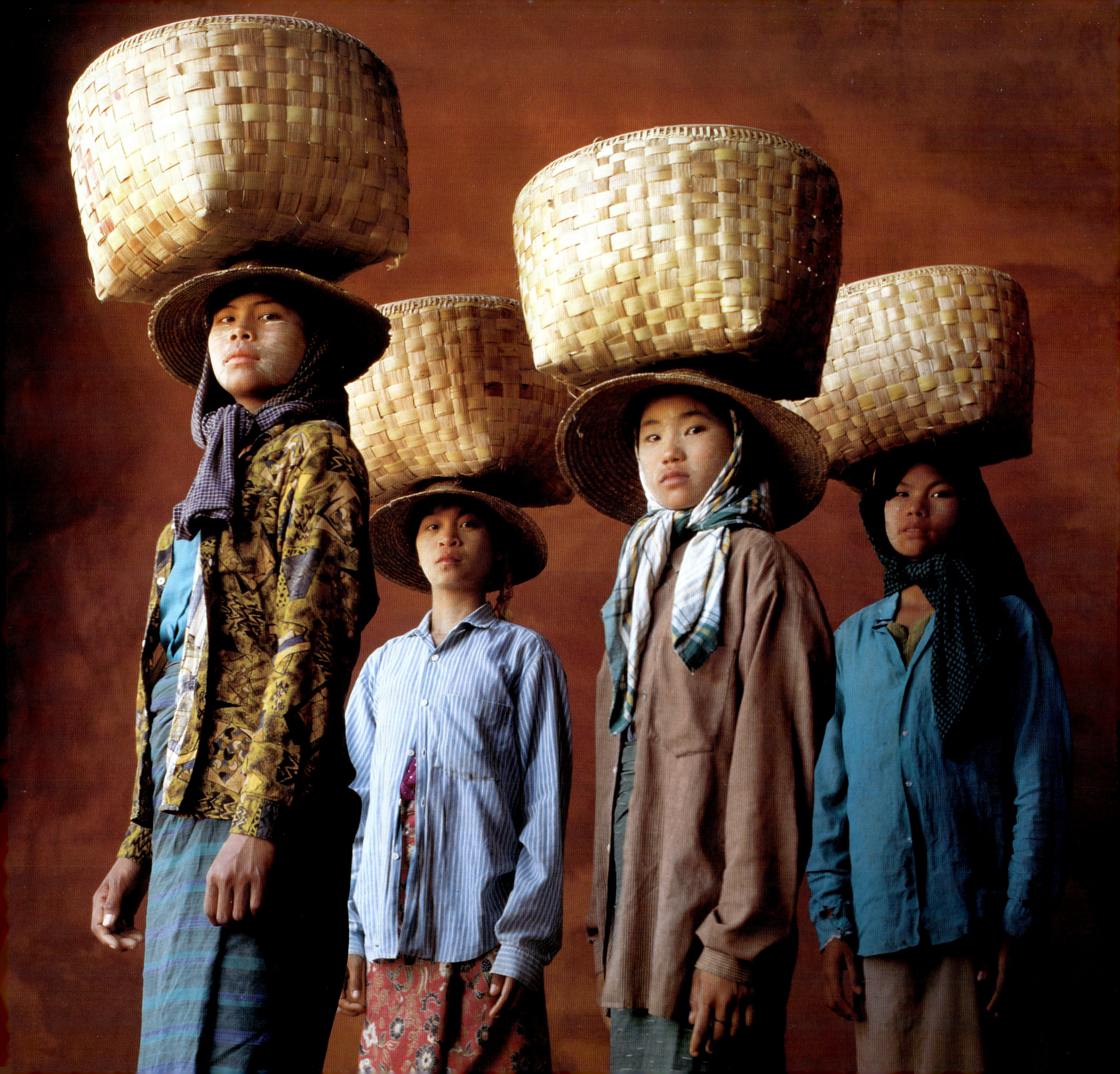

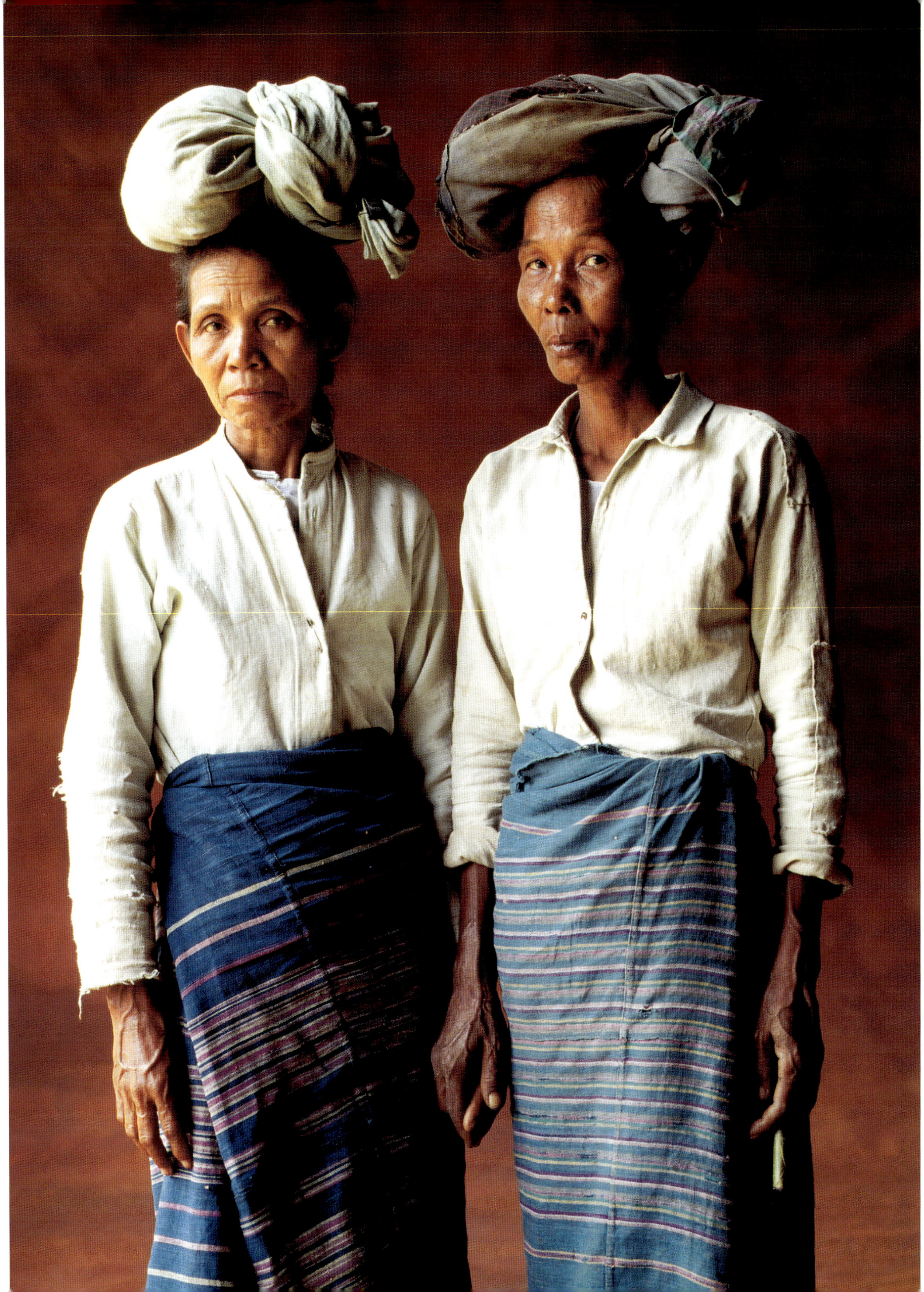

DAW MYA AYE, FIFTY, AND DAW THE TIN, FIFTY, BAMAR. NATKHAYAIN, MYANMAR.

Daw Mya Aye and Daw The Tin are wearing the traditional dress for women in Sagaing province. They wear white blouses and longyis (a wrapped garment worn by both men and women) fastened around the waist. When walking to the fields, they carry their belongings in bundles on their heads. The cheroot, smoked as often by men as by women, cannot be missed.

OPPOSITE:
MOE KAING, SIXTEEN, STUDENT, BAMAR. MOKSOBO, MYANMAR.

During harvesting season in January, students join their parents to collect the paddy that turns Sagaing province into a golden field. Moe Kaing carries the basket in which she brought the paddy to the winnowing stand, where her sister separates the paddy from the chaff.

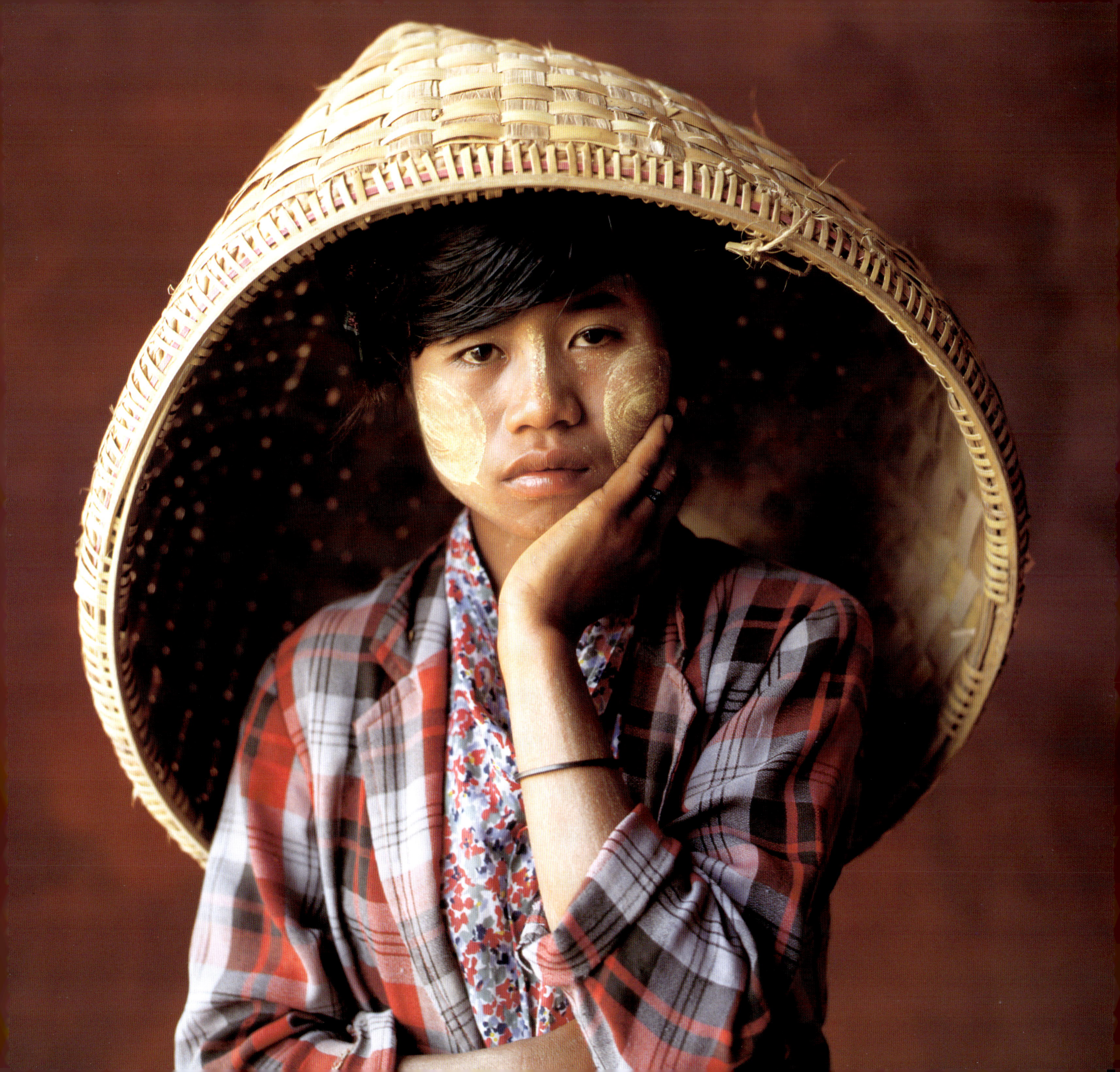

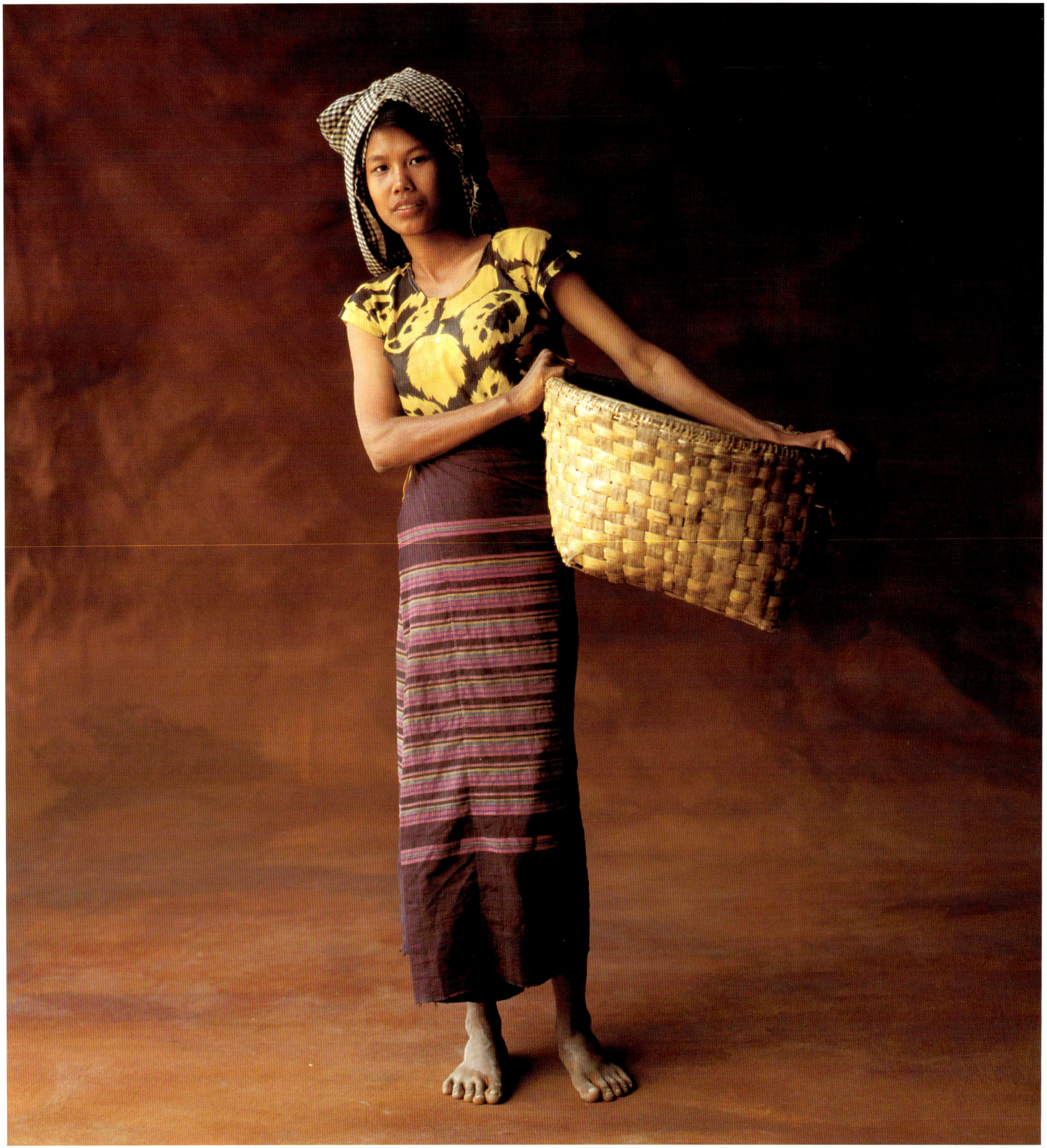

MA TINTIN AYE,
TWENTY-ONE, BAMAR.
NATKHAYAIN, MYANMAR.

Ma Tintin Aye had been winnowing paddy since the morning and was returning home after the day's harvest, singing and taunting the young men who drove the oxcart that brought them back.

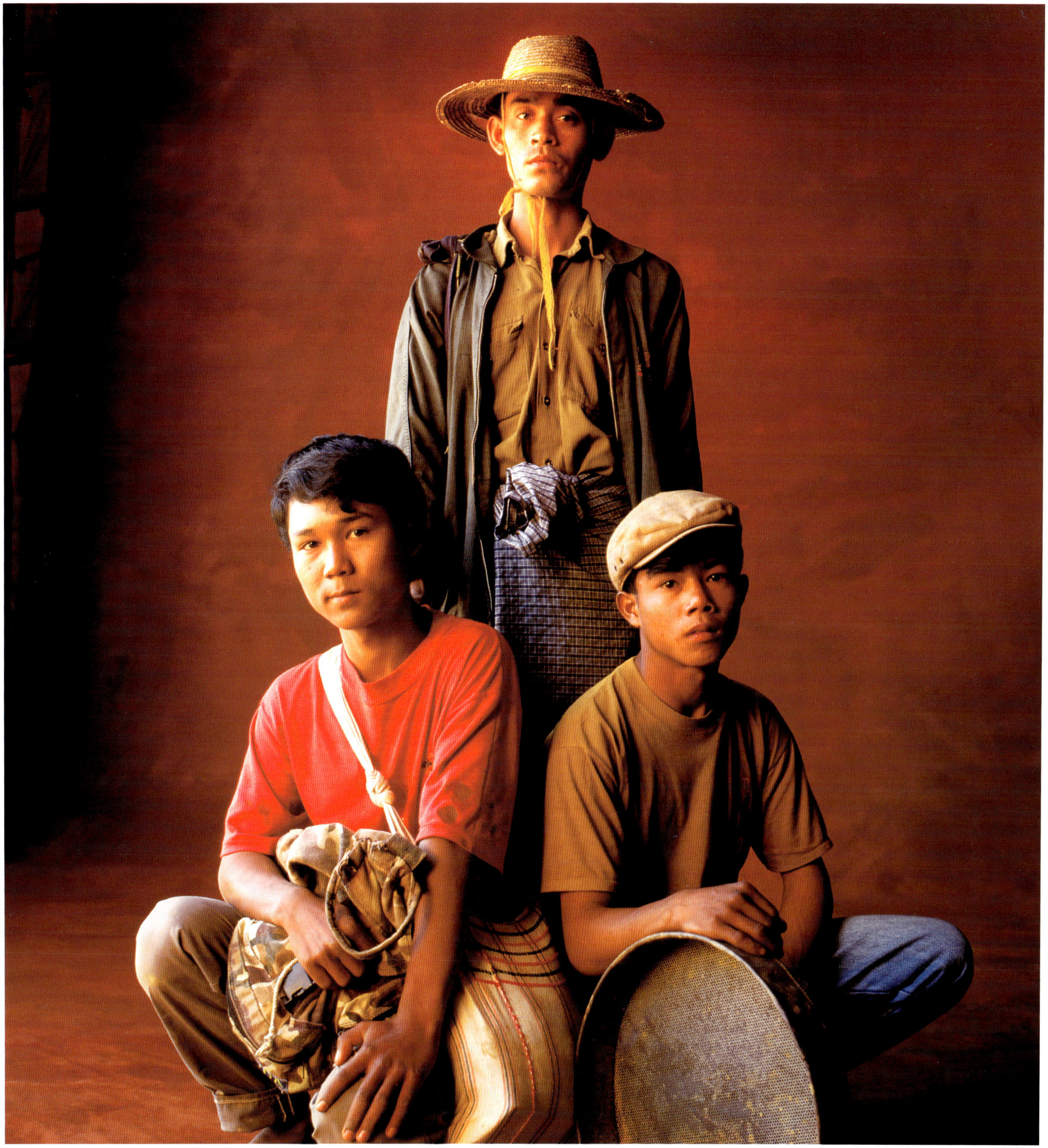

LEFT TO RIGHT:
AUNG WIN, TWENTY-ONE; MYANAING, TWENTY-FIVE; AND JO LIN, SEVENTEEN; MINERS, BAMAR. MOGOK, MYANMAR.

Aung Win, Myanaing, and Jo Lin work up to twelve hours a day washing soil in the ruby pits, which belong to influential ruby barons. The miners spend their free time panning on their own in the small rivulets in the vicinity, hoping for a big find in the midst of the tiny splinters that wash down abundantly.

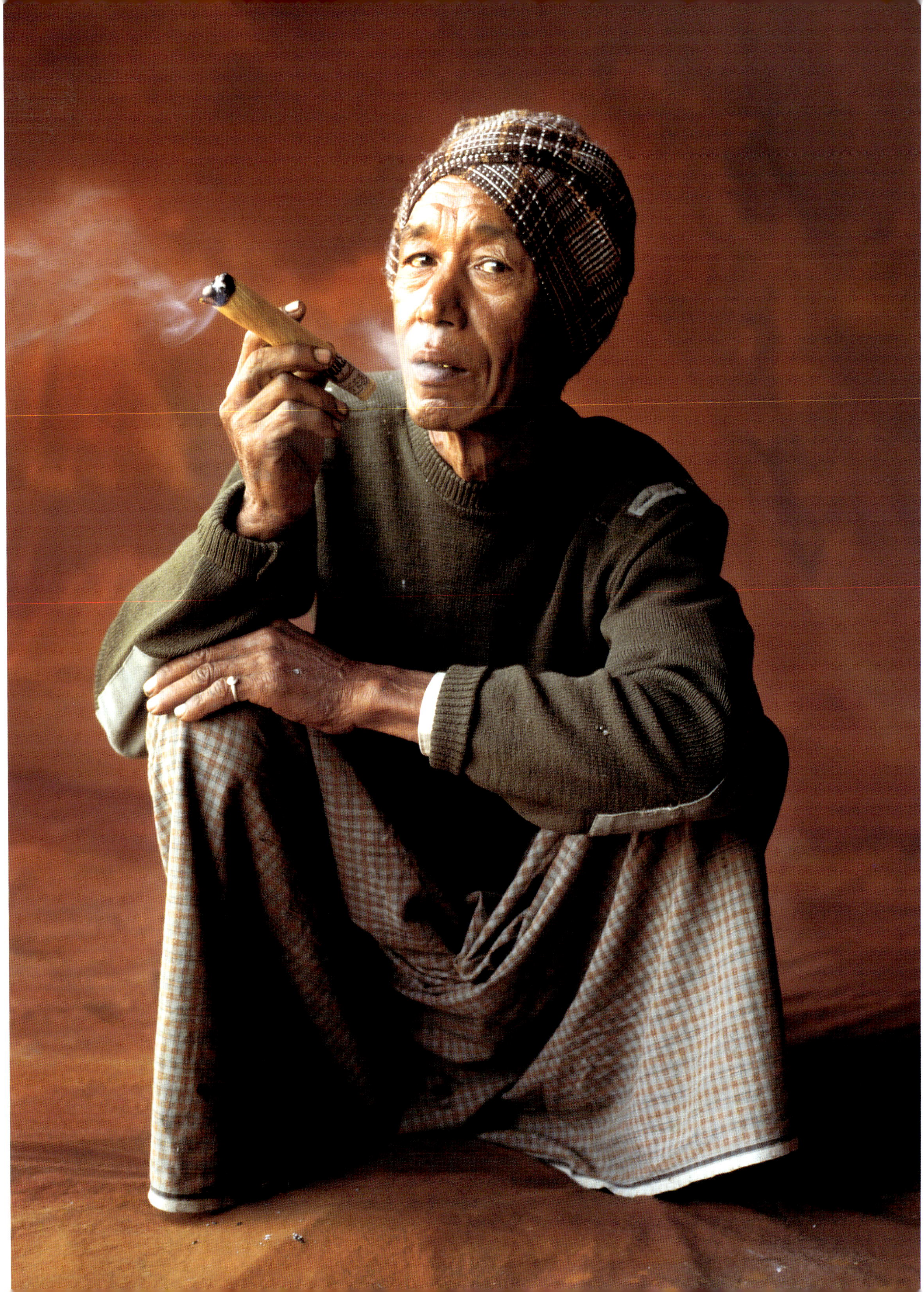

U TUN SHAW, FIFTY-SIX,
FARMER, BAMAR.
NATHKAYAIN, MYANMAR.

U Tun Shaw is a farmer in the small village of Nathkayain in Sagaing province, north of the Ayeyarwady's bend. He wears a longyi and smokes the proverbial "whickin' white cheroot."

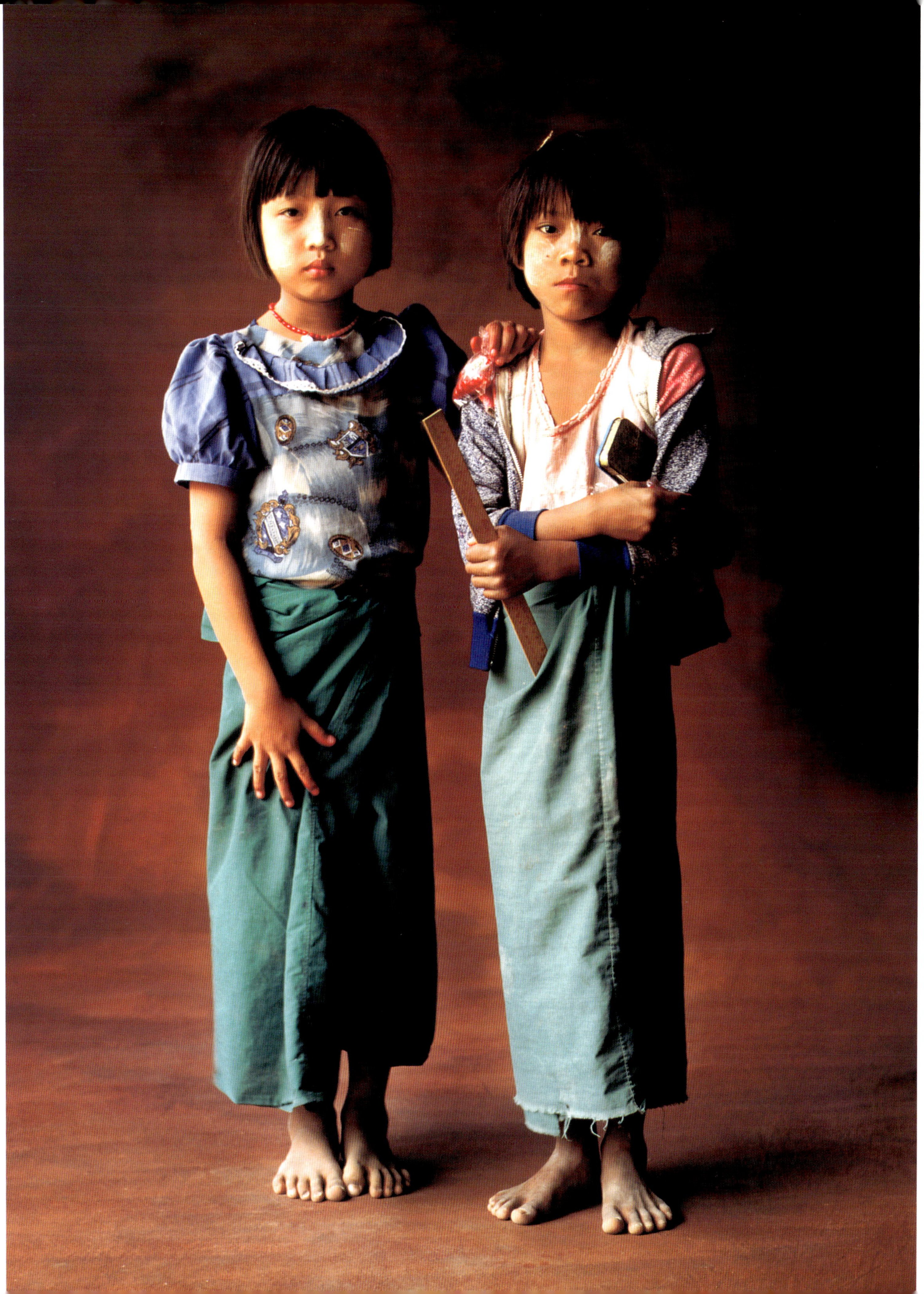

MA NADUSA, SEVEN,
AND MA PUSEWIN, EIGHT,
SCHOOLCHILDREN, BAMAR.
NATKHAYAIN, MYANMAR.

Both Ma Nadusa and Ma Pusewin are schoolchildren in the small farming village of Natkhayain, in Sagaing province. One of their duties is to take care of their younger brothers and sisters while their parents are working in the fields.

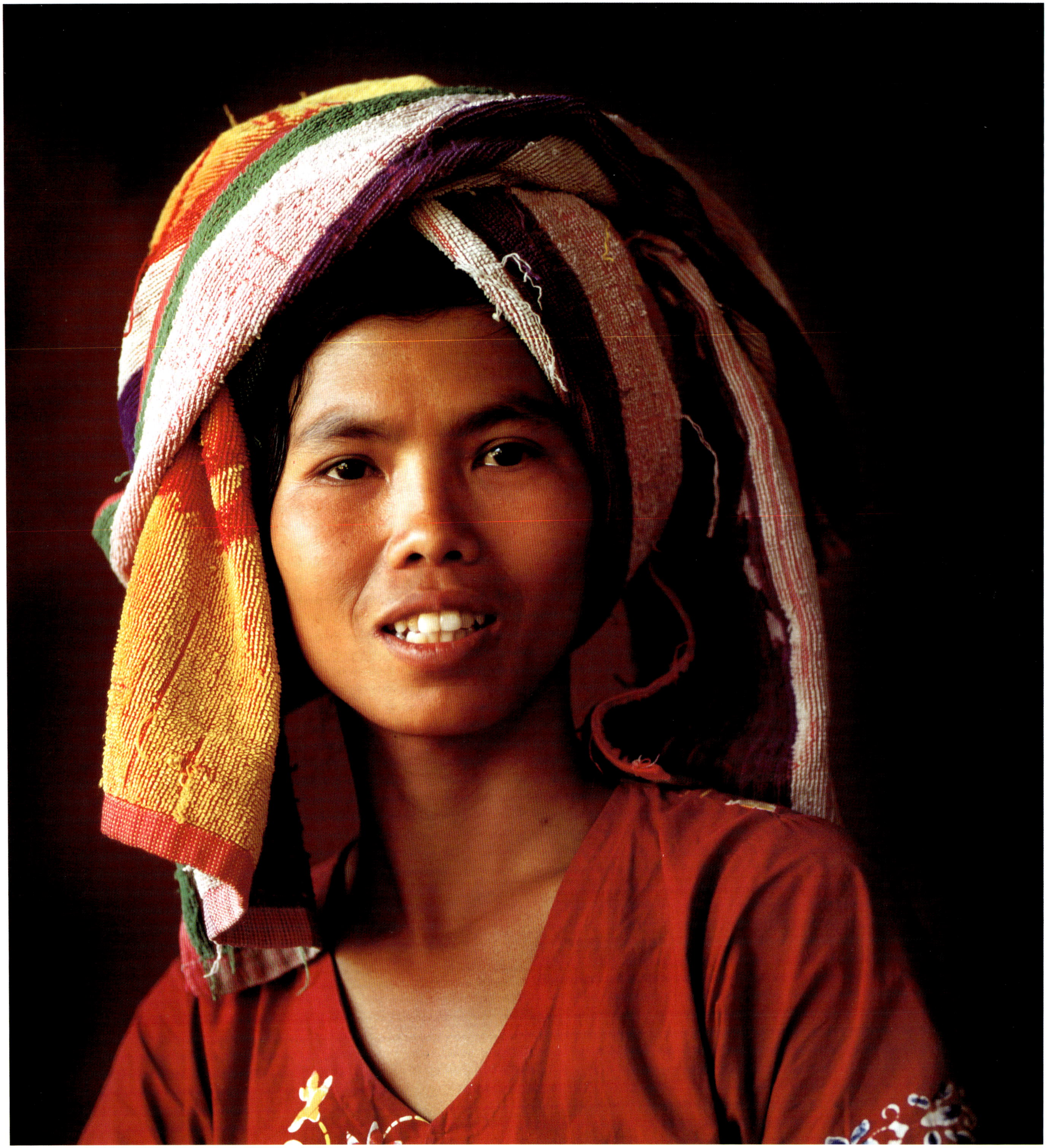

MA AYE NGWE, TWENTY-TWO, BAMAR. NATHKAYAIN, MYANMAR.

Ma Aye Ngwe visibly radiates the strength of this predominantly earth-bound nation of farmers. Most people in Myanmar still live in rural areas and earn their living by growing rice.

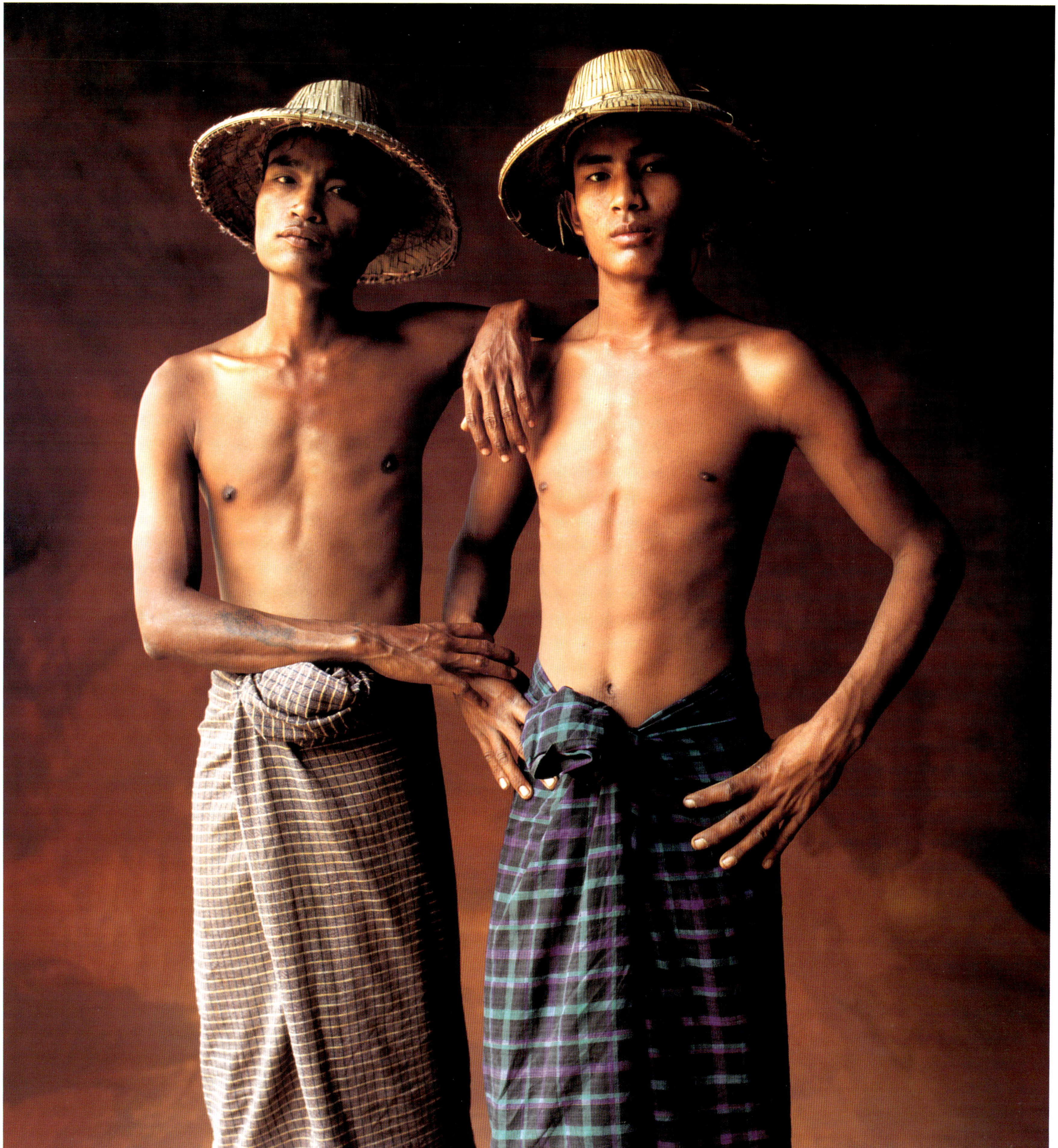

MAUNG HLA, THIRTY, AND MAUNG MINAY, TWENTY-ONE, OXCART DRIVERS, BAMAR. NATKHAYAIN, MYANMAR

Maung Hla and Maung Minay prefer loading and driving carts to the backbreaking work of planting and harvesting the paddy fields.

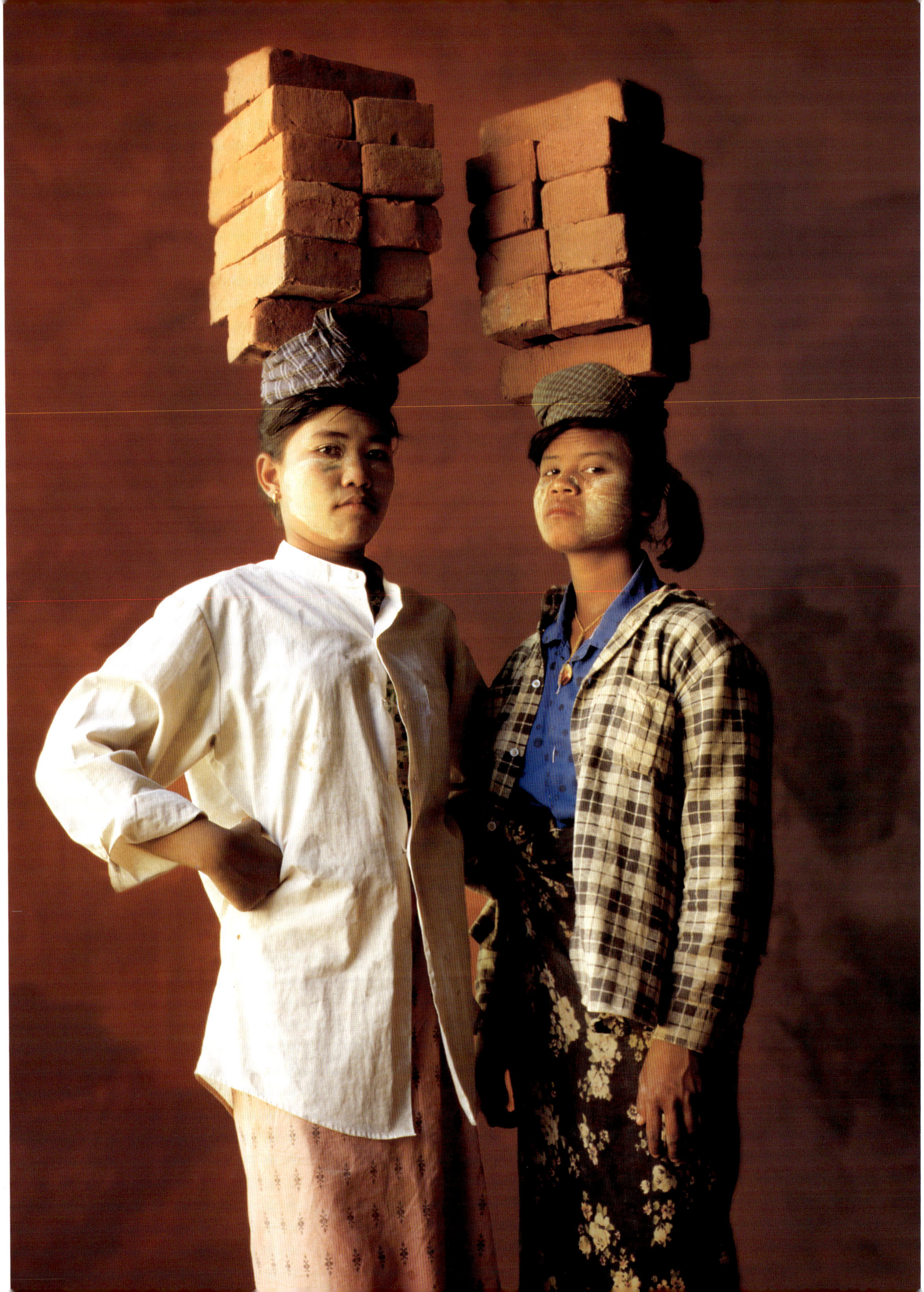

MA PAW NYEIN, SEVENTEEN, AND MA OHNMAR, SEVENTEEN, CONSTRUCTION WORKERS, BAMAR. SAGAING, MYANMAR.

Ma Paw Nyein and Ma Ohnmar were carrying bricks to a Sagaing construction site. As in other Southeast Asian countries, women and men in Myanmar share physically demanding labor. A yellow paste called *thanaka* is used to beautify the face and protect the skin from the sun; pale faces are considered beautiful.

OPPOSITE: NATAMI, FORTY-FIVE, LISU. PAIN PYIT, MYANMAR.

Natami is married to a Lisu farmer. She was returning home from collecting firewood. As the hills to the east of Mogok in Shan State have been depleted of trees, collecting wood often requires a daylong trek.

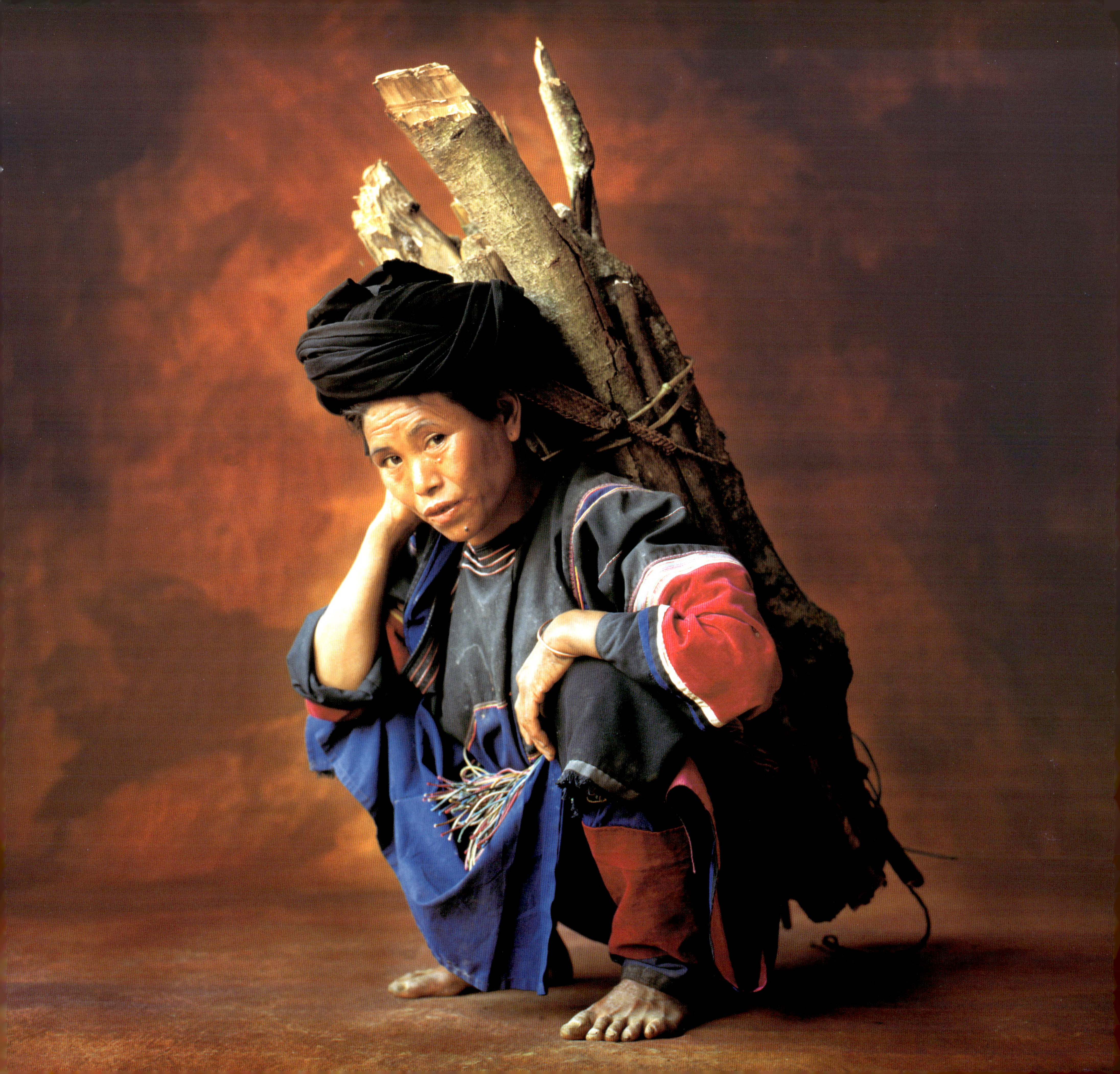

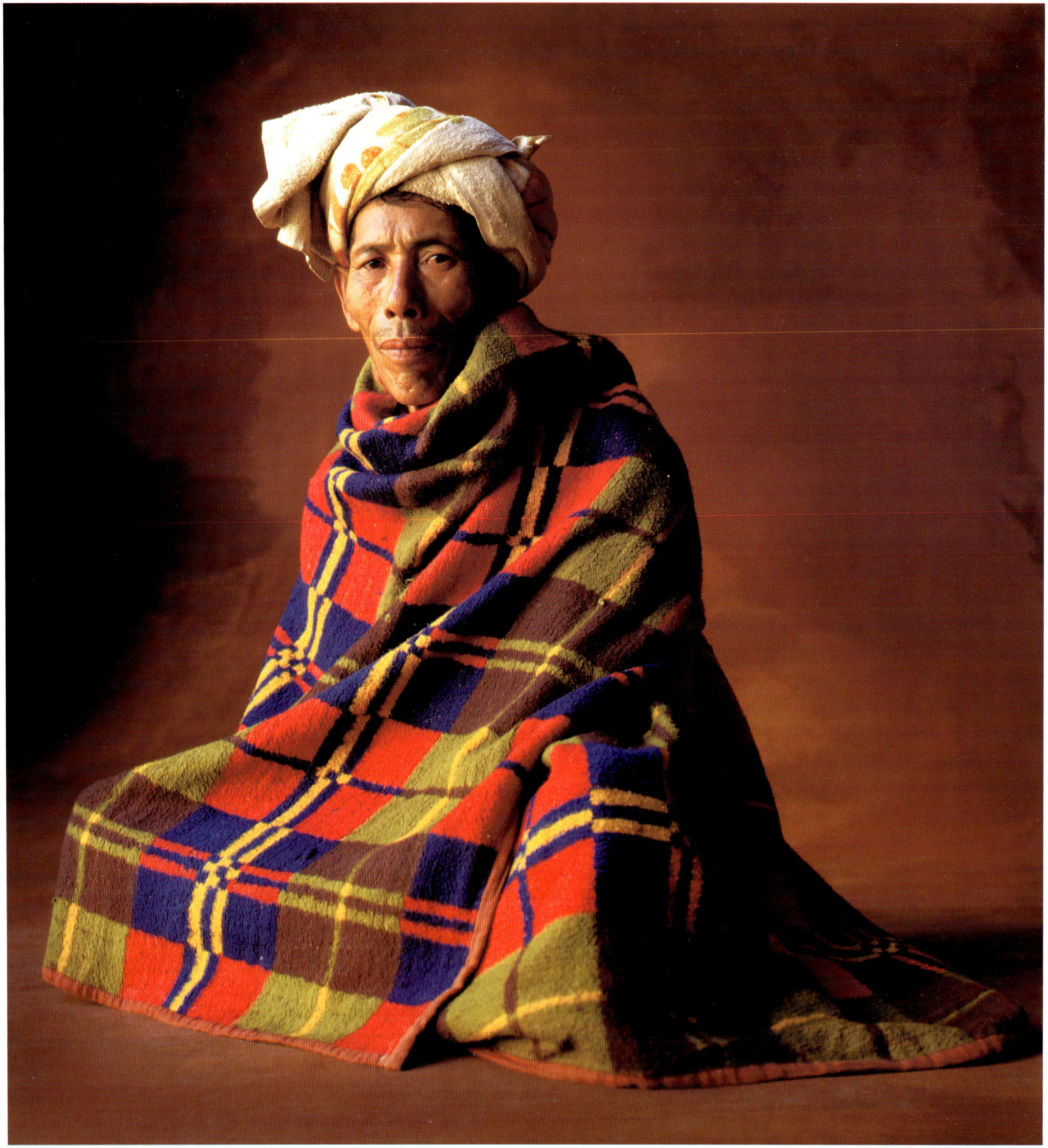

IL TUN SHIN, FIFTY-SIX,
BAMAR, FARMER.
SAGAING, MYANMAR.

Il Tun Shin is a farmer in a village not far from Sagaing. He wears a towel arranged in the form of a *gaung baung*, the ancient Burmese headdress whose material and particular style distinguished the different classes in the former Ava kingdom.

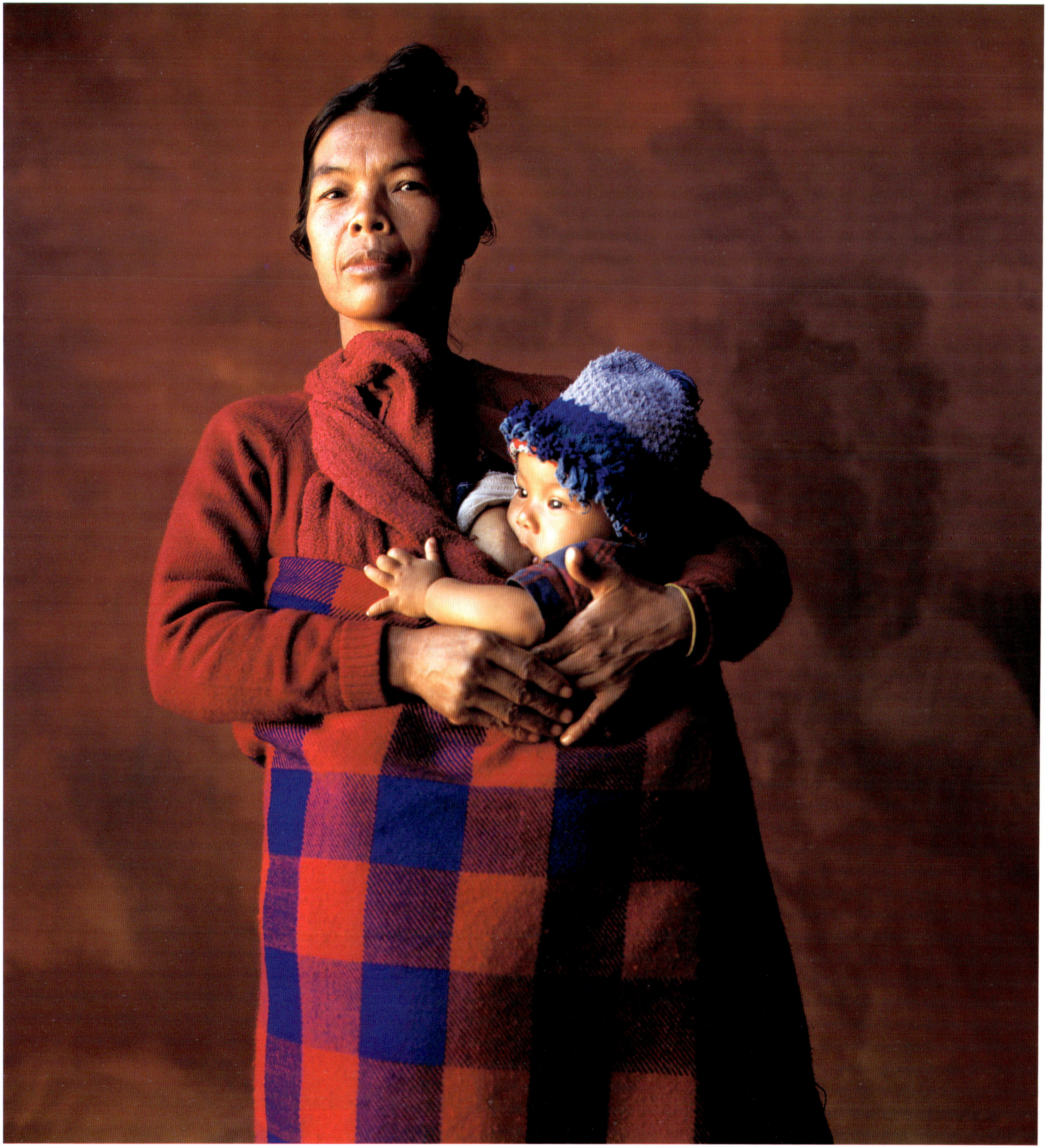

HMUNKITKAI, FORTY-THREE, WITH BABY LALDUHMUAI, SIN CHIN. FALAM, MYANMAR.

Hmunkitkai and her baby, Lalduhmuai, are Sin Chins living high up in the Chin Hills along the border of the Indian state of Manipur. For the last couple of decades, the Chin Hills have been off-limits to foreigners. The Sin Chins have minimal contact with the world beyond the hills. They are also deeply religious Baptists in a country that is more than 80 percent Buddhist with serious tensions between the two religious groups.

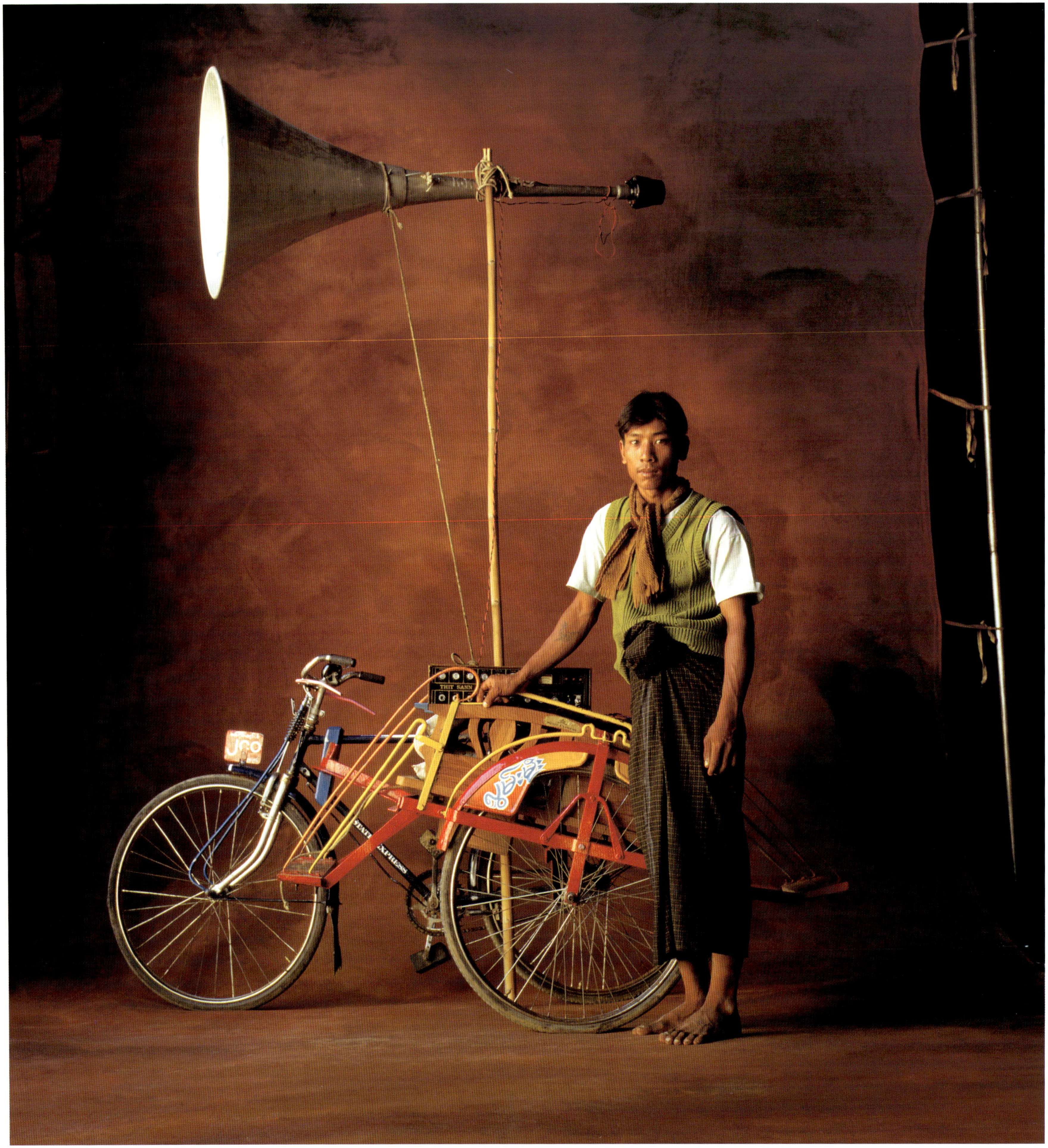

AYE KO, TWENTY-SEVEN, BAMAR, TRISHAW DRIVER. SAGAING, MYANMAR.

Aye Ko earns his living by driving announcers through the town. His trishaw is equipped with an ancient loud-speaker and a vintage tape recorder.

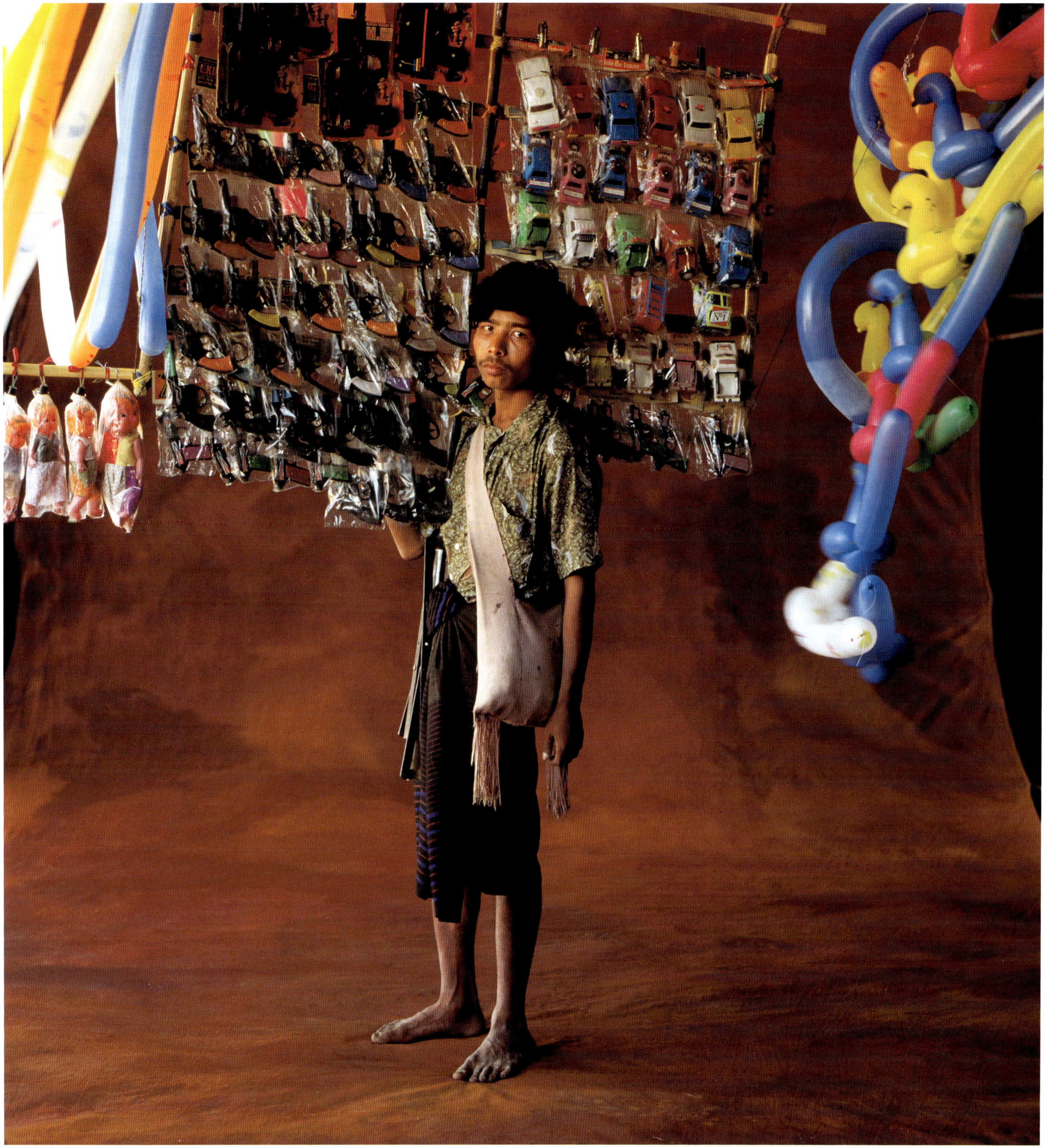

TUN U, TWENTY-TWO,
BAMAR, VENDOR.
MYITKYINA, MYANMAR.

Tun U sells balloons and small gadgets for children in the market of Myitkyina. His business flourishes during the annual Manao Festival in January, which attracts thousands of Kachins from the hills along the Chinese border. Returning, they bring inexpensive toys to their children back home.

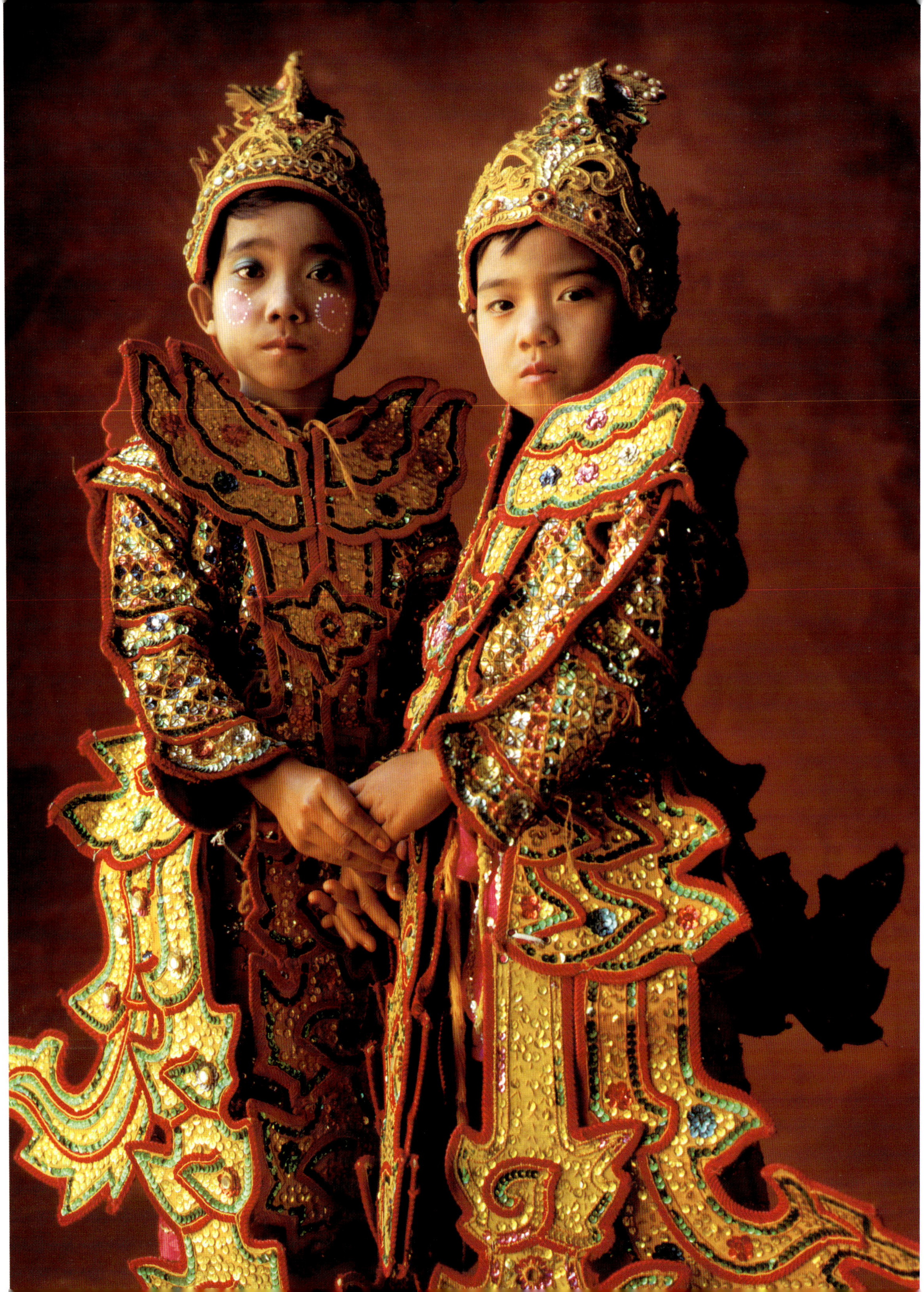

MYINT MYINT THAN, NINE, AND AYE AYE SUNG, SEVEN, BAMAR, SCHOOLCHILDREN. SAGAING, MYANMAR.

Myint Myint Than and Aye Aye Sung are dressed as *devas* (gods) or *nats* (spirits). According to Myanmar mythology, there are thirty levels above or below the level of human beings. Those above our world are inhabited by *devas* and *nats*.

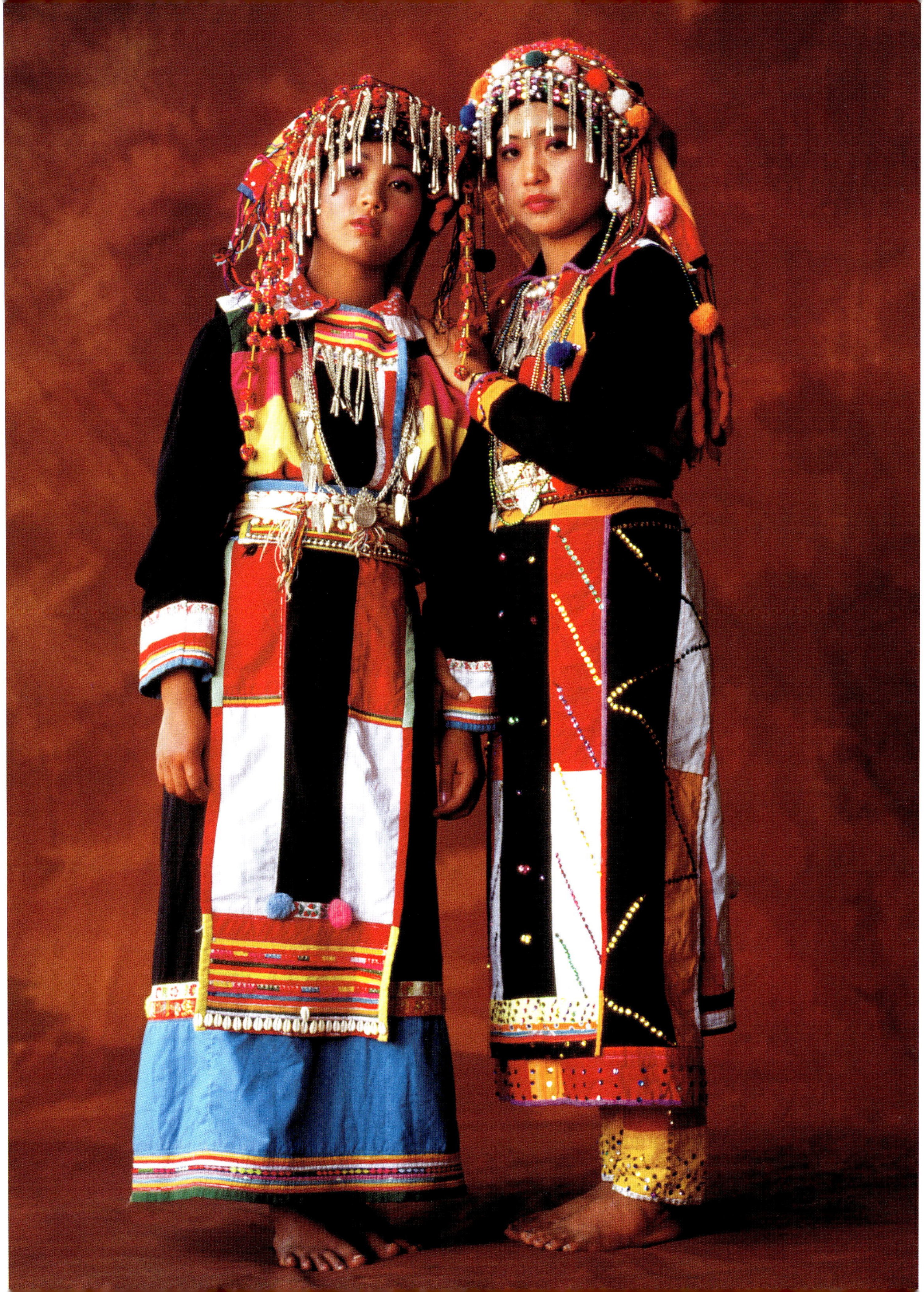

SI MI, TWENTY, AND LASHOWLAY, NINETEEN, FLOWERING LISUS. MYITKYINA, MYANMAR.

Si Mi and Lashowlay came to the annual animistic Manao Festival in their most colorful costumes, signifying that they are unmarried. The Manao festival attracts many young women and men, making it an important matchmaking event.

MABAI, TWENTY-FIVE, PADAUNG.
HUAY PU KANG, THAILAND.

Mabai belongs to the last generation of true "giraffe-women," though one can see girls as young as five wearing their first brass rings.

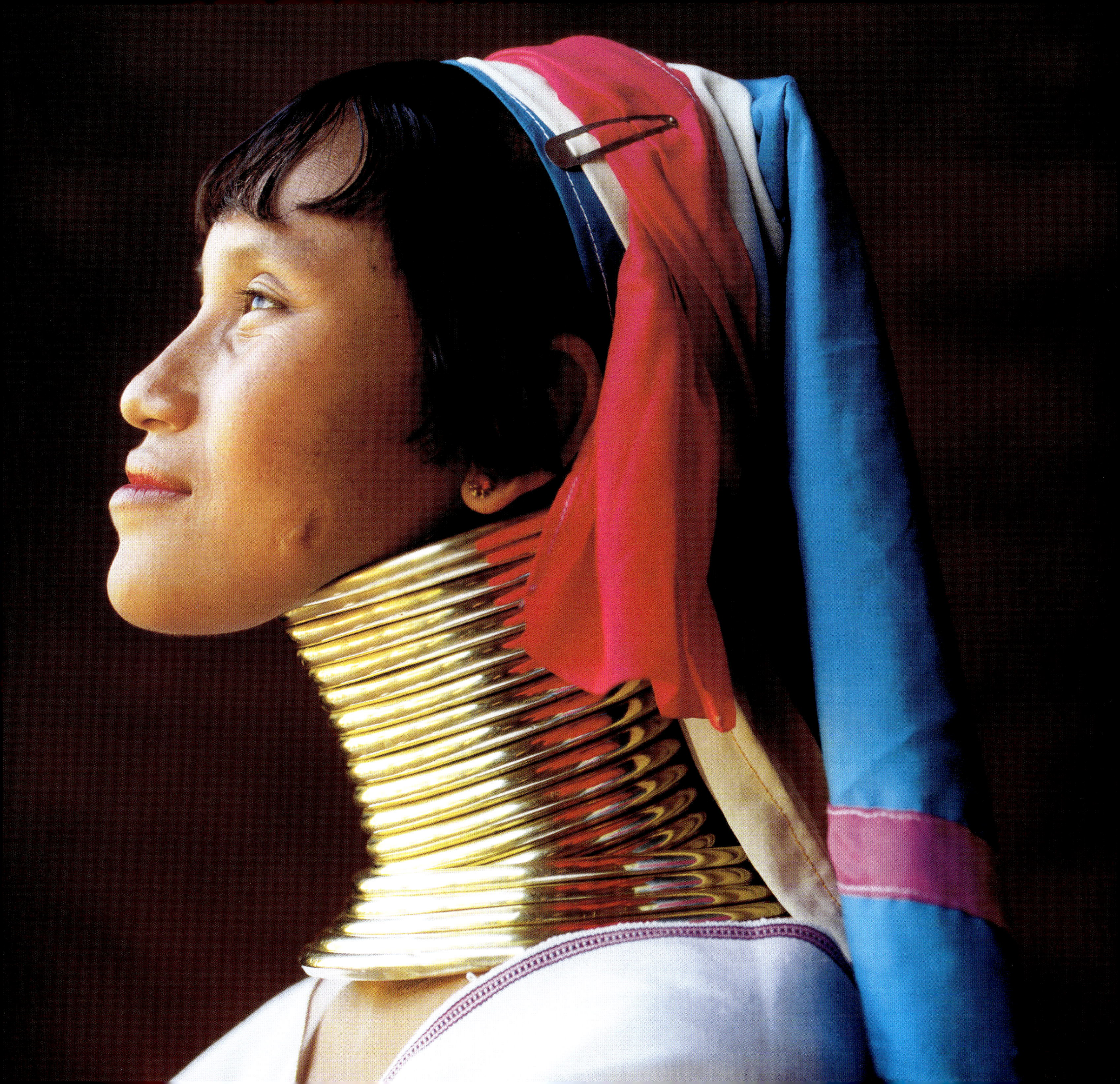

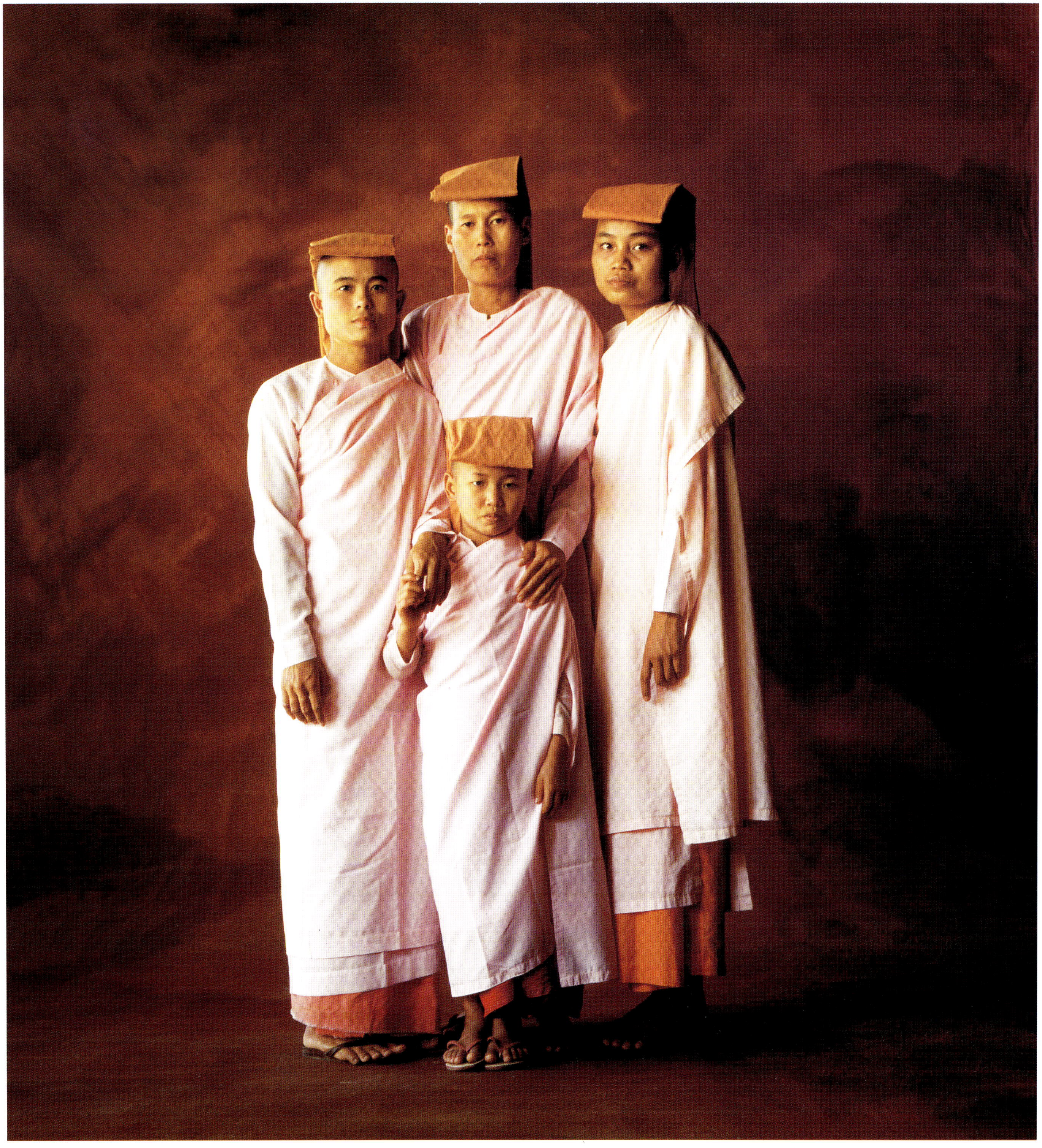

LEFT TO RIGHT:
MA KUTAMA, THIRTY;
MA NANTHA THIRI,
SEVENTEEN; MA SAWANA,
TWENTY-SIX ; AND MA
KELADI, NINE (CENTER),
BUDDHIST NUNS.
SAGAING, MYANMAR.

Ma Kutama, Ma Nantha Thiri, Ma Sawana, and Ma Keladi are nuns at one of the many small nunneries located in the shade of huge trees on the slopes of the Sagaing valley. Little Ma Keladi comes from a large family and was brought to the nunnery at age six.

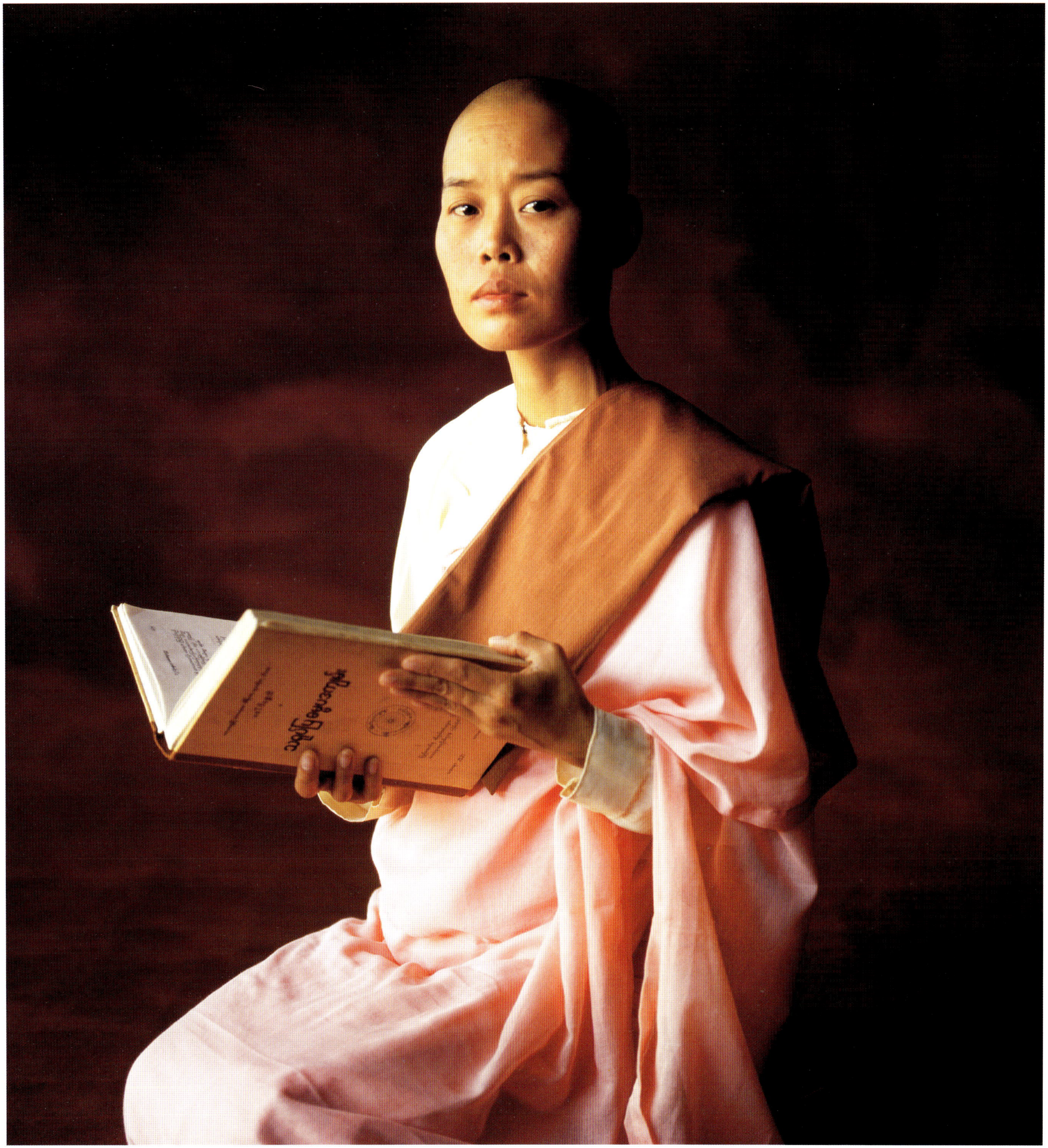

MA EGA, THIRTY-THREE, NUN, KAYIN. SAGAING, MYANMAR.

Ma Ega is a Kayin Buddhist nun. Religious customs determine that both monks and nuns shave their heads, although nuns do not subscribe to all of the 227 monastic rules that *pongyis* (monks) observe.

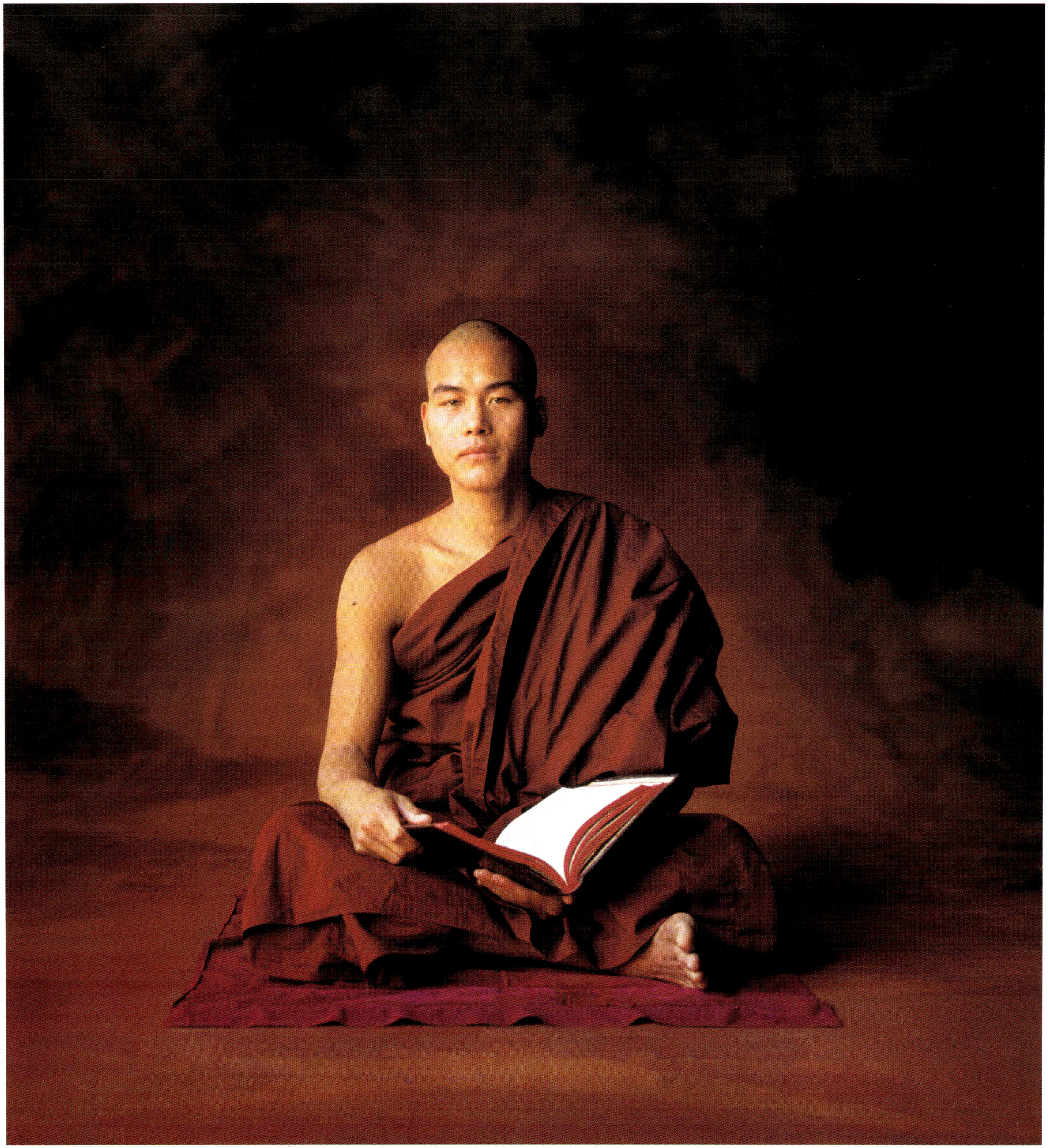

ASHIN U KOSALA,
TWENTY-TWO, MONK.
AMARAPURA, MYANMAR.

Ashin U Kosala studies the Buddhist scripture at the Maha Ghanda monastery in Amarapura. He has just become a fully ordained monk, and intends to spend the rest of his life in the *sangha* (brotherhood of monks).

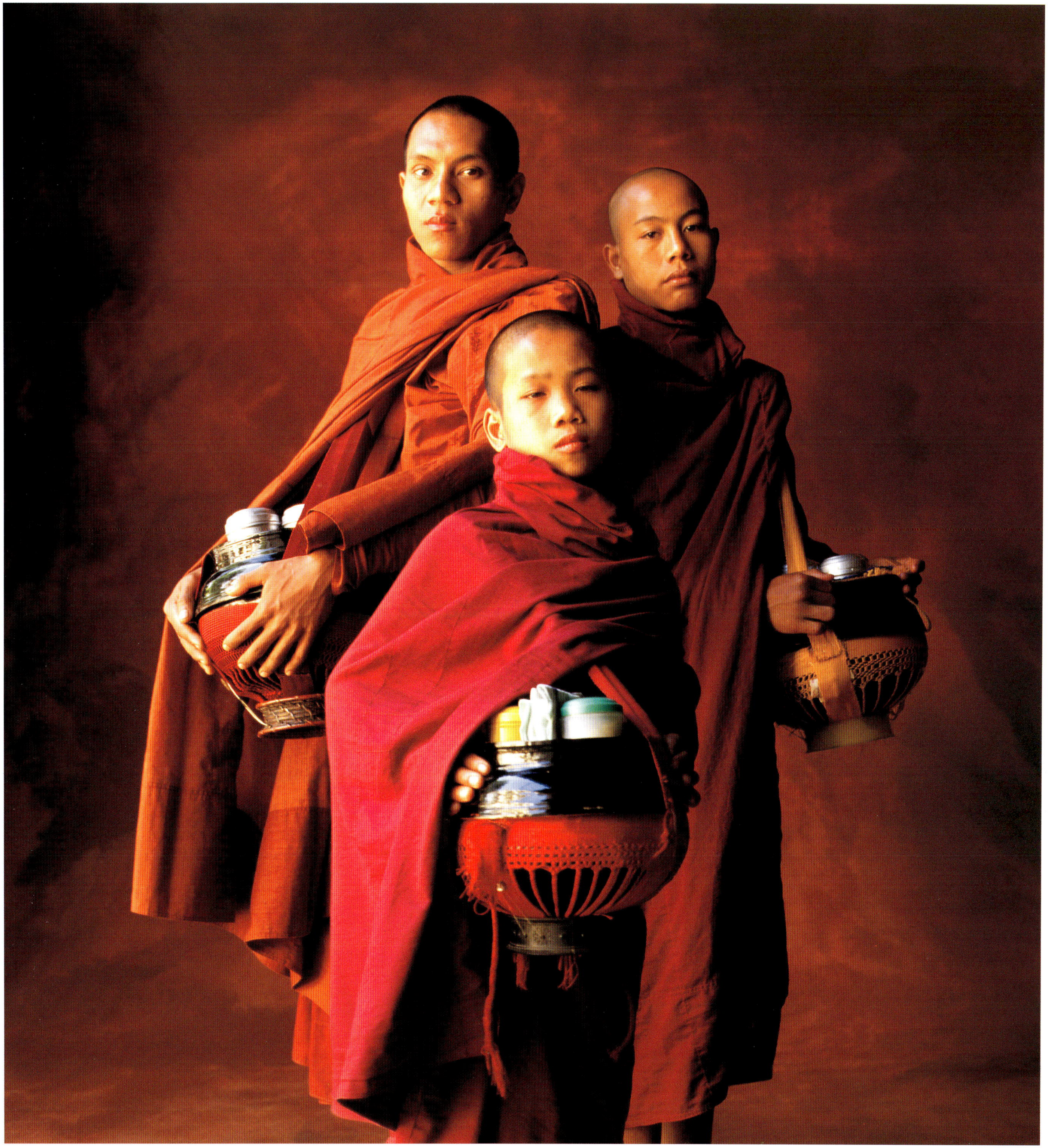

LEFT TO RIGHT:
IL WANNA THIRI, TWENTY-FIVE; SHIN YEWARAT, EIGHTEEN; AND U KWA THAN HLA, TWENTY-SEVEN; MONKS, BAMAR. SAGAING, MYANMAR.

Nearly every young Buddhist Myanmar male spends a certain amount of time in the religious order. Initiation can take place at any age, preferably during the rainy season.

U GUSALA, SIXTY-SEVEN, BAMAR, MONK. AMARAPURA, MYANMAR.

U Gusala was initiated as a full-fledged monk thirty years ago. Since then he has spent most of his waking hours in meditation. He gets up at four in the morning and has his last meal of the day before noon. During the photography session he remained in the same position without the slightest movement for nearly two hours.

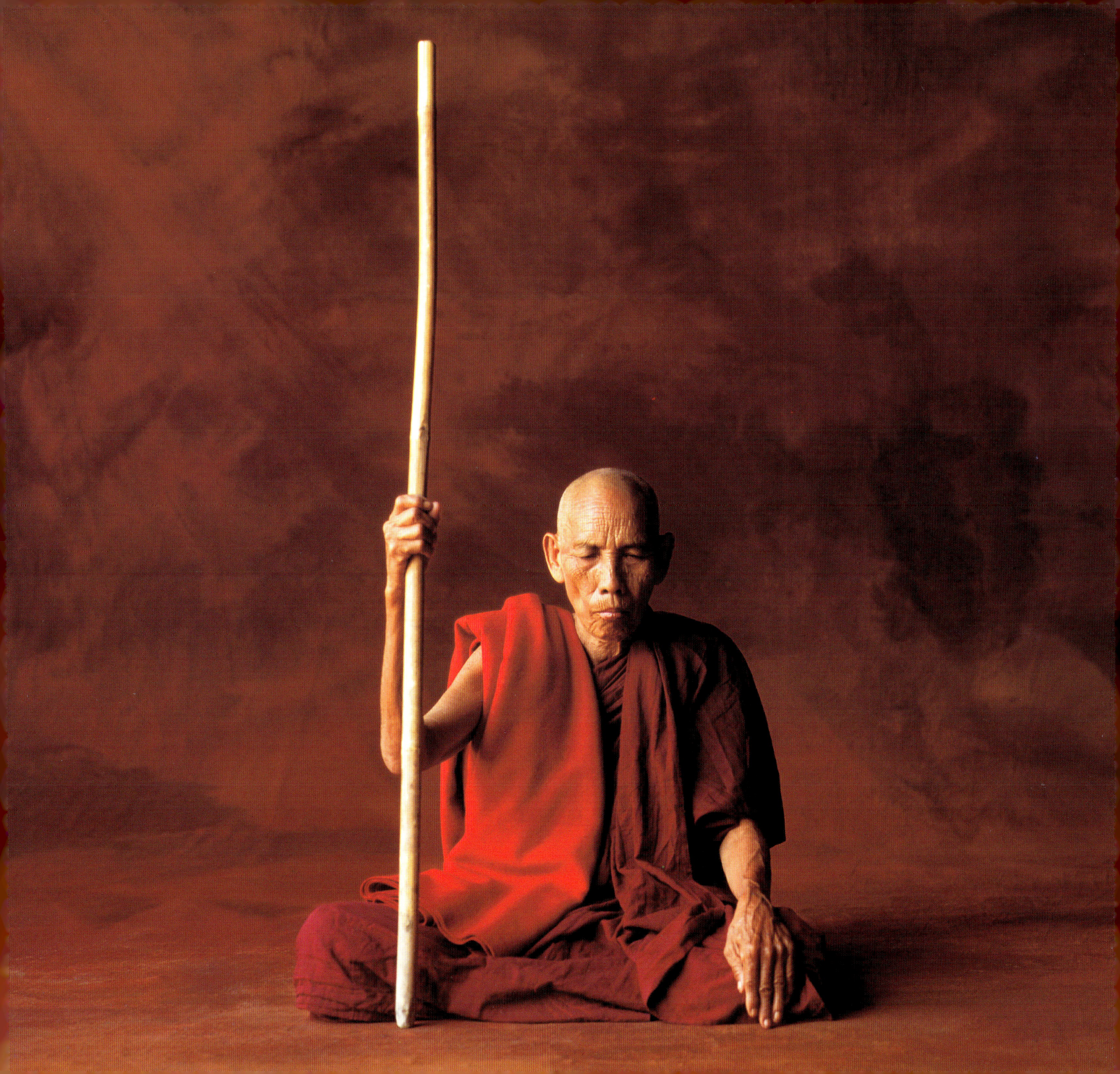

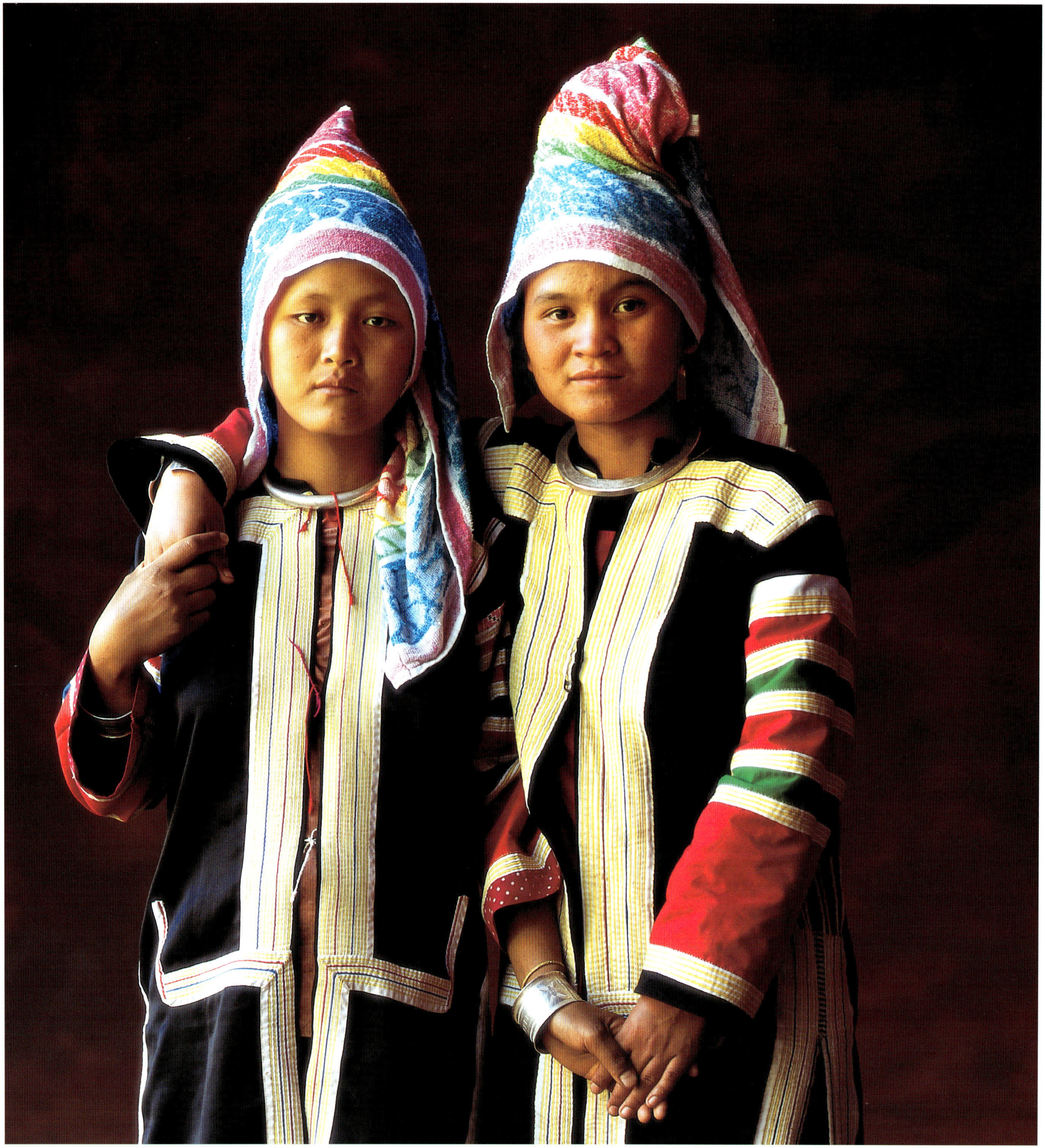

NAUE, EIGHTEEN, AND NAKA, SEVENTEEN, LAHU. JABO, THAILAND.

Naue and Naka still wear their national dress, but this tradition is not likely to withstand the influx of modernity which has accelerated tremendously over the last decade. Tourists now visit their village, and industrial goods are slowly replacing those once produced by hand by the people of their community.

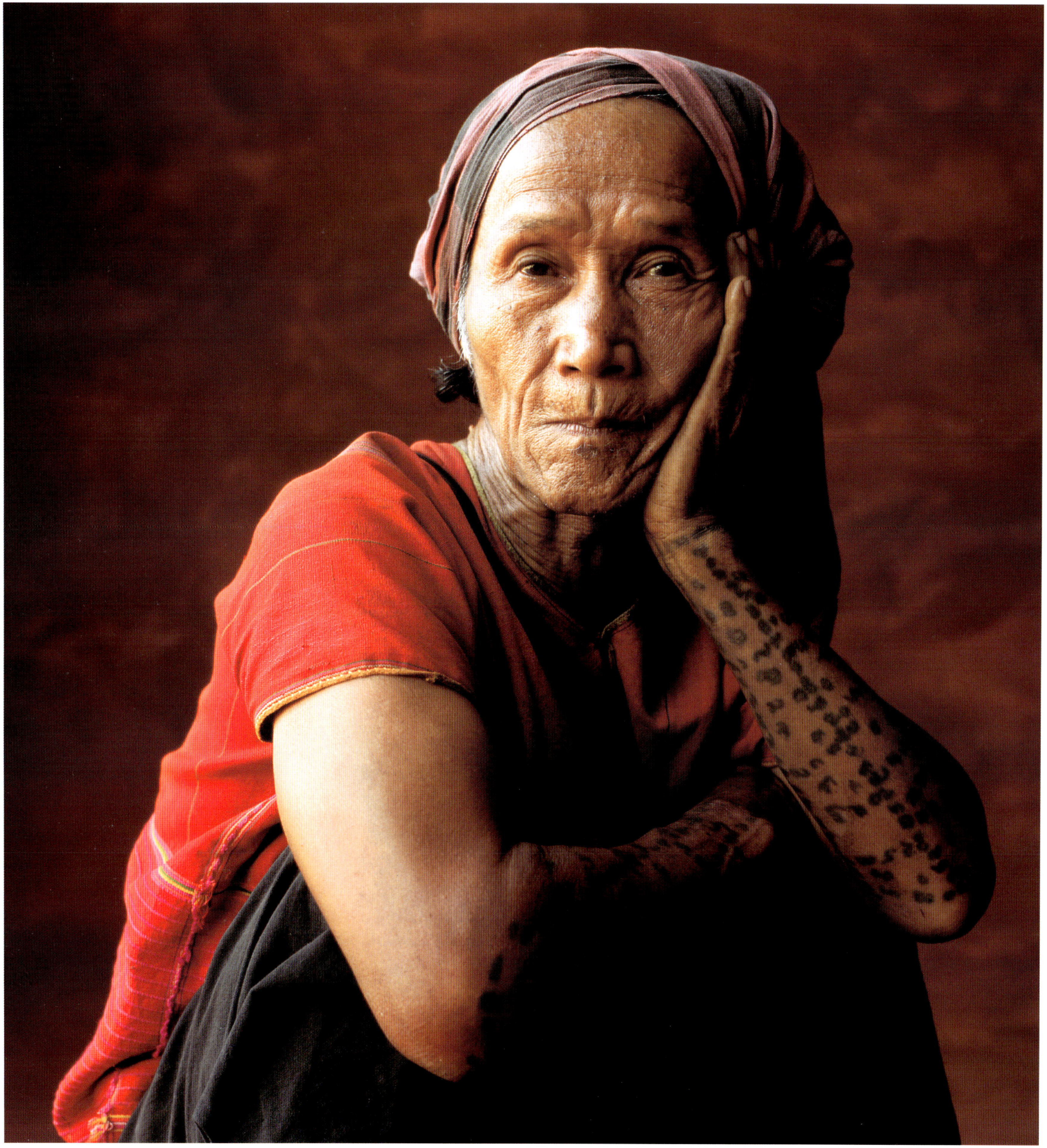

OEJE, EIGHTY, WHITE KAREN. BAN HUEY KAW, THAILAND.

Oeje is a White Karen who lives in Thailand, not far from the Myanmar border. Karens are spread along the hills on both sides of the frontier. The tattoos on his arms are not only adornments, but are believed to give the wearer special powers and fend off evil spirits.

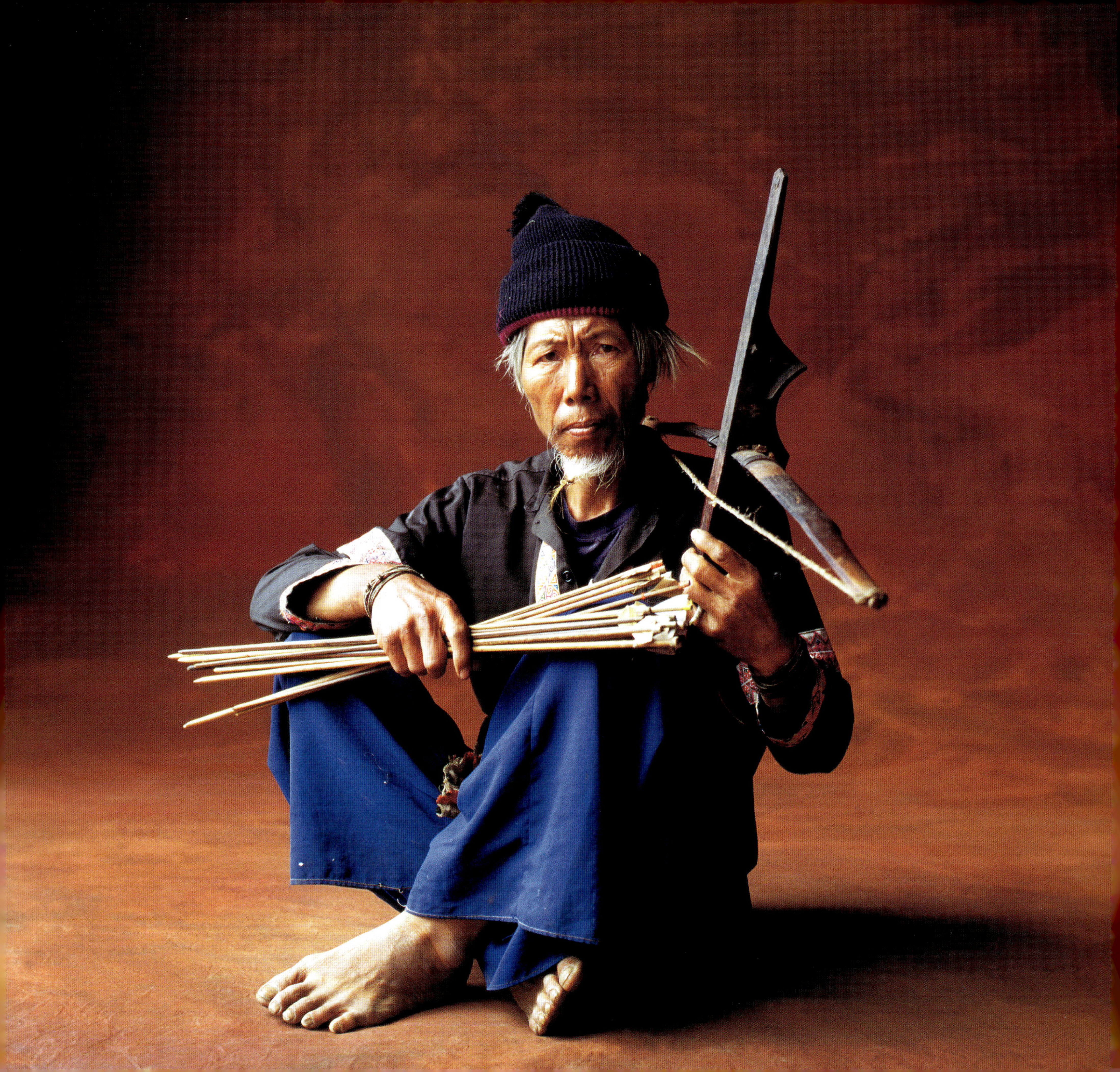

OPPOSITE:
JUE DAETUO, FIFTY-EIGHT, FARMER, HMONG. DOI PUI, THAILAND.

Jue Daetuo is a Hmong farmer in the hills of northern Thailand. The Hmongs can be found along the entire stretch of hills that run from Myanmar through Thailand and Laos to Vietnam.

LAU CHENG SAE TUNT, SIXTY-ONE, HUNTER, HMONG. DOI PUI, THAILAND.

Lau Cheng Sae Tunt is a permanently settled Hmong. His people, who reside as far away as Vietnam, have gone through major struggles as a result of the Vietnam war. Many of them became refugees and ended up settling in the United States.

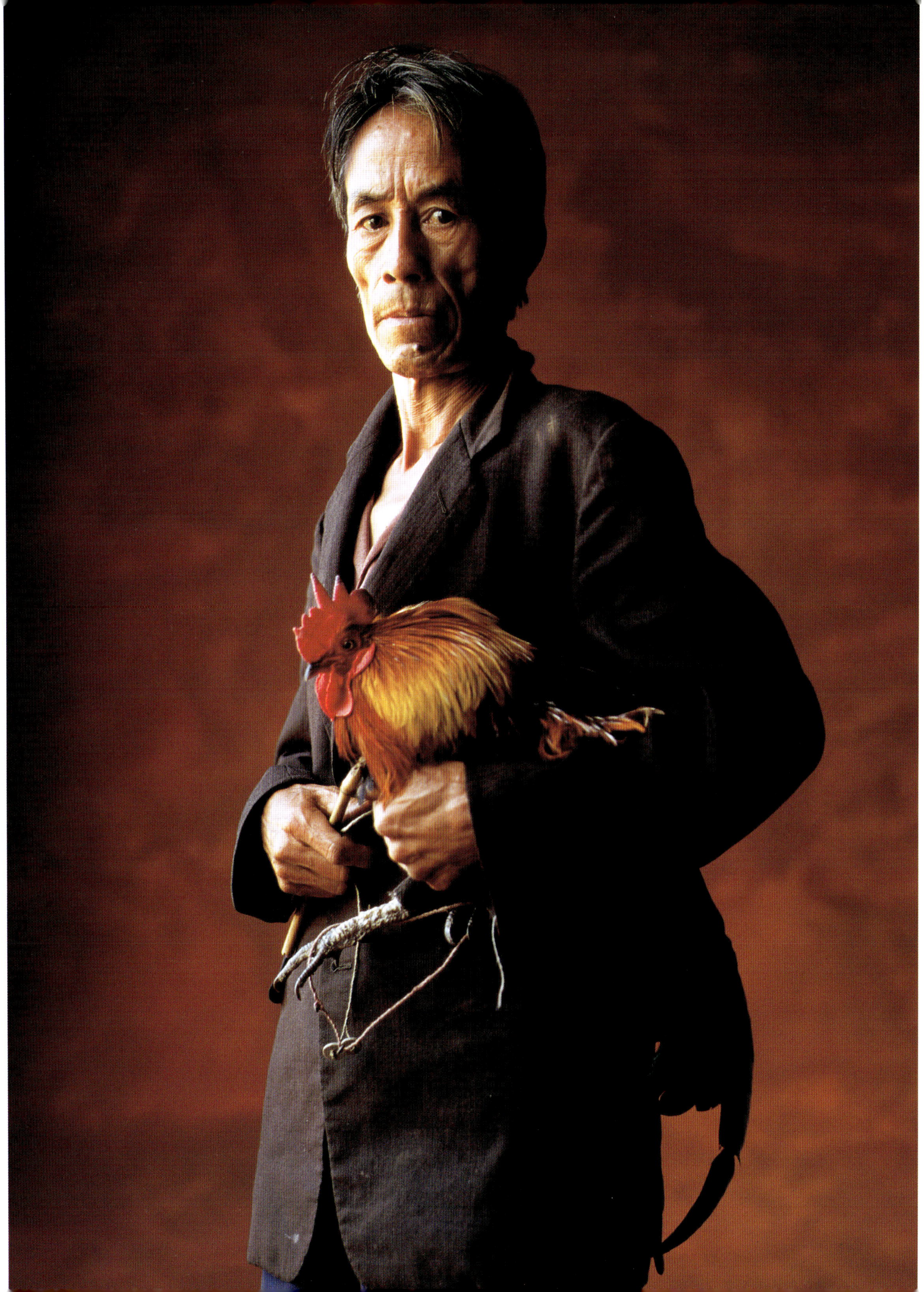

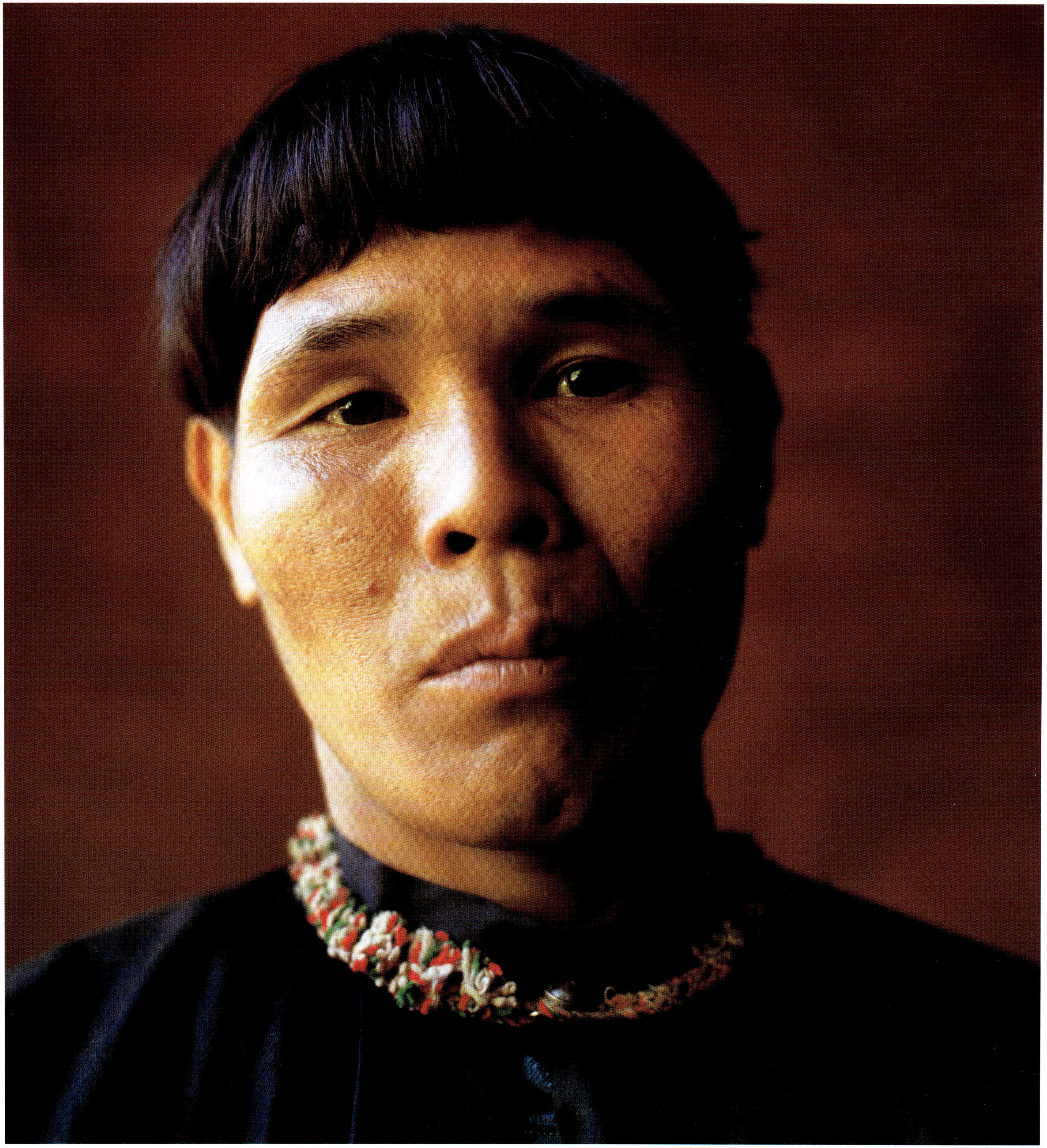

DADA, FORTY, FARMER, LAHU. JABO, THAILAND.

Together with his wife, Dada works the small plot of land that feeds his family. They live in a remote village in the hills of northern Thailand; it is nearly impossible to earn any money beyond what they make from selling their excess produce.

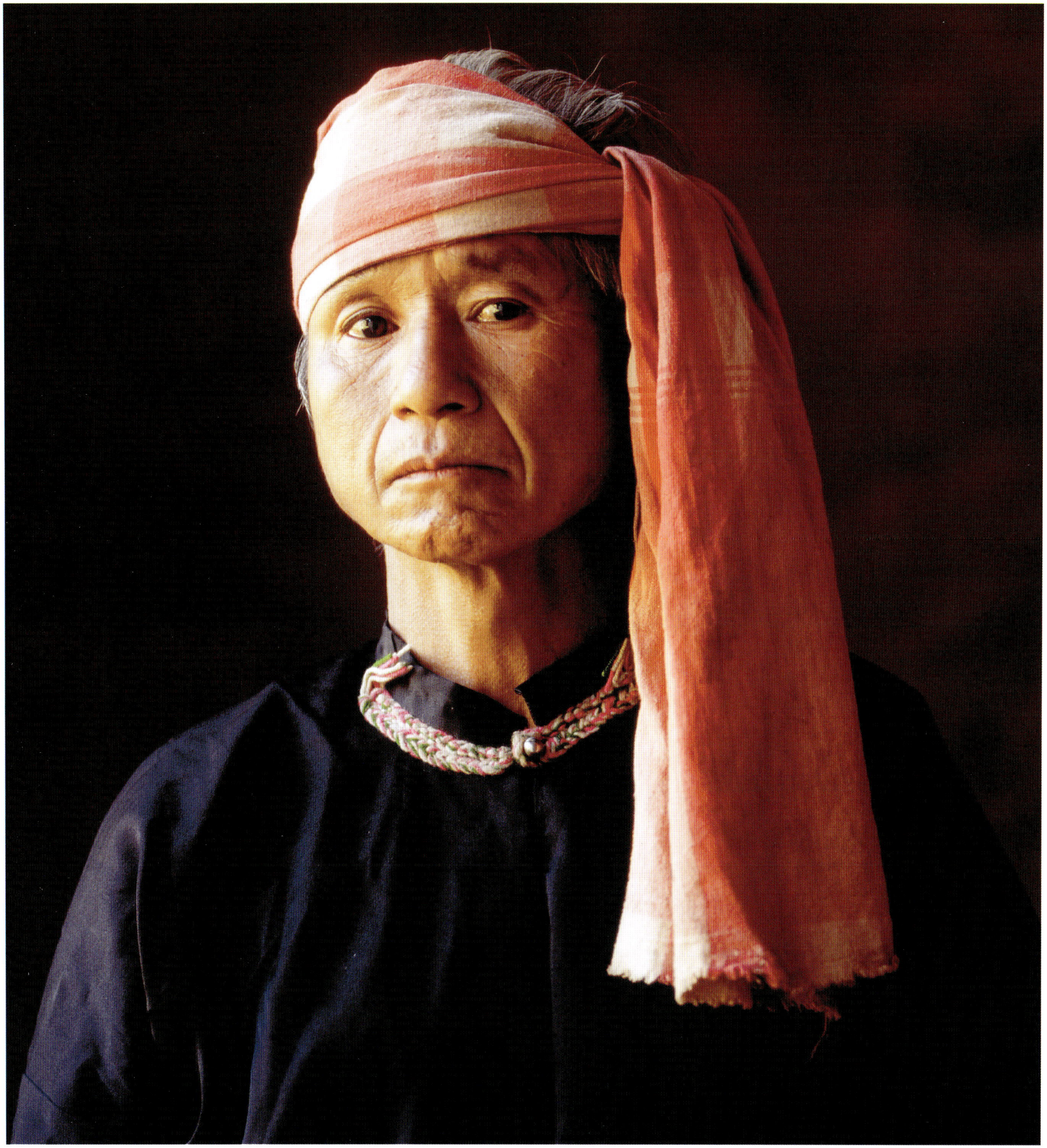

CHUN, SIXTY-THREE, FARMER, LAHU. JABO, THAILAND.

Chun follows the same lifestyle as his forefathers did. Most older Lahus cherish their simple way of life. Traditionally, they believe in a Man-God with magical powers.

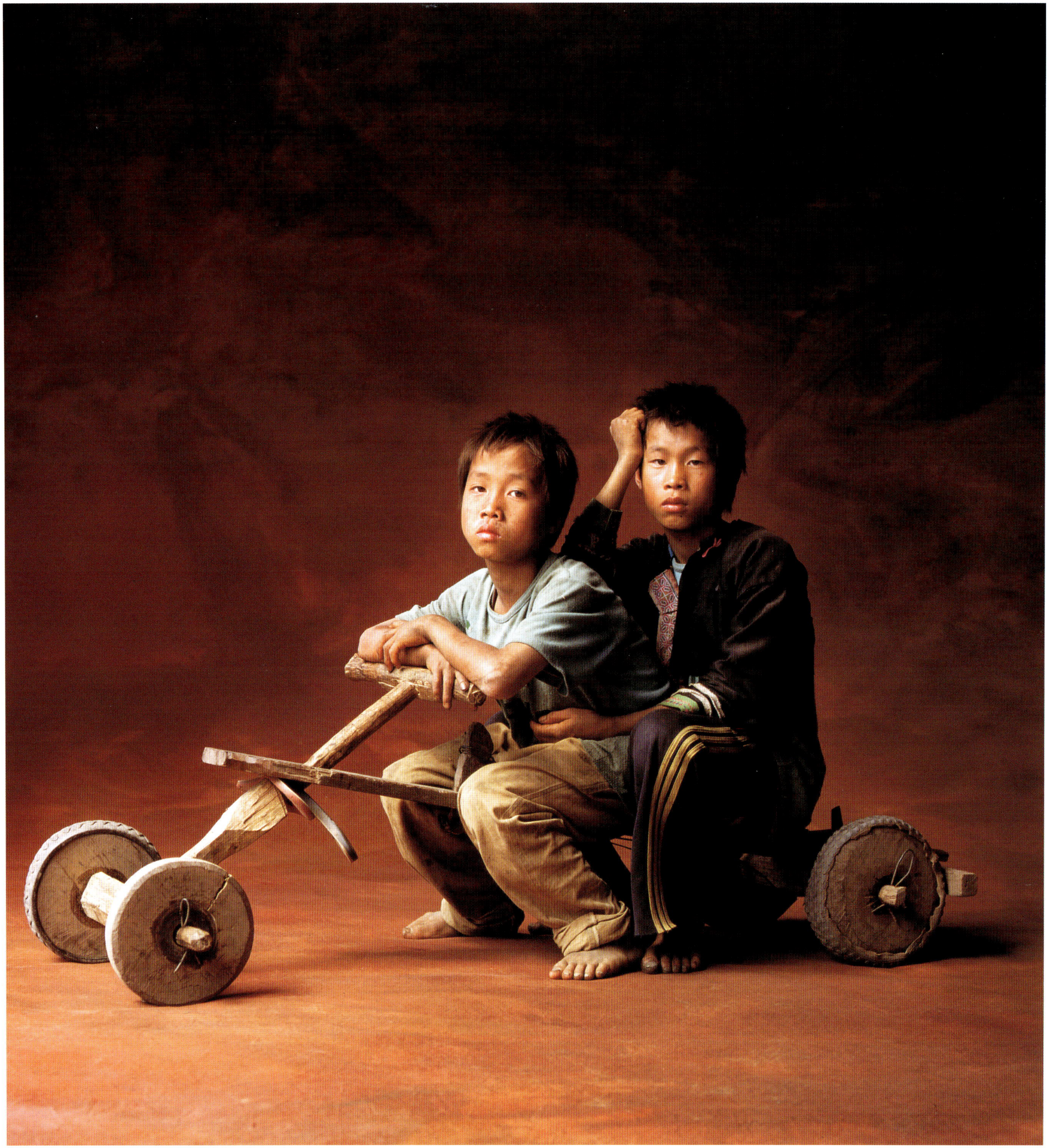

PENG, THIRTEEN,
AND LI SAE YOUING,
TWELVE, HMONG.
DOI PUI, THAILAND.

Peng and Li Sae Youing live in the hills of northern Thailand. Running this handmade go-cart along the rough tracks of their village is their favorite pastime.

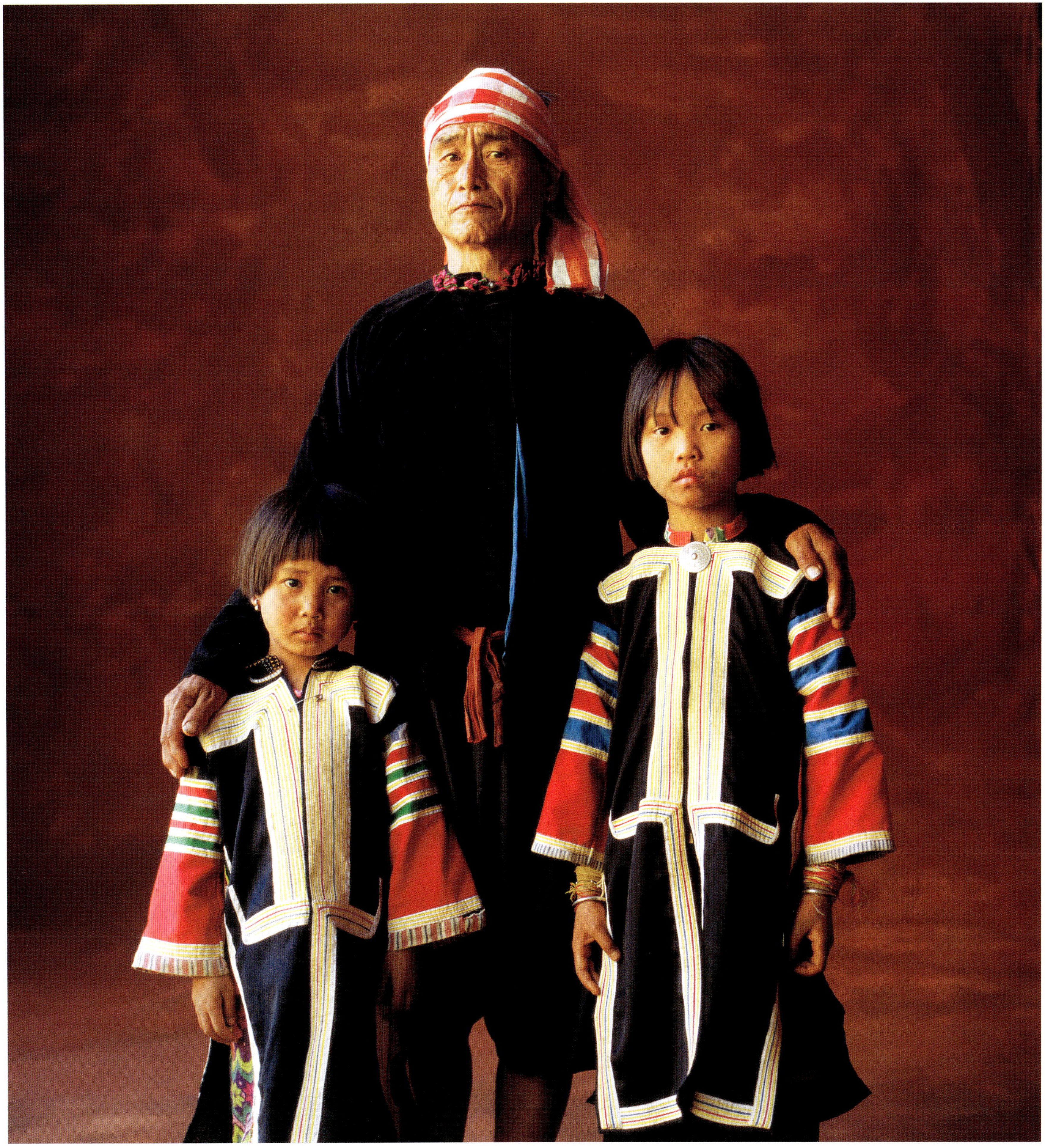

LEFT TO RIGHT: NAPHO, SEVEN; JAKA, FIFTY-NINE; AND KANJANA, NINE; LAHU. JABO, THAILAND.

Jaka, a Lahu farmer, is proud of his daughters, Napho and Kanjana. Though Jaka grew up in the tribal tradition, his children attend a government school.

FOR CENTURIES THE TRIBES OF THE GOLDEN TRIANGLE HAVE BEEN ON THE MOVE—A SLOW MOVEMENT THAT TOOK A GENERATION FOR A STEP FURTHER SOUTH. NOW IT HAS COME TO A SUDDEN HALT, AND WITH IT THE HEAVEN THAT SPANS THEIR WORLD COMES CRASHING DOWN, BURYING FOREVER THEIR IDENTITY AND ORIGINAL LIFE-STYLE.

MOEMOE, SEVENTY-TWO, AKHA.
BAN KOAE, THAILAND.

Moemoe lives in Ban Koae on the Thai side of the Thailand/Myanmar border. There is no road that enters her village; goods are transported on mules. Moemoe has rarely left her hillcrest home; she smokes an opium pipe, a tribal custom.

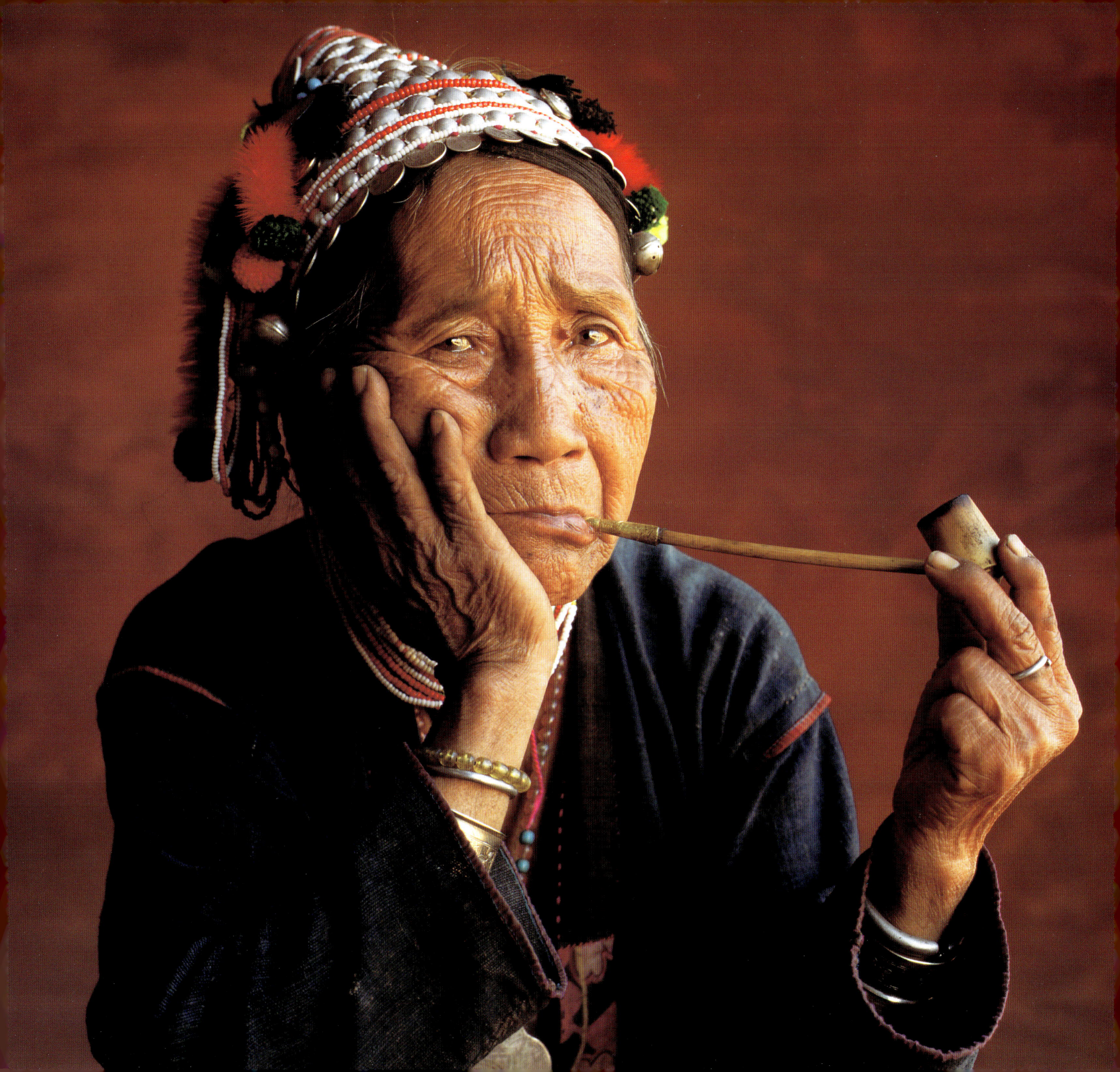

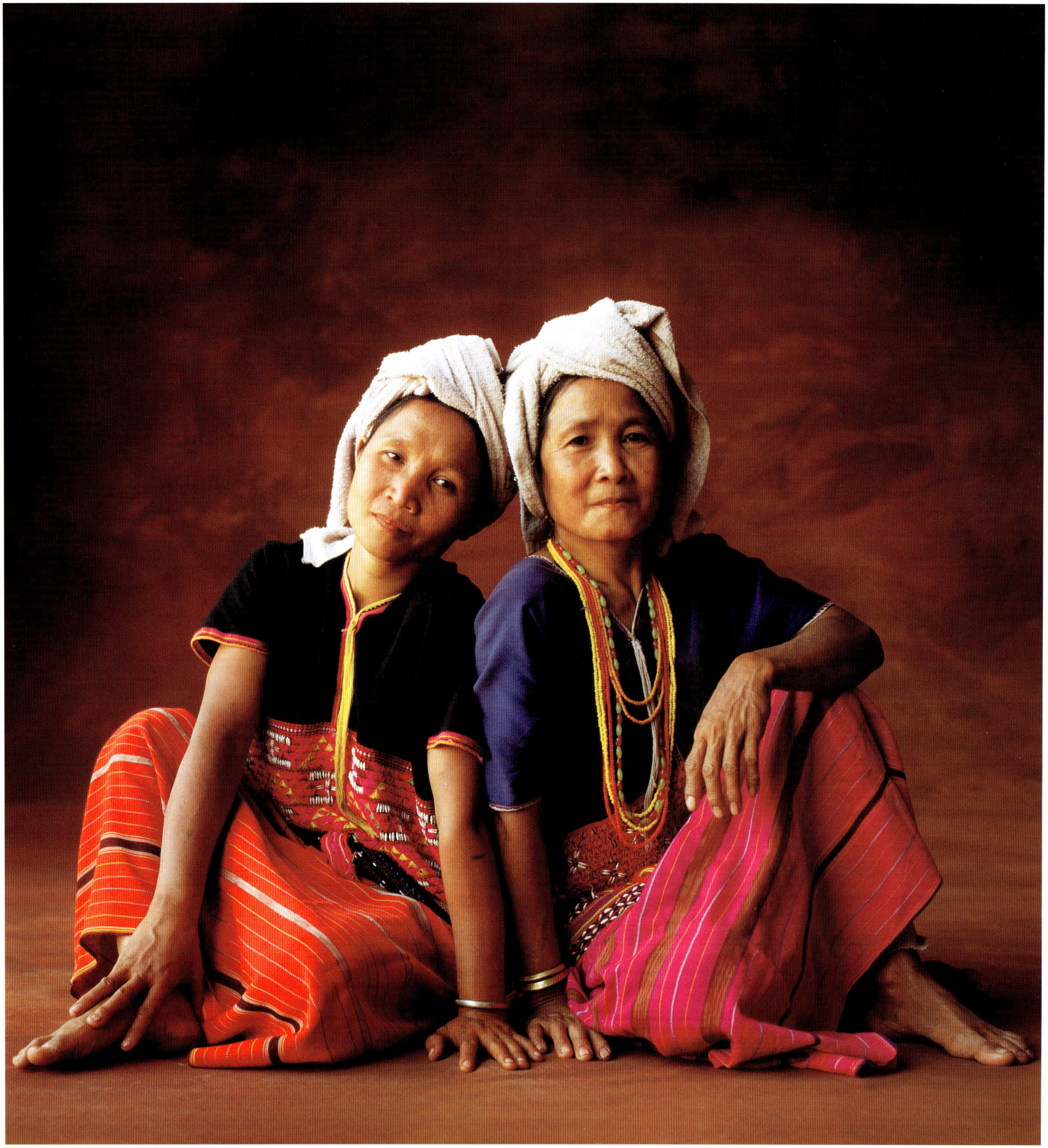

TORTARE, THIRTY-EIGHT, AND NOSHISHI, FIFTY, WHITE KAREN. BAN HUEY KAW, THAILAND.

The White Karen of northern Thailand are also known as the Sgaw Karen, "the Karen that live in the hills." Seventy thousand Sgaws live in Thailand. The majority of the Karen, however, some 2.7 million, live in Myanmar. Though the Karens' war with the Myanmar government continues, the Thai Karens are at least spared the ravages of war their cousins experience across the border.

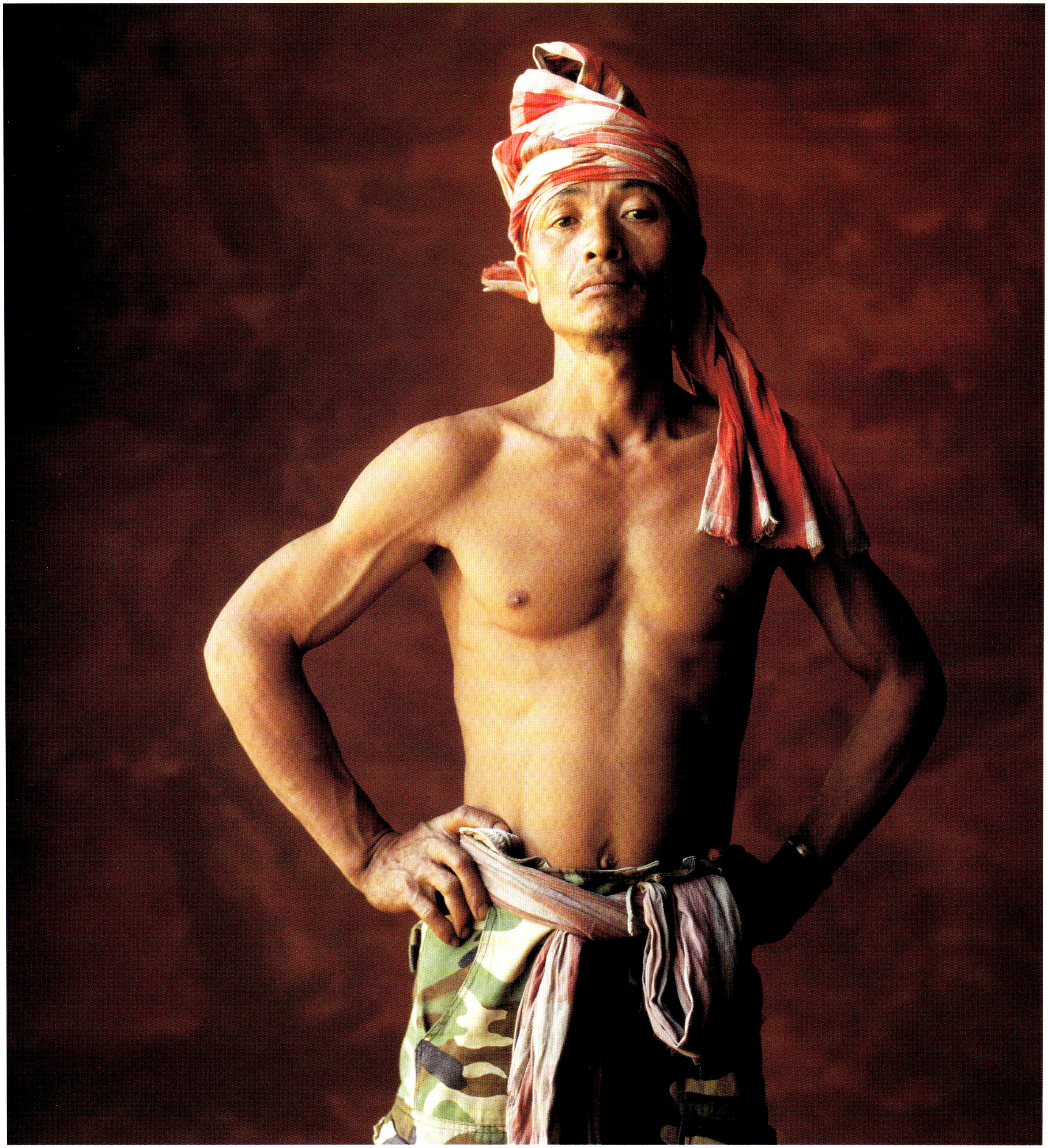

JAMSUI, FORTY-FIVE, FARMER, WHITE KAREN. BAN HUEY KAW, THAILAND.

The Karen are a predominantly Christian tribe in the two strictly Buddhist countries of Thailand and Myanmar. For years the Myanmar Karen fought for the right to have an independent state. Jamsui's generation has experienced some of the hardest struggles as a result of this conflict.

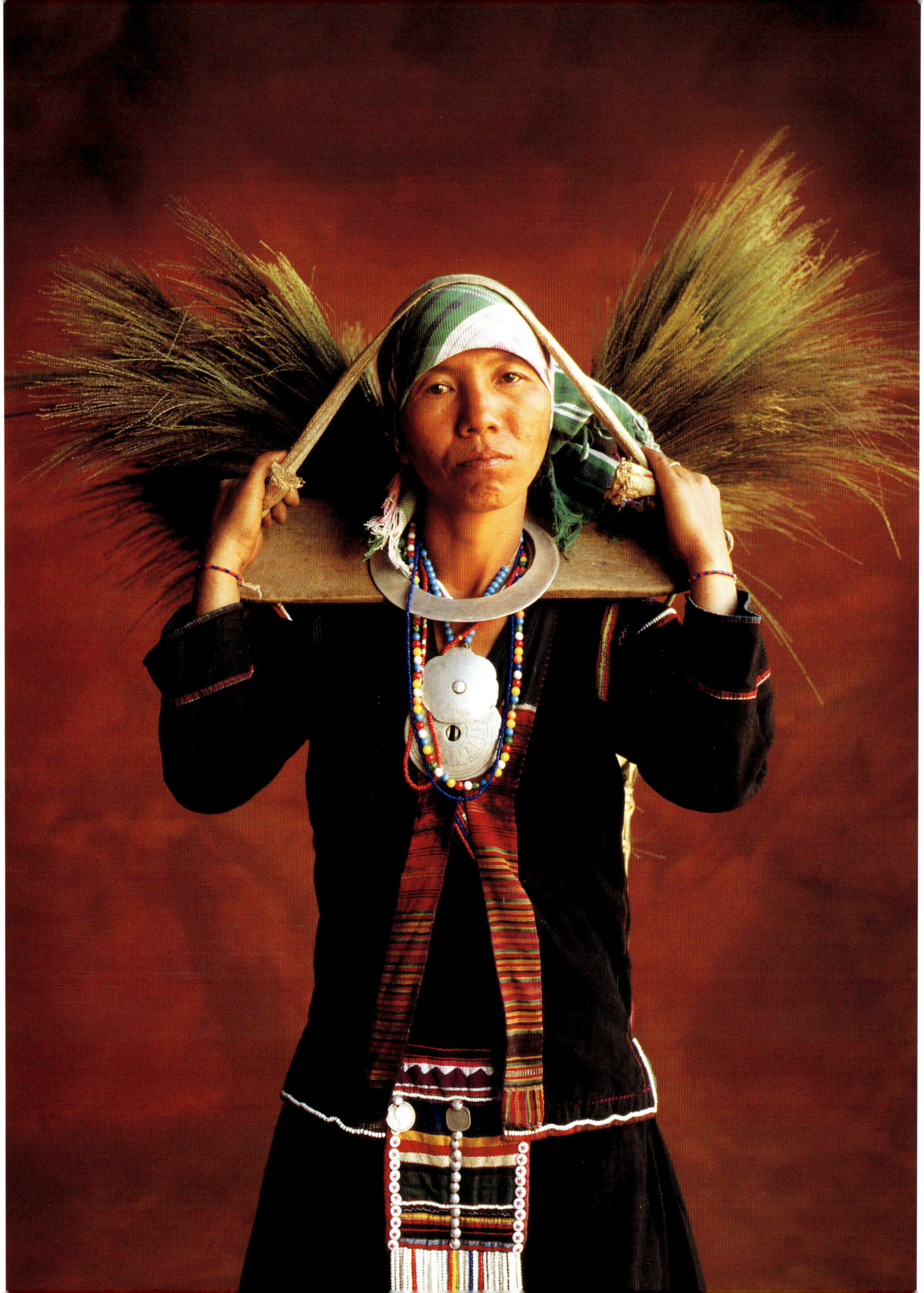

ALEMO, THIRTY-SEVEN, AKHA. BAN KOAE, THAILAND.

Alemo is dressed in the Akha national costume; all she lacks is the typical conical headdress. She came from the fields with a basket full of freshly cut crops. The Akha national dress is one of Thailand's most colorful.

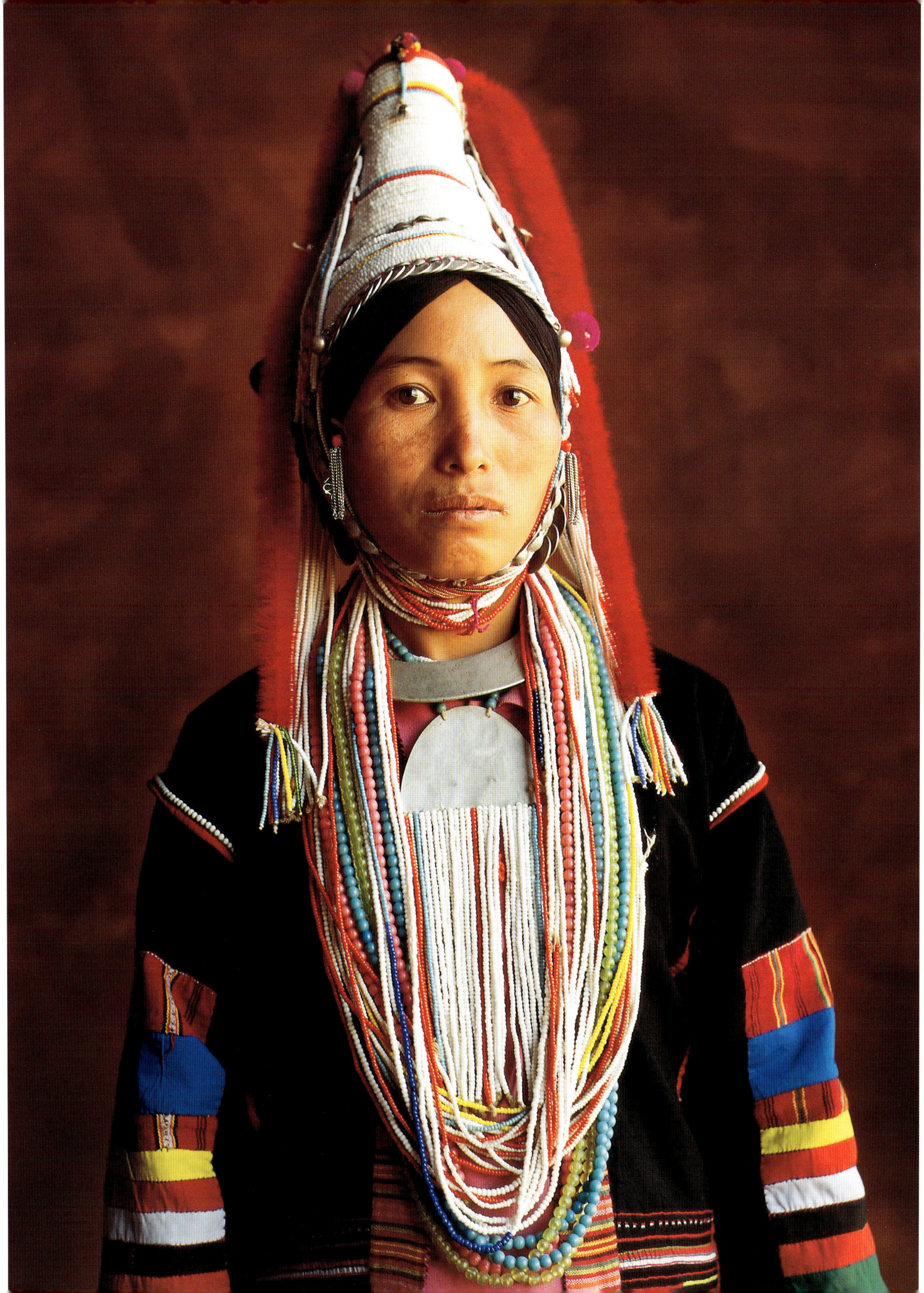

MICHU, THIRTY, AKHA.
BAN KOAE, THAILAND.

Michu is a married Akha woman living in the hills of northern Thailand. The women put a lot of effort into sewing and stitching their dresses. Their typical headdress makes them instantly recognizable whenever they appear in one of the lowland markets.

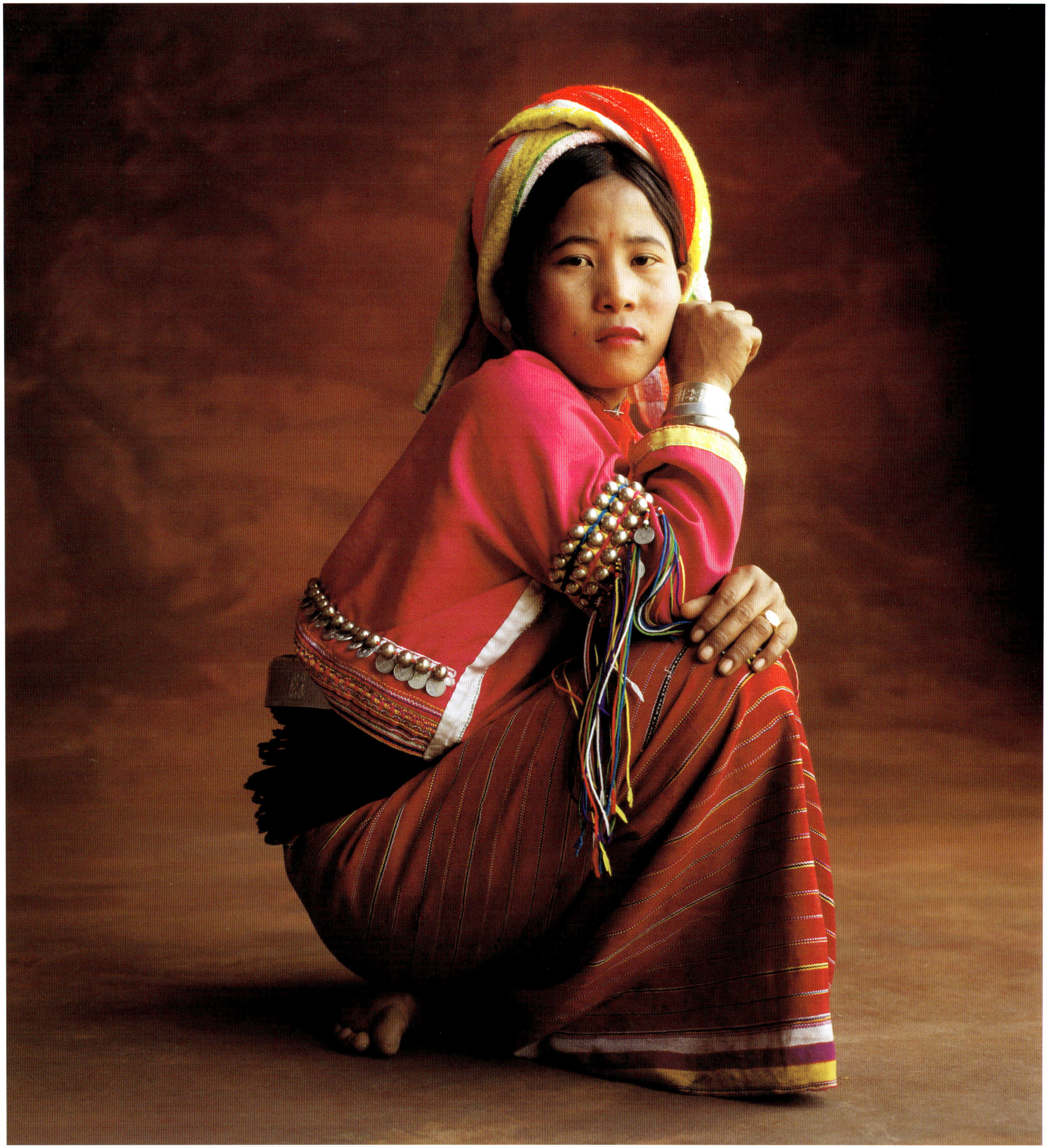

JERNG, TWENTY, PALAUNG. BAN HUEY MAK, THAILAND.

The Palaungs belong to the Mon-Khmer speaking people of the Golden Triangle. Their main settlements are in Myanmar, around the town of Kalaw in Southern Shan State.

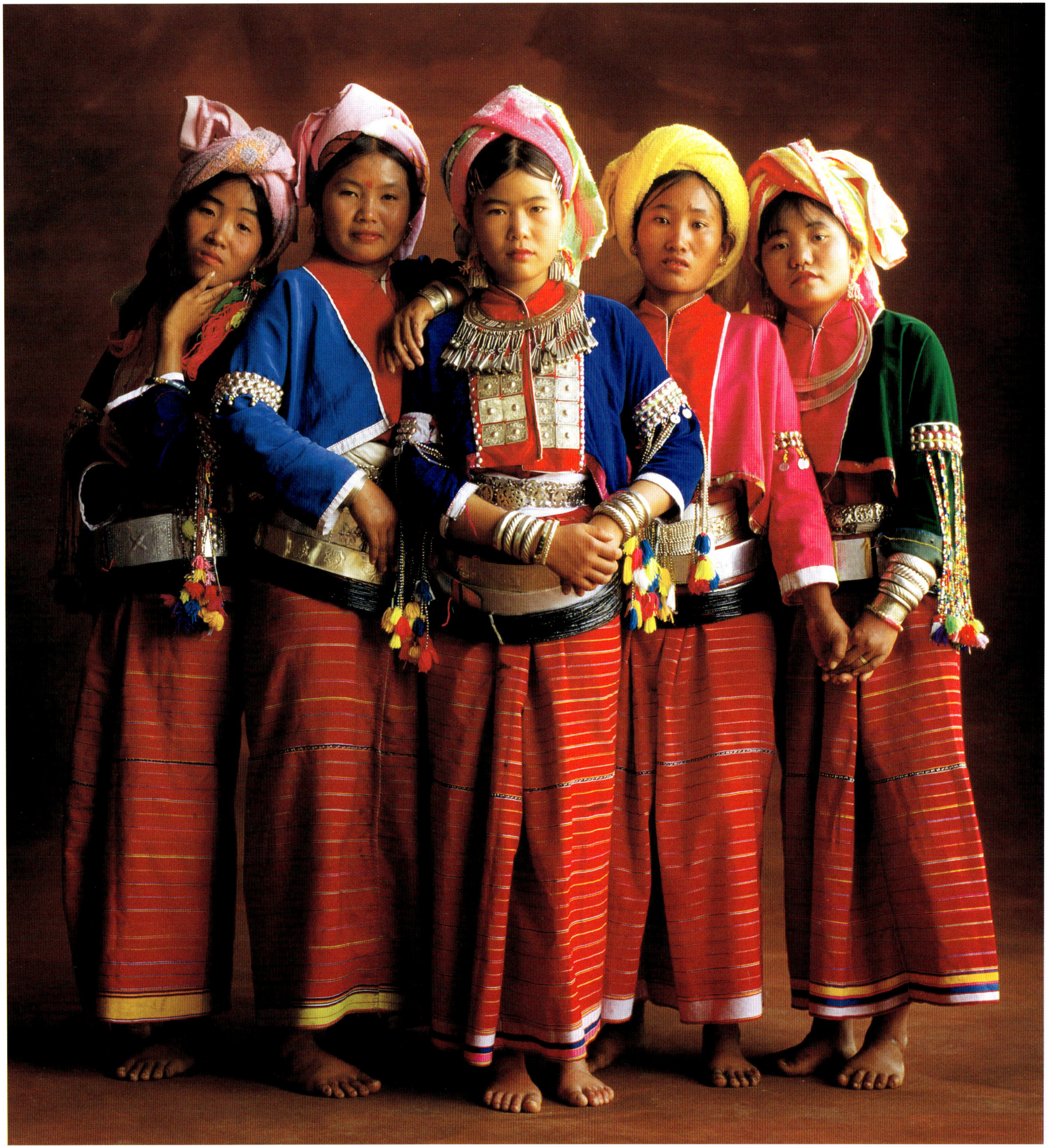

LEFT TO RIGHT: NOD, TWENTY; LU, TWENTY-TWO; JIM, SIXTEEN; LEE, TWENTY-EIGHT; AND TUATONG, EIGHTEEN; PALAUNG. BAN HUE MAK, THAILAND.

Nod, Lu, Jim, Lee, and Tuatong dress daily in their colorful national costume. These women appeared joyous and content working in the fields or in their Palaung village in the remote Thai hills.

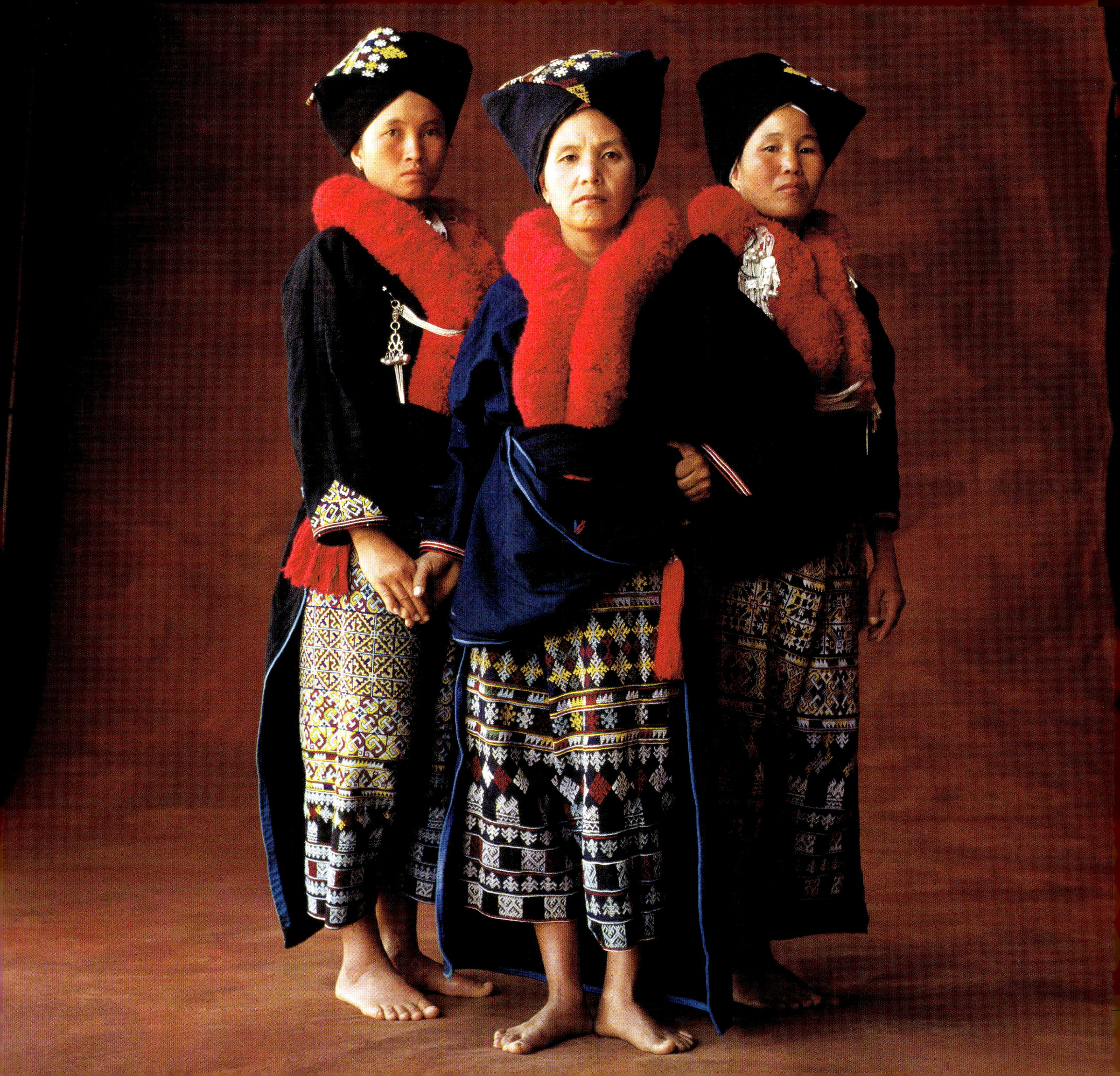

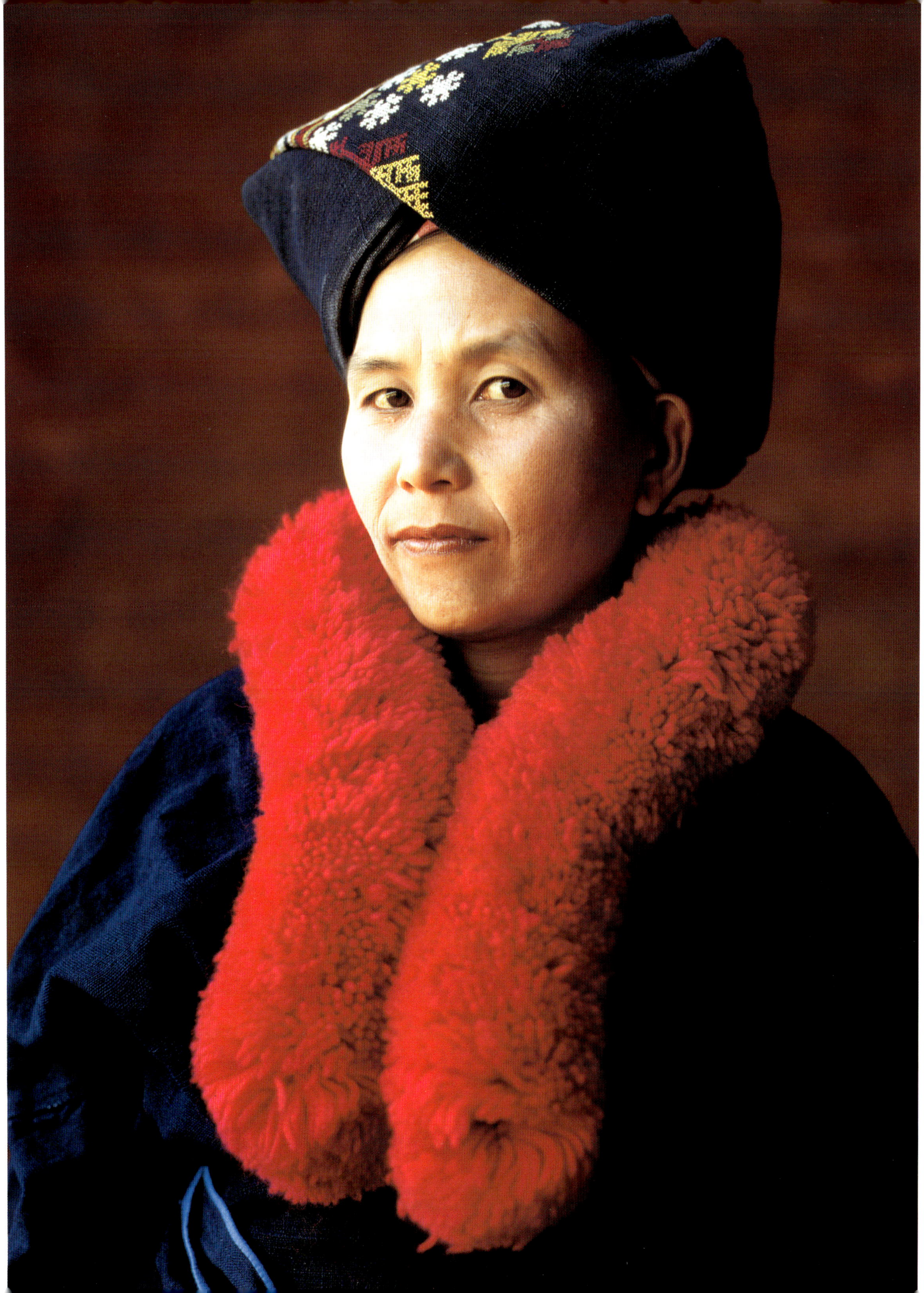

OPPOSITE: YIN LIN, TWENTY-TWO; FANG YEN, THIRTY; AND NAI CHING, THIRTY; YAO. HUEY CHOMPHOO, THAILAND.

Yin Lin, Fang Yen, and Nai Ching come from the village of Huey Chomphoo in the hills to the north of Chiang Mai. The Yao are still intimately related to the people of southern China. They enjoy communal festivities, during which the entire tribe feasts upon a freshly slaughtered pig.

FANG YEN, THIRTY, YAO. HUEY CHOMPOO, THAILAND.

Fang Yen is proudly wearing her national dress. Her village has been reached by a road that leads to the world beyond the hills. It now has a small shop where she can buy the materials she needs to produce her garments.

EPILOGUE

Human dignity has gleamed only now and then and here and there, in lonely splendor, throughout the ages,a hope of the better men, never an achievement of the majority.

—*James Thurber*

In spite of its universal usage in our upcoming one-world culture, human dignity remains an ill-defined concept. It serves many masters and always reveals the mind of the user. While in a materialistic sense dignity has become nearly identical with pride, in political parlance it connotes the upholding of human rights. In its minimal but basic meaning it depicts the straightened back of a person confronting the unconquerable; attempting to be fearless in the face of a destiny beyond his or her reach and influence. It is people's understanding of their place in the universe that gives them dignity. In this understanding, humankind sees itself as neither all powerful nor as being completely at the mercy of its instincts.

In prehistoric times, human dignity emerged as the strength that prevented mankind from succumbing to or being overwhelmed by awesome natural phenomena. Facing danger with courage and defending one's offspring with cleverness made prehistoric people realize that they possessed a consciousness that does not exist in other species. As long as they felt themselves to be an integral part of nature, they drew their dignity from transforming their immediate surroundings to their advantage and never exceeded the boundaries of necessity. With the consciousness of an equality in intellectual and spiritual dimensions, the sense of dignity has changed.

Five to three thousand years ago, during the age of the sages, this change became apparent. Until then, people perceived themselves as being in an environment for which there were only names for the most imminent manifestations. At once, in Greece, the Middle East, India, and China, a similar set of ideas sprung forth; ideas which, when seen without their religious connotations, spelled the same unalterable truth. Humankind started to understand itself as being object and subject of the universe at the same time. As an object we are mortal, fleeting and dispensable. As a subject we realized the ever-present eternal power with which we are endowed during our lifetimes. This contradictory mixture and its thoughtful application provided humanity with a new understanding of dignity—with the ability to be proud and devout at the same time.

Some two-and-a-half thousand years ago, the Buddha, who then lived in the Indian province of Maghada, was able to encapsulate the concept of true human dignity in eight simple precepts. In doing so, he laid the foundation of a culture that has since influenced the world for a much longer period than Christ's sacrifice and appeal for compassion. He created a world culture that draws its power from dignity. Dozens of highly civilized realms across mainland and insular Asia came and went. Without Buddha's charismatic insight they might as well have remained in the Dark Ages. His basic ideas found their way to the Middle East, where they flourished again in a monotheistic form. History then was the periodic shifting of the emphasis of how compassionate men and women saw themselves—either as objects or as subjects in the universe, driven either by devotion or action. Monasteries and battlefields marked the events. Nothing much has changed since then. No new idea has altered this understanding. The dually active and compassionate man has yet to create his realm. We are still suspended between heaven and earth.

With the reappearance of this ancient view in a Christian environment during the Renaissance, the ground was laid for the Age of Enlightenment. Enlightenment stood on three columns: the liberation from despotic social systems, the development of natural sciences, and the strengthening of the individual's moral ground. In the minds of the advocates of Enlightenment the three were interlinked. Only in a free society consisting of self-respecting people could individuals find the happiness and fulfillment they were in search of. During the eighteenth century the thought that a free society could still be based on mentally enslaved individuals was unacceptable. It was also unthinkable that by exploring natural and social sciences mankind's very survival could be endangered.

With science now replacing religion as the yardstick for our actions, a new understanding is dawning. Its pitfalls are many and varied; humankind's survival will depend on its outcome. Only if we live without violating nature, in an intellectual setting that reflects a universal reality; only if we are not thoughtlessly rebelling against unalterable facts; only if we accept that we are not more than participants, can we succeed.

THE DIGNIFIED VERSUS THE VIRTUAL MAN

Seen after two hundred years of stunning achievements, Enlightenment has so far handed us the tools to subjugate nature. We are on a winning streak, not accepting any cautious reservations. The successes are too convincing. A casual glance at the state of humankind at the beginning of the third millennium shows that democracy has become a power that is changing the political structures on a global scale. It is liberating millions of oppressed people who now contribute with vigor to what has become our obsession: material development.

However, looking more closely we can see that political liberation is parallel with a new subjugation to a world-unifying set of ideas that does not know which direction to follow except the propagation of democracy and a global market economy. Its solitary aim is to facilitate the manufacture and distribution of an ever-increasing number of new products. To function, it needs a basis of similarly thinking and feeling buyers, a mass of uncritical consumers who produce the added value necessary to develop new products. The primary duty of the media is to synchronize the perceptions of the world as a great marketplace, making people into useful consumers.

Artists of all kinds—poets, composers, musicians—have been able to express the nameless something that we all carry within us; a hinting of the secret of existence. It has no constant form, like a light that illuminates and warms. Mass media has difficulty depicting this vague entity. Unique values such as human dignity find no place in a multimedia world that is tied to the laws of a capitalist system.

To live without paying heed to man's ephemerality, thinking that conquering the world materially will create the happiness we all strive for, ignores the fact that great civilizations can only flourish if they are not violating the basic laws of nature. The inconsideration, egotism, and avarice that drives an uncontrolled market can furnish short-lived successes, but this is in opposition to the true quality that surrounds us. Such a state in human development is a sign of the disappearance of the dignified and the appearance of the virtual person.

We lose contact with reality if we live removed from nature, if we don't feel the wind against our skin, if we don't stand in awe looking into the starry night, aware of our common destiny. Our forebearers who lasted the night by the light of a chip of pine wood could not escape the truth that settled on them night after dark night. It kept them from assuming privileges and taking advantage of seemingly inexhaustible resources. Their idea of nature was grounded, thus they understood their true place in the natural world. It was such a setting that made them realize and accept the flux that surrounds us—that ever-changing quality that is central to true self-understanding.

Compared with theirs, modern life seems shallow and alienating. We cover it minutely with actions, events, and distractions, hide inconsistencies away behind the walls of medical institutions and prisons. It is a virtual world based on distorted perceptions that we have constructed. It is so overpowering that the average person would immediately shy away or simply deal with it as he or she is used to—by changing the channel or consulting a psychiatrist.

When we look back in history we often wonder why people could not see the contradictions of their time. We are in a similar situation. The facts and contemporary values that are constantly thrown at us cannot be seen as being just another inconsequential ideology. They block our vision. In this *circulus virtiosus* the individual is again disappearing as a liberated body, as it disappeared in times of political despotism. Now, however, the overwhelming force we face is not invested in a dictator. It rests in our innocent belief that conquering and exploiting nature without compassion is to our advantage. We unassumingly pick the fruits as a God-given privilege. The currency we pay with is the upright back—the trademark of the free, unbiased, dignified human being.

The signs are becoming increasingly more obvious that the actions that reflect this asssumed privilege will make us and future generations suffer in a yet unprecedented dimension. This suffering will occur individually by making us subservient to the uncontrolled forces of a free market, and as a species by (proverbially) destroying the fertile soil that feeds us. All this has roots in our having forgotten that the authors of Enlightenment and their forerunners, the Greek, Middle Eastern, and Asian sages, have always put the greatest emphasis on the development of the individual as an independent, compassionate, and responsible being—on his or her ability to become moral and virtuous.

DIGNITY AND COMPASSION In contrast to pride, dignity can only flourish in an altruistic environment. Pride thrives on power, material success, possessions—the tools to control one's environment. Dignity on the other hand is based on the human's ability to suffer, to understand that there are unalterable conditions that must be accepted. Grasping deeply that we are an integral part of nature and not its master is a pre-condition to dignity. In the absence of this, the fleeting notion of pride will replace dignity in our every gesture.

Virtue, the word that has lost ground in the modern perception of the world, means that we are aware of a quality that empowers the very roots of our existence. Today, dealing with it has become too bothersome when most of the things we strive for are mundane. They demand one's full attention to remain informed. There is just no time left to bother ourselves with virtue.

A society that follows short-lived aims rarely plans beyond the living generation's growing needs and does not follow a set of values that generates dignity. This existence involves a mundane philosophy that excludes responsibilities for the state of humankind. By its very definition it asks no more about man's raison d'être in a timeless manner, and is a dead end. The devastating absence of true dignity in the abyss of modern metropolises is a valid sign that we do not apply the lessons that history can teach us.

Thus, the learned men and women during the first half of the last century might have truly been the last universally educated ones. They might have been at the high water mark of individual development. These were thoughtful, virtuous, highly responsible people for whom history still meant more than the stringing together of realms and genealogies. For them, mental development was the measure for assessing change.

Global communication and transport have now reached the last pockets of isolated lifestyles—of worldviews that in the past have had a cross-cultural fertilization effect. Whenever nations took a wrong turn and followed a path of self-destruction, these pockets of alternative values took over and healed the wounds of man's megalomania. Today the countries of the South, by copying the West's questionable success story, are throwing their inherited knowledge overboard faster than they can substitute it with new values that are in harmony with their environment and their precarious ecological situation. The outcome is a generation of culturally dispossessed individuals.

Looking at the populace of the megacities of the South, our "enlightened" perception of success is still the same as the former colonial perspective. We look at them without compassion; not as humans but as they are cold-heartedly depicted and discussed in the media, as immigrants and the source of cheap labor. Once market economy laws are internalized and anchored as "universal" in our mind, compassion becomes an unnecessary burden. We dispose of it, and with it we dispose of our dignity. There can be no dignity without compassion, as there can be no true laughter without joy and no vision without light.

During most of humankind's history, oppression of man by man was the rule. Under such circumstances no emancipation could take place without bloody and mostly ill-designed revolutions. Today we stand more than two hundred years after the drafting of the Constitution of the United States, after the Encyclopedists' outcry for justice, more than fifty years after the Declaration of Human Rights and oppression is still the rule of the day. This time it functions under the cover of necessary market adjustments. Most people living today have no chance to live in dignity. Since dignity is not a marketable product, it is not on the list of anticipated objectives. Western culture is now so deeply involved in the amassment of worldly goods that the compassionate outlook has been moved to the back burner. Only if it does not threaten our ability to consume do we give it a chance to enter our mind. Just one unbiased look at the distribution of wealth makes it clear that most people populating this globe at the beginning of the third millennium live substandard lives that prevent them from using their inborn abilities. When people are unable to live dignified lives it prevents humanity from accessing its full potential. The Encyclopedists' promise of Enlightenment remains yet to be fulfilled.

THE SEARCH CONTINUES Searching for human dignity has brought us to regions where the rapid transformation of man's perception of himself over the last fifty years has had minor impact. These are regions where, in a Rousseauan sense, people still live off the fruits of what they have sown themselves, and with which they are as satisfied as their ancestors were; regions where the social and political system has not yet transformed the structure of the tribe or the village. Such places are rare today, as are people who follow a trade with tradition and pride. They cling to their small world because it offers them recognition and dignity, because it still connects them with the unfathomable.

Once the sluice gate is opened, the peasant who saw himself as an accomplished farmer, a venerated head of a family, a man suspended between heaven and earth, will see himself as a man clothed in rags, uneducated, poor, helpless, and lacking all the necessities to survive in a global economy. In reality nothing much has changed, he has just lost his dignity in a society based on material gain. Photographing people who have not yet succumbed to this view means taking live photographs of the past, recalling what once has been. Then dignity is not controversial anymore; it becomes perceptible to the onlooker who is not yet spoiled by a materialistic classification of his fellows. The dignity that emanates from these photographs is a reminder of what our society direly needs to preserve. They show what is at the heart of the Bill of Rights, what the Declaration of Human Rights really defends—dignity, the violable essence that makes us human.

ACKNOWLEDGEMENTS

All things are interconnected. This book is the outcome of the efforts of a variety of people, each of whom has left his or her mark. Imagination, moral support, creativity, and foresight are the invisible factors, the backbone, on which any project such as ours thrives. More people than can be mentioned on this page have contributed to it.

Sabine and Renate, whose names do not appear on the title page, have to be mentioned first and foremost. They have been with us every step of the way. They have gone through all the hardships with us, and we have also shared the joy and fun of traveling with them. They brought the female aspect to what otherwise would have been a tiresome male adventure. Without Sabine's limitless optimism and her professional acumen, we would have given up more than once, and without Renate's imperishable joy of life—not to mention the culinary feats she accomplished in the midst of nowhere—it would have been half the fun.

Then there is Pia who should have been with us, but someone had to stay back home to take care of the children. She volunteered, and she knows how grateful we are for that. The little surprises she packed into our equipment boxes spoke of her foresight and anticipation of what was awaiting us.

Our dependence on local support was high, but we were fortunate to always find the right people on the spot. In Ethiopia it was Aki Haddis, the half German, half Ethiopian tour operator who seems to know every inch of the country. Our drivers: young Getu, who never let us down, and Sirak, this mountain of a man, were more than drivers—they have become friends. And then there was Workayu; like Sirak he was a handsome, intelligent, and incredibly tough son of his country. He died of an unknown illness while we were back in Germany. We will never forget him.

In the wilderness along the Omo it was Susan and Nassos Roussos who cheerfully offered us their camp as a base. Without it we could never have worked in peace and security. Later, with the Borana, it was Jordan Holtam of Care and Cheru Duba, the learned Borana liaison, who made our camp in this unsafe region possible. For being able to stay with the Samburus we are ever grateful to Malcolm Gascoigne, the exemplary Scotsman who shares his life with them and who offered us his Yare Camp in Maralal as a base.

Without Kailash Parashar in Pushkar we would have drowned in the crowd of pilgrims and visitors. His assistance and influence in the region created the space and support we needed to work; otherwise we might have ended up as just a couple of camera-wielding tourists. We would never have been able to travel with the nomadic Rabaris had not our guide, Manga Sumar, a wizard in local dialects, been with us. And in Delhi it was Baljeet Malik in whose Raj-style domicile we could recreate from the arduous hours on top of the Sis Ganj Sahib. But neither photographing in Gujarat nor at the Sikh's sacred temple would have been possible without the assistance of Christiane Brosius, who shared her professionalism and her love for things Indian.

Over the years during which we came to Myanmar and Thailand there were numerous people who assisted us. Here we can only mention a few; the others will know of our gratitude. Being able to travel to the still war-torn Kachin province would not have been possible without the support of the then Myanmar ambassador in Bonn, Win Aung. M.C. Myo Min and Tin Aung Myint made sure it didn't end in disaster. Of the different liaisons who accompanied us on our subsequent trips it was Hubert Ca Lian Rhang in Kalemyo who helped us through our travels in the Chin Hills and Aung Hlatun who was with us at the Manao Festival in Myitkyina. They both did much more to ensure the success of our project than they were assigned to.

Our special gratitude goes to Saw Po Sha, our Christian Karen liaison and friend who provided moral support as well as being a tireless guide and interpreter. Our trip along the Myanmar border of northern Thailand would never have been possible without Thawach Surathep, our friend Khun Ti. Himself an ardent traveler, he knew what we were looking for and where to find it. He was more than a guide, he was a core member of the team. We have to thank Klaus Walkhoff, who also came with us to the Chin Hills, and Manfred Schaupp, the high-tech wizards who understood our vision. They constructed the state of the art studio that allowed us to do professional photography in regions traditionally reserved for 35mm cameras.

The support from home and along the way could not have born fruit if our idea had not found a sympathetic publisher. We found this in Michael E. Hoffman of Aperture, the dean of American photographic design. His enthusiastic support, and the competence of Aperture's publishing, production, and design specialists made this book what it is. Our thanks go to Michael E. Hoffman and Michael Sand, who led us through the publishing details, Phyllis Thompson Reid, who supervised the project, and to Michelle Dunn Marsh, who designed the book.

Last but not least, the photographs would not have their brilliance without Dick Wenzel, who tirelessly developed and brought the right touch to them, and Holger Goertz, who perfected the digital scans.

All of those mentioned, and the many that have gone unmentioned, have contributed, were invaluable, and have made this book possible. Thanks to all of them—all things are interconnected.

—GÜNTER PFANNMÜLLER AND WILHELM KLEIN
Frankfurt / Koh Samui

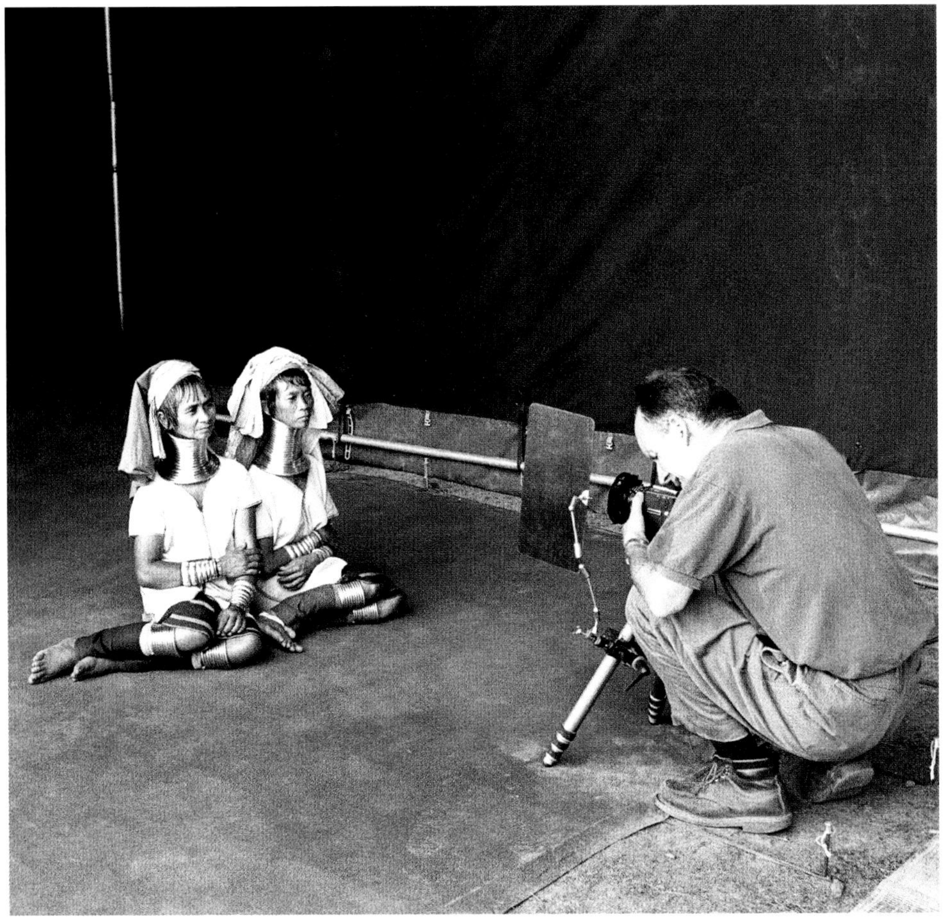

GÜNTER PFANNMÜLLER PHOTOGRAPHING TWO PADAUNG WOMEN AT HUAY PU KANG.

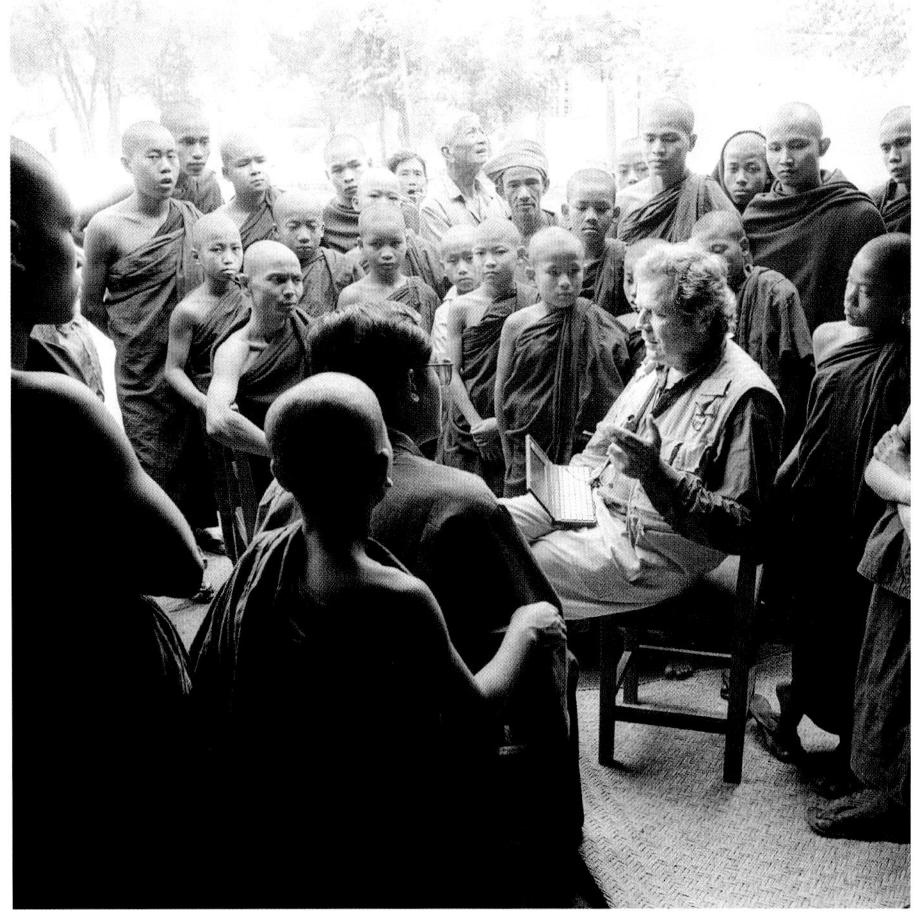

WILHELM KLEIN WITH YOUNG MONKS AT THE MAHA GHANDA MONASTERY, AMARAPURA.

Library of Congress Catalog Card Number: 00-103557
Hardcover ISBN: 0-89381-912-3

Design by Michelle Dunn Marsh

Printed and bound by Sing Cheong Printing Co. Ltd., Hong Kong

The staff at Aperture for *In Search of Dignity* is Michael E. Hoffman, Executive Director; Phyllis Thompson Reid, Editor; Stevan A. Baron, V.P., Production; Lisa A. Farmer, Production Director; Meredith Coeyman, Editorial Work-Scholar

Aperture Foundation publishes a periodical, books, and portfolios of fine photography and presents world-class exhibitions to communicate with serious photographers and creative people everywhere. A complete catalog is available upon request.

APERTURE CUSTOMER SERVICE: 20 East 23rd Street, New York, NY 10010. Phone: (212) 598-4205. Fax: (212) 598-4015. Toll-free: (800) 929-2323. E-mail: customerservice@aperture.org

APERTURE FOUNDATION, INCLUDING BOOK CENTER AND BURDEN GALLERY: 20 East 23rd Street, New York, New York 10010. Phone: (212) 505-5555, EXT. 300. Fax: (212) 979-7759; E-mail: info@aperture.org

APERTURE MILLERTON BOOK CENTER: Route 22 North, Millerton, New York 12546. Phone: (518) 789-9003.

Visit Aperture's website: www.aperture.org

Visit Günter Pfannmüller's website: www.pfannmueller.de

Aperture Foundation books are distributed internationally through:

CANADA: General/Irwin Publishing Co., Ltd., 30 Lesmill Road, Don Mills, Ontario, M3B2T6. Fax: (416) 445-5967.

UNITED KINGDOM, EIRE, SOUTH AFRICA: Aperture c/o Robert Hale, Ltd., Clerkenwell House, 45-47 Clerkenwell Green, London, United Kingdom, EC1R OHT. Fax: (44) 207-490-4958.

WESTERN EUROPE, SCANDINAVIA: Nilsson & Lamm, BV, Pampuslaan 212-214, P.O. Box 195, 1382 JS Weesp, Netherlands. Fax: (31) 29-441-5054.

AUSTRALIA: Tower Books Pty. Ltd., Unit 9/19 Rodborough Road, Frenchs Forest, Sydney, New South Wales, Australia. Fax: (61) 2-9975-5599.

NEW ZEALAND: Southern Publishers Group, 22 Burleigh Street, Grafton, Auckland, New Zealand. Fax: (64) 9-309-6170.

INDIA: TBI Publishers, 46 Housing Project, South Extension Part-I, New Delhi 110049, India. Fax: (91) 11-461-0576.

To subscribe to the periodical *Aperture* write Aperture, P.O. Box 3000, Denville, New Jersey 07834. Toll-free: (866) 457-4603. International subscriptions: (973) 627-2427. One year: $40.00. Two years: $66.00. Add $10.00 per year for international orders.

FIRST EDITION
10 9 8 7 6 5 4 3 2 1